Ancient Sins ...
Modern Addictions

Ancient Sins ... Modern Addictions

A Fresh Look at the Seven Deadly Sins

R. SCOTT SULLENDER

CASCADE *Books* • Eugene, Oregon

ANCIENT SINS ... MODERN ADDICTIONS
A Fresh Look at the Seven Deadly Sins

Copyright © 2013 R. Scott Sullender. All rights reserved. Except for brief quotations in critical publications or reviews, no part of this book may be reproduced in any manner without prior written permission from the publisher. Write: Permissions, Wipf and Stock Publishers, 199 W. 8th Ave., Suite 3, Eugene, OR 97401.

Cascade Books
An Imprint of Wipf and Stock Publishers
199 W. 8th Ave., Suite 3
Eugene, OR 97401

www.wipfandstock.com

ISBN 13: 978-1-62032-690-9

Cataloguing-in-Publication data:

Sullender, R. Scott.

    Ancient sins . . . modern addictions : a fresh look at the seven deadly sins / R. Scott Sullender.

    xviii + 180 pp. ; 23 cm. Includes bibliographical references.

    ISBN 13: 978-1-62032-690-9

    1. Substance abuse—Religious aspects. 2. Compulsive behavior—Religious aspects. 3. Deadly sins. I. Title.

BL625.9.R43 .S50 2013

Manufactured in the U.S.A.

Contents

List of Illustrations   vi

Acknowledgments   vii

Introduction   ix

1. What Is Addiction? An Overview   1
2. Pride: Self-Absorption and Self-Deception   22
3. Envy: A Problem in Community   43
4. Anger: A Cycle of Resentment, Rage, and Violence   64
5. Sloth: Apathy and Lack of Motivation   84
6. Greed: A Problem of Excess   105
7. Gluttony: Being Hooked on Consumption   126
8. Lust: An Obsession with Sex   151
9. Some Concluding Thoughts   170

Theological Postscript: What is Sin?   173

Bibliography   177

Illustrations

Figure 1	Chemical/Behavioral Components of Addiction	4
Figure 2	The Addictive Cycle	16
Figure 3	Cycle of Rage/Violence	70
Figure 4	Human Needs and their Distortions	88
Figure 5	Cycle of Sexual Addiction	160

Acknowledgments

I WISH TO THANK the many people, clients, friends, and congregants who have shared with me their struggles with the various types of addictions. I have learned a lot from you and hope that together we have walked a pathway to greater freedom. I wish to thank my partner and spouse, Linda, who has been so patient and supportive of my writing aspirations. I wish to thank my colleagues at San Francisco Theological Seminary, who have encouraged me with helpful feedback, and the seminary itself for giving me the necessary time and financial support to finish this project. This book is dedicated to all who long to be free from the modern slavery of addiction.

Introduction

OVER THE PAST FORTY years, I have met with hundreds and hundreds of individuals and families in my practice as a psychologist and certified pastoral counselor. Most of them have been in great pain—emotional pain, relationship pain, spiritual pain, and sometimes physical pain. The pain people suffer has often been due to sin, whether their own sin or the sins of others. Sometimes people do things or fail to do things that lead to their own suffering. They are sinners. Other times, people and families are in pain because of the sins committed by others. They are sinned against. Sometimes, it is a combination of both. On still other occasions, suffering has been caused by evil or by the nature of life itself, complicated by sin. Over the years, I have become a keen observer of sin, of its various manifestations and complications. You might say I have become an expert on sin, perhaps even a "sin doctor"! On occasion, my colleagues have joked with me, "People learn a lot about sin when they come to see you, Scott. Some of them are becoming better sinners." I do not intend for people to become better sinners. They can usually do that pretty well by themselves. But I do want people to learn about sin—how it works, how it enslaves us, and how we might keep ourselves free from its power.

The task of keeping ourselves free from sin is not an enterprise that concerns many modern secular people. Yet, if I change the language and talk about personal growth or becoming free from addiction, modern people may in fact resonate with this enterprise. For centuries, humans—pre-modern and modern—have struggled with addictions, hurts, inner conflicts, suffering, and the challenges and joys of the human experience. In a religious context, we use religious language to talk about such dynamics. In a secular context, we tend to use the language of psychology or addiction recovery to talk about the same processes. People of faith talk about their "walk with the Lord," about sanctification, about facing their demons, or about their spiritual growth. Secular people talk about personal growth, about facing their shadow side, about individuation, or about recovery and

Introduction

self-acceptance. Both language systems are useful at times. Both ways of conceptualizing human growth have contributed insights to our common enterprise of becoming more whole and more free. By resurrecting in this book the language of sin and temptation, I hope to recover some valuable insights that have been lost in our rush into the worldview of psychology. In addition, I hope to set up a dialogue in which these two perspectives on humanity's struggle can contribute to the common goal of helping ourselves and our loved ones live more fully and freely.

In this book, I propose to look at the traditional Seven Deadly Sins in the light of modern psychology and addiction recovery literature. I hope to highlight the obvious—that these Seven Deadly Sins are still around and still destroying lives just as much as they did in past centuries. In fact, two of these seven—lust and greed—are enjoying their best years ever! I hope to convince you that your own spiritual health is not fully achieved unless or until you gain some freedom from these tempting snares. I will offer you some practical suggestions for how to fight these sins, especially in a culture that increasingly promotes sin. I will remind you of some of the traditional virtues and spiritual disciplines that our forebears found useful in combating sin.

The categorization of the Seven Deadly Sins emerged in a culture quite different from the world we live in today, although, as I will suggest, the list still offers us some universal insights about human nature. Between approximately 500 and 1500 CE in Western Europe, Christianity permeated every aspect and facet of human culture and civilization. In this intensely religious age, the human journey was seen as a struggle between good and evil, between sin and virtue, a struggle upon which hinged the destiny of one's soul. In the early centuries of Christianity, wise religious leaders of the period identified seven out of all the possible sins that they considered to be the most powerful and most difficult to defeat—in short, the most deadly. The traditional list of the Seven Deadly Sins dates back to the fifth century, but some consider the list to have scriptural roots in the exorcising of seven demons from Mary Magdalene in Luke 8:2 (interestingly, the use of the term "demon" is suggestive of an addictive process). The Seven Deadly Sins appeared in slightly different orders until the medieval period, when the list was codified and widely embraced. The concept permeated the spiritual lives of believers for hundreds of years. It was talked about in sermons, referred to in morality plays, and served as the subject of many a spiritual retreat or pilgrimage.

Introduction

Looking through the lens of modernity, we tend to see this effort to classify sin as legalistic, if not downright silly. "Sin is sin is sin," some of us might say. Why make such fine distinctions? Others might be repulsed by the moralistic tendencies embedded in such efforts to categorize sin. Yet, I believe that the tradition of the Seven Deadly Sins was actually born in a context of compassion, not unlike the context of my contemporary counseling office. Behind the written words are hundreds of years of pastoral ministry with and for people caught in the pain and suffering of sin. Born of a desire to help others, the pastoral caregivers of medieval Christendom tried to identify the most deadly of the human vices. You might say that the system of the Seven Deadly Sins was one of the first attempts at creating a diagnostic system, a way of labeling and thus understanding what was wrong with a given suffering soul who entered the church seeking relief. Indeed, it was commonly thought in those days that every individual had an inborn vulnerability for one of the Seven Deadly Sins; so priests and other religious caregivers attempted to match an individual's personality type with a particular spiritual weakness. In the language of that era, preachers and priests taught that Satan assigned a particular demon to each of us at our birth, a demon designed to exploit our unique spiritual weakness. In turn, thankfully, we were also assigned a guardian angel whose job it was to protect us, guide us, and prevent us from falling into that particular sin or any other vice.

In keeping with my proposal that the Seven Deadly Sins evolved in the context of pastoral care, in a context of compassion rather than of moralistic legalism, it is helpful to note that Christian teachers of that era also identified virtues that corresponded to each of the Seven Deadly Sins. They encouraged parishioners to resist the temptation of a particular sin by practicing and embracing that sin's "saving virtue." For example, by practicing humility, a person could avoid or fight against the temptation of pride. By practicing patience, he or she could learn to control a quick temper, the sin of anger. In modern psychological terminology, we might say that the concept of the saving virtues was the first attempt at a treatment plan. And for each saving virtue, there were various spiritual practices—prayers, readings, rituals—that were designed to strengthen or cultivate that virtue within the person. So now we have the whole sequence that most modern psychologists are familiar with—diagnosis, treatment planning, and methods—all implemented by the local priest or spiritual director, the medieval equivalent of a psychotherapist. In its day and for its age, this list of Seven

Deadly Sins and their corresponding seven virtues was a useful tool in facing the challenge of facilitating psychological and spiritual growth.

When the Reformation arrived in the sixteenth century, Protestant leaders rejected the classification of sins, arguing that such lists represented the over-legalization of Christianity. Such lists only encouraged believers to buy and sell sins, confessions, and penances, they said. Psychologically, the classification of sins allowed people to compare sins and thus rationalize or make excuses for their immoral behavior by saying, "Well, my sin is not as bad as yours." Protestant reformers argued that all sin is equally reprehensible to God. Protestants have continued to place a strong emphasis upon the concept that we are all sinners who are incapable of saving ourselves, much less of helping others overcome sin. The task of "sanctification" (being made holy) is pointless until we confess our utter helplessness before God and receive, by faith, the gift of salvation. According to this view, the problem of sin can only be addressed through repentance and acceptance of Jesus Christ as Lord and Savior.

Yet, by placing such a strong emphasis upon the concept of "justification" (being saved by faith alone), Protestants have tended, with the exception of some contemporary mainline denominations, to ignore the importance of sanctification. To put it another way, evangelical leaders give the impression that once we are saved (once we accept Jesus Christ as our personal Lord and Savior), there is nothing more for us to do. Further, salvation is mistakenly thought of only in terms of freedom from the consequences of sin—guilt and death—instead of in terms of freedom from the sin itself. Becoming *saved* is mistakenly portrayed as the end in itself, instead of the beginning of a life-long journey of *being saved*.

Many of my counselees have been tragically hurt by their naïve assumption that once they became a Christian, they would be free from sin. Some Christian leaders promise as much. This is the cornerstone of evangelical theology, reflected, for example, in a line from the hymn "How Great Thou Art": "He bled and died to take away my sin." My experience, however, has often been the opposite; when we find faith in Christ, our struggle with sin may become all the more intense, not less so. Sometimes only after we are saved, and begin to see with the eyes of faith, do we realize how fully entrapped by sin we were and perhaps still are. Or is it that old Screwtape turns up the heat on new Christians in an effort to win them back to the dark side?

Introduction

The classification of sins and their corresponding virtues reminds us that salvation is more than a one-time, once-and-for-all decision. Salvation is also a life-long struggle with sin and, conversely, a life-long struggle to embrace the virtues of faith. In the process of sanctification, lists such as the Seven Deadly Sins can still be helpful guides. Christians need to be taught to avoid sin by becoming more self-aware and by understanding better how sin works because, after all, sin is very deceptive in its dynamics. Christians can also be encouraged to practice various spiritual disciplines and, through those disciplines, cultivate in themselves the necessary saving virtues that fortify the soul and move the believer ever so gradually toward the likeness of Christ.

You will notice that I have used some traditional Christian language related to the concepts of temptation, sin, and even demons. Maybe you are a bit uncomfortable with this language. You are not alone. Modern psychology does not have much use for this way of seeing the human struggle. As Karl Menninger pointed out in his 1973 book *Whatever Became of Sin?*, psychology has changed the paradigm in the twentieth century for how we understand human failings. We now have a psychological understanding of sin. Sin, if that is the right word in a secular age, is the result of inner forces, unmet inner needs, bad genes, unresolved traumas, and unresolved conflicts from our families of origin, and thus the idea is that if we can only understand these dynamics, we can change our lives for the better. Increased self-awareness leads to salvation—that is the promise of psychotherapy.

The temptation/sin model looks at human failings a bit differently, seeing our failings as the result of outside forces, of "powers and principalities" that seek to tempt us, to lead us astray and ultimately destroy us. In this model, the source of our problems is outside of ourselves, and yet we have a clear choice. With every temptation, there is an implied moral choice, a choice between good and evil. So, what is the cause of our various human failings—forces within or forces outside of ourselves? And what is the role of human will in determining our fate? Are we the victims of our psychological issues or do we make moral choices? I suggest to you that the traditional Christian temptation/sin perspective on human failings still has its strengths, its "virtues," if you will. When combined with the psychological models of the contemporary secular age, we will have a fuller picture of human sin and virtue.

I grew up in the 1950s in a mainline Protestant church in what was then suburban Los Angeles. The preachers and teachers in my home congregation talked about sin, but life seemed simpler then. I believed that sin was bad and that I was forgiven for my sins, but as I look back on my spiritually formative years, the sins of my childhood and youth seem pretty minor, comparatively speaking. Generally, I was a good boy . . . maybe a little too well-behaved for my own good.

Throughout my adult years, however, as a pastor and then professional psychologist, I have tried to assist people who are struggling with more complicated sins. In my counseling office, I have worked with people who have actually killed others, whether intentionally or unintentionally; people who have destroyed their lives and the lives of others through drugs, alcohol, and/or food; people who have been so consumed with rage, jealousy, and revenge that they have ended up in prison; people who have let their lust destroy relationship after relationship; people who have been addicted to the acquisition of wealth at all costs; and people who have been so hopelessly caught in such sins that they have wanted to or actually attempted to end their own lives. These are not unusual problems for a contemporary psychotherapist serving an urban population. Nevertheless, the experience has had a profound effect on my spiritual journey.

As a result of my practice, over the years I have become more impressed with sin, with its power, its complexity, and its deceits. I have concluded that we in the mainline churches do not talk enough about sin. This is why, in part, I have chosen to write this book. At the same time, let me also say that even as I have become more impressed with sin, I have concurrently become more impressed with God's forgiveness and grace. What amazing grace it is that washes away such hideous sins as those that plague us humans! So I have also concluded that most of us who call ourselves Christians have no idea of the true depth of God's grace. Grace is a far more profound, deep, and truly radical spiritual truth than most Christians ever imagine. Sadly, for some this radical grace only becomes real when they are delivered from their slavery to one of the Seven Deadly Sins. Often, it is the recovering addict, the pardoned prisoner, the loved adulterer, or the once terminally ill patient—in short, the forgiven sinner—who truly understands the meaning of grace.

The traditional Seven Deadly Sins are *pride, envy, anger, sloth, greed, gluttony,* and *lust*. Certainly, the human capacity for sin is endless. We could identify hundreds upon hundreds of sins, if we were inclined to be so obsessive. These seven were considered to be the worst! They were thought to be the worst because they were particularly difficult to resist and particularly difficult to free oneself from. They were also considered the worst because they are the root sins from which so many other sins spring. For example, from the sin of anger springs violence, an increasingly common problem in our time. From the sin of lust springs rape, pornography, prostitution, and adultery. Greed can lead to cheating, lying, property crimes, and/or betrayal.

These Seven Deadly Sins are mostly sins of the mind. They are mental, not behavioral. They are a different category of sin than the sinful deeds we do. Jesus pointed out in his Sermon on the Mount (Matt 5:21–31) that many sins, like murder and adultery, begin in the mind, with what we think. Our thinking then leads to our behavior or, to paraphrase, "Sinful attitudes lead to sinful deeds." There is certainly a tradition that suggests that a sin is not a sin until it is a deed—you cannot hold me accountable for my thoughts! The tradition of the Seven Deadly Sins takes a different perspective, suggesting that there is continuity between what we think and what we do. Sin begins in the mind, in what is called by modern psychologists the obsessive thinking process. That is where the battle is won or lost. So, resisting the snares of these seven sins was traditionally considered essential to the success of one's earthly spiritual walk.

Our spiritual ancestors called these sins "deadly." They did so because these seven were considered more serious, more life-threatening in nature than most other sins. They often contribute to or lead directly to death. They also are more likely to lead directly to the death of the soul, i.e., pulling us further and further away from a saving relationship with Christ, preventing us from true and free worship of the living God. Yet, more than all this, I believe that the precise meaning of deadly is captured best by the modern word "addictive." These seven sins are all addictive in nature. As noted, these sins begin in the mind with addictive or obsessive thinking. Then, once acted out, they have a way of driving us to sin again and again and again; they are repetitive or compulsive behaviors. Addictive sins are, as we know from modern addiction recovery literature, quite capable of enslaving the human spirit and killing our psychological and spiritual freedom as children of God.

Because of what I have just described—that these sins are the worst, that they are addictive, that they are the root sins for so many other sins, and that they begin in the mind—some well-meaning people of faith over the centuries have thought it impossible to master these sins while living in this corrupt, tempting, and at times evil world. Thus was born one of the

Introduction

motives for the monastic movement and other set-apart Christian communities. By removing ourselves from the temptations of this world, we might be better able to avoid the snares of these seven sins by living a purer, more righteous life. For some people it may indeed be necessary to relocate, to remove oneself from a sinful world, but for most people, for most believers, we must somehow learn to "fight the good fight" and to "work out [our] salvation with fear and trembling" (Phil 2:12b NRSV) while living in the world instead of being removed from it. This fight is also what this book is about—equipping us to fight the good fight with sin and win.

Are these Seven Deadly Sins still around? You betcha! In fact, one could argue that they are doing quite well—actually flourishing in our increasingly post-Christian culture. Every year, the Seven Deadly Sins are still leading millions of souls, sometimes along with their families, to ruin. They are flourishing in part because Western culture has turned so blatantly amoral and sometimes outright evil. They are flourishing among Christians in part because Christians are so poorly armed with knowledge of these sins and of the spiritual disciplines that protect against them.

I suppose we modern Christians could challenge this list of seven sins. Are these seven still the most deadly, the most serious of sins? After all, there is a huge cultural gap between the medieval Christendom of Europe and the twenty-first-century Christianity of the United States. Perhaps as culture, history, and the human psyche have changed over the centuries, other sins have become more deadly, more tempting, and more destructive. Some people have argued that power needs to be included in a modern list of the Seven Deadly Sins. Others have suggested that deceit should make the top seven. Over the centuries, the list of the Seven Deadly Sins has actually varied some, reflecting different times and subcultures. So it would be perfectly appropriate to suggest a revised list for our times. What would you add? Keep that question in the back of your mind as you read this book; don't jump to a conclusion yet. Let's let these classic seven speak for themselves first.

In summary, in this book I invite you to look with me at the traditional Seven Deadly Sins through a new lens. Our effort will be to understand these sins in light of modern psychology and modern culture. Are these sins still deadly? And if so, in what ways are they deadly? How does the modern concept of addiction help us understand the dynamics of these sins? What precisely is the relationship between the Seven Deadly Sins and addiction? How can serious followers of Christ recognize these sins, avoid

Introduction

them, and protect their children from them? Finally, what are the corresponding virtues that we could develop in ourselves in order to prevent these deadly sins from taking away our freedom? Before we address each of the Seven Deadly Sins individually, I will update you, in chapter 1, on the nature of addiction as it is best understood today.

Reflection on these questions will be intriguing to Christian readers, since the concept of the Seven Deadly Sins is clearly a Christian tradition. Further, these issues will be of interest to Christians who want to be informed psychologically. Personally, my social location is as a European-American male from a largely progressive Protestant church tradition. More importantly, I approach this topic from the perspective of having been a practicing psychotherapist/pastoral counselor for the past forty years. Clearly, these issues may be approached from historical, theological, and anthropological perspectives. I welcome comments and feedback from people who approach this topic from perspectives other than my own.

This will be a difficult book to read without taking it very personally. Coming face to face with our sins (or addictions) is not a fun experience. Each of us has our struggles with sin and virtue. Each of us has our victories and our defeats in the realm of spiritual warfare. You may discover, too, like our ancestors did centuries earlier, that each of us has an Achilles heel— one or two sins to which we seem to be especially vulnerable, that seem to pester us year after year in our lives. If reading this becomes a difficult process for you on an emotional, spiritual, or personal level, please consult with your pastor or a pastoral counselor or spiritual director. These are not easy struggles. Above all else, surround your study with times of prayer. Sometimes the more we learn about sin, the more the Evil One turns up the heat on our souls. So bolster yourself with prayer and may the grace of our Lord Jesus Christ be with you!

R. Scott Sullender, PhD
San Anselmo, California

1 What Is Addiction?
An Overview

OVER THE PAST SEVENTY years or so, the number of people struggling with one or several kinds of addiction has exploded, especially in Western culture. One can certainly argue that addictions have been around since the dawn of humanity. Yet, the incidence and severity of addictions in recent decades are so high that in most professional circles addictions are considered to be the most significant mental health or behavioral problem in the United States, with the possible exception only of depression. In some ways, addiction has become the disease of our times. Every year millions upon millions of dollars are lost due to decreased productivity, medical costs, law enforcement expenses, and treatment programs related to addiction. Yet these costs pale in comparison to the human tragedy of lost lives, destroyed families, and abused and neglected children resulting from addiction. In my view, our children are the true and most tragic victims of this epidemic—the abused, neglected children, the mentally and developmentally disabled children, the emotionally deprived and abandoned children. In the face of these circumstances, our political, religious, and academic leadership seems to be helpless, clueless, and/or prone to simplistic answers that have failed to stem the growing tide of addictions. At another level, the very culture that decries drug abuse with one voice promotes it with another voice. The United States has embraced a culture that promotes addictive processes, in part because addiction feeds the economic system.

In the last twenty-five years, the problem of addictions has increased in both quantity and quality. The incidence and severity of addictions has increased and, at the same time, the variety and scope of addictions have also expanded. One hundred years ago, the primary addictive problem was alcohol abuse. Alcohol addiction received considerable national attention, as manifested in the temperance movement and the eventual enactment and repeal of the 18th Amendment to the U.S. Constitution. Addictions to substances other than alcohol were relatively unknown or were confined to a subculture or minority of the population. Today, substance abuse and drug addiction have become commonplace across the entire spectrum of society. As I already noted, alcoholism and drug addiction currently border on being the largest mental health or behavioral health problem in our nation. The only addiction that has substantially decreased in the last generation is nicotine addiction, largely due to investment of the medical community in the anti-smoking campaign and to a massive educational and media program.[1] It is an oddity of our times that one can watch an American television advertisement promoting beer drinking, only to be followed by an advertisement warning of the dangers of smoking cigarettes. On the one hand, we promote addiction; on the other hand, we discourage it.

Over the last seventy years or so, the definition of addiction has substantially broadened. In the middle decades of the twentieth century, we were primarily concerned with alcohol and drug addiction. Today, we include in our definition of addicts compulsive gamblers, compulsive shoppers, people with eating disorders, heavy smokers, sex addicts, and rage-aholics, to name just a few. Correspondingly, today we have addiction treatment programs for pathological gamblers and for people with anger problems and sex problems, along with the long-standing and widely increasing intervention programs for alcoholism and drug addiction. The biggest change in the last few decades has been in the recognition of the power of and problems associated with behavioral addictions, in contrast to the addictions that come from the ingestion of a substance. Today we incorporate behavioral addictions along with the traditional chemical addictions into a larger theoretical framework called addiction studies or addictive dynamics.

Addiction studies began with the study of just one type of addiction—alcoholism. Thus, what was learned about addiction was learned in the context of alcoholism. Soon, this knowledge was applied to the treatment of other addictions, first drug addiction and then various other kinds of substance abuse as well. As this happened, our collective eyes opened. We began to see more clearly that one can become addicted to a wide variety of

---

1. It should be noted that although cigarette usage has declined in the United States in recent decades, its use is growing around the world.

What Is Addiction?

chemicals. Suddenly, addiction problems showed up everywhere. Today we recognize addictions to nicotine, prescription medications like pain pills, illegal drugs like heroin or cocaine, and even commonly available substances like sugar. By the 1980s we came to see clearly that one can become "hooked" on an activity as well as a substance, and the concept of behavioral addictions was born. Behavioral addictions, which is the term I prefer, are also known as "activity addictions" or "process addictions," in contrast to chemical addictions or substance abuse. Today, compulsive gamblers, workaholics, sex addicts, rage-aholics, and even compulsive shoppers are recognized as having a type of behavioral addiction. Now we can see clearly that alcoholism is but one example of a broader problem: addiction. Some have even pushed the envelope further by suggesting that there are "positive" addictions, addictions that are socially recognized and supported, like addictions to exercise or even to religious activities. Clearly, addictive dynamics are nearly universal among humans, particularly among people influenced by Western culture. So, now clinicians wonder if the difference between psychologically well people and addicts is not that the latter are addicts and the former are not, but rather that some people just can't manage their addictions while others can. In the very broadest understanding of the term, no one is addiction-free.[2]

Since the definition of addiction problems has expanded so widely, the term "addiction" has lost some of its meaning. Drug addiction and compulsive shopping have many common dynamics, but clearly drug addiction is far more addictive and far more powerful than compulsive shopping, as destructive as the latter problem might be for some people. Thus, some scholars have argued for a more narrow use of the term addiction so that it refers only to those addictions that are primarily, but not exclusively, physiological in nature. Some refer to these classic addictions as "true addictions" because they build a physiological tolerance. The term "compulsive behaviors" has come to be employed to describe addictions that are

---

2. This line of thinking argues for an approach to addiction treatment called harm reduction. Since addictive dynamics cannot be entirely eliminated in humans, advocates of harm reduction argue that in many cases the best approach is to take measures to reduce the harm of addictions, like substituting a less destructive addiction for a more destructive addiction. In this book, I will be arguing for a spiritually based recovery approach to addiction that addresses the underlying dynamics that transcend all of the various kinds of addictions, although I see a place for harm reduction measures as a first step toward a fuller recovery.

primarily, but not exclusively, behavioral in nature (these are also called activity addictions or process addictions).

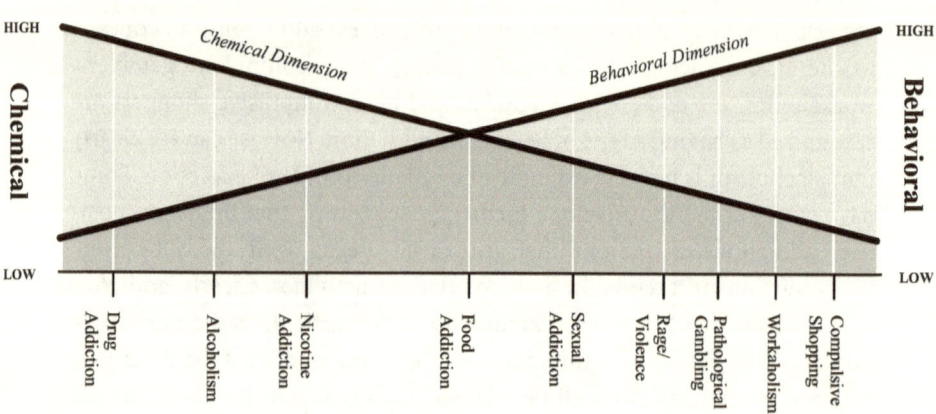

Figure 1
Chemical/Behavioral Components of Addiction

Addictions can be classified along a continuum (see Figure 1) based on the relative mixture of behavioral or chemical components. At one end of the spectrum there is drug addiction, which is probably 90 percent chemical and 10 percent behavioral. Probably the most physically addictive drug on the planet right now is methamphetamine. At the other end of the continuum there are addictions like compulsive shopping and workaholism, which are 90 percent behavioral and 10 percent chemical. Because addictions exist along a continuum, even the most physiological of the addictions have behavioral components, and even the most behavioral of the addictions are characterized by chemical changes in the brain. Addiction is always a whole-person disorder. Addictions always include physiological and behavioral elements, as well as mental, relational, and spiritual components.

Professionals who work with addicts of all kinds, as well as people who have personally struggled with addiction issues, often reach the same conclusion: the addiction dynamic transcends its substance/activity. They notice, for example, that most people these days are poly-addicted, using and abusing one or several types of substances and/or activities at the same time. Further, they note that addiction problems run in families. The grandfather was an alcoholic, but the son is a drug addict, while the grandson grows up to be an over-achieving workaholic. The drug of choice has changed over the years, but the addiction dynamic remains, passed from one generation to the next generation. Similarly, many recovering addicts go from drug to drug or activity to activity. For example, a recovering alcoholic has not drunk alcohol for years but smokes heavily and drinks coffee by the gallon. Another person stops smoking, only to gain weight. Another takes a forced vacation from their addiction to work and withdraws into depression. And still another person stops gambling, only to take up compulsive day trading on the stock market. The once over-eater becomes a compulsive jogger. Even the recovering alcoholic can become addicted to AA meetings! We have seen it all. Dr. Gerald May called this substituting of one addiction for another "reforming our behavior" instead of "transforming our desire."[3] The latter approach, in his view, involves addressing the real problem, the addictive process or the displaced desire. This realization, that the addictive dynamic transcends the drug of choice, raises certain questions: Is addiction a larger disease, a larger problem than the particular substance or activity employed? Or, to rephrase the question, what do all addictions have in common and in what ways is each addiction unique?

So, the relevant question in the literature on addiction studies is this: Is there such a thing as an addictive personality? In other words, are some people just vulnerable to addictions, regardless of the type of addiction? If we bring together people representing all of the various types of addictions and analyze their personality traits, would they be similar in certain ways? If so, did those similarities exist prior to the onset of the addictive behavior or were those dynamics created by the addiction itself? The term "dry drunk" speaks to this issue. Dry drunk refers to an alcoholic who has stopped drinking but still behaves like an alcoholic, still has an alcoholic personality. I tend to be of the opinion that there is such a thing as an addictive personality—that some people are by temperament, genes, or family upbringing more vulnerable than other people to addictions. Some people have, as the phrase goes, the psychological and physiological "soil of addiction."[4] We might say that the seeds of addictions grow easily in certain psychological soils. The particular kind of addiction depends on the availability or popularity of particular drugs or activities in one's social and cultural environment. Once an addiction-vulnerable person starts abusing

---

3. May, *Addiction and Grace*, 146.
4. See Clinebell, *Understanding and Counseling*, 65.

a substance or an activity, he or she gets hooked much more easily than most people and, correspondingly, has a much more difficult time getting clean and sober. Furthermore, once a person becomes hooked, the features of the addictive personality are intensified and reinforced by the addictive process itself.

This wider vision of what constitutes addiction has also enabled us to see that we have thought too narrowly about the "high" associated with the addiction. Highs can come in varied forms. We recognize the buzz people get when they drink. We see the intense highs that speed users get when they pop pills. But gamblers get a high, too. Sex addicts get highs. Even runners talk of the runner's high. Granted, some of these highs are more powerful than others and thus more addictive, but all involve the same or similar chemical changes in the brain. We now know that chemical changes in the brain, or mood changes, can be triggered by a variety of factors or processes. In 1985, two researchers in brain chemistry, Harvey Milkman and Stanley Sunderwirth, proposed three different types of highs—arousal highs, satiation highs, and fantasy highs.[5] An arousal high is associated with excitement, as in an adrenaline rush, and with activities such as gambling, engaging in sports, or using drugs such as methamphetamine. A satiation high gives a person the feeling of being full, relief from pain, and escape from stress. Many people feel contented and relaxed when they drink alcohol or smoke marijuana. The fantasy high, according to these authors, comes later, when people relive their addiction rituals in their minds. A typical example of a fantasy high would include a sexual fantasy or a triumph high. Personally, I think that fantasy highs are just a vicarious arousal high. A more legitimate third type of high, in my experience, is the trance high. Typically, a trance high is induced by a computer or television screen.[6] Prolonged viewing creates a mental condition we describe as being zoned out. This high functions like other highs, providing an escape from a reality that is otherwise painful or boring. (The rapidly growing problem of

---

5. See Milkman and Sunderwirth, *Craving for Ecstasy*, and also their more recent work, *Craving for Ecstasy and Natural Highs*.

6. The concept of a trance as a high helps support the idea of Internet addiction. The possible existence of an Internet addiction disorder has been widely talked about in the popular literature, but the American Psychiatric Association, author of the *Diagnostic and Statistical Manual of Mental Disorders*, has yet to recognize it as a psychological disorder. Interestingly, government officials and professionals in South Korea have recognized Internet addiction as a legitimate disorder and are alarmed by its growth among Korean youth.

cybersex is a unique mixture of both a trance high and an arousal high.) Trance highs are certainly habit-forming at the very least and can be addictive under some circumstances.

So our eyes have been opened. What began seventy years ago as a focus on the perils of alcoholism has evolved into a much wider, more diverse, and more serious study of addiction. This broader approach to the subject of addiction has led to research to identify the core elements of addiction. Are we dealing with one disease or many diseases? Why does addiction affect some people more than others or look different in different people or across the spectrum of addiction problems? Craig Nakken has suggested a helpful metaphor.[7] He has likened addiction to cancer. There are different forms of cancer, just like there are different types of addiction. Yet all of the various cancers have common dynamics, common stages, common traits, and maybe even a common origin. So, what are the common traits, common themes, and common dynamics shared by all addictions, across the board?

Common Features of Addiction

Mood Change

What do different addictive substances or activities have in common? The first answer is that they all have the ability to produce a positive and pleasurable mood change. Any substance or activity can become addictive if it creates a positive mood change in the individual. Substances or activities that do not cause mood changes are non-addictive. Thus, milk is not addictive, but wine is. Sexual encounters create a mood change. Heroin creates a mood change. Gambling creates a mood change. Even anger creates a mood change. All of these mood changes occur in the brain. Recent studies in brain functioning have described how the dynamics of addiction are sustained by brain chemistry. At the level of the brain, the dynamics of addiction are fairly similar from addiction to addiction. In fact, one could suggest that from the brain's point of view one addiction looks about the same as another, although addictive substances or activities do tend to focus on particular, corresponding neurotransmitters. Abnormal levels of dopamine, for example, can be caused by a variety of factors—an ingestion of a chemical or a highly intense activity or even a fantasized version of

---

7. Nakken, *The Addictive Personality*, 2.

the same activity or substance. Regardless of the type of high, the common result is that we feel better, at least momentarily.

All of which begs another question: What are we changing our mood from? Or, what are we trying to escape from? Perhaps we are seeking relief from boredom and/or depression. Depression, in fact, is related to addictions, and it is no accident that the depressive disorders, along with the addictive disorders, are the two most common psychological problems of our time. Perhaps, too, we might be uncertain of ourselves, insecure, lacking confidence. So a drink or a pill gives us confidence, maybe even a backbone. The confidence we receive may be an exaggerated confidence, a grandiosity, a feeling that we can do no wrong and that we are somebody now, not nobody. Under the spell of such false confidence, we can make foolish, impulsive decisions. Just ask any gamblers about their experience of being high off of a couple of wins.

All of us know what it is like to be stressed, nervous, worried, or in pain. The mood change or high we are trying to gain in this situation is relief, a feeling of calm, a sense of being satiated or full. This explains why some people smoke marijuana to mellow out. Others have an after-work drink to relax. Still others play computer games or watch television or overeat as a way of relaxing, of self-soothing, and of feeding the inner nervous child.

All mood changes occur in the brain. The chemistry of the brain is altered so that we have a sensation of being better or different. In this sense, substance abuse does not act much different than a prescribed mood-altering medication. This is why we sometimes refer to a drug abuser as self-medicating. The use or abuse of certain substances can be understood as an attempt to treat one's depression with an arousal high or one's anxiety with a satiation high. All of this brings us back again to the interrelationship between depression and substance abuse. Untreated depression is growing, especially among children and teenagers, and many clinicians see the growing incidence of substance abuse among teens as representing an attempt to self-medicate depression. The irony, of course, is that substance abuse, especially in the form of alcoholism, only makes the depression worse.

We become addicted to substances or activities that create a positive mood change of some kind or degree. That mood change is responding to an emotional need. We use the substance or activity as a way of escaping an unpleasant feeling, such as feelings of pain, low self-worth, boredom, rejection, failure, perfectionism, and hundreds of other feelings. Addictive

What Is Addiction?

behaviors can also be used to avoid or cope with certain painful relationships or social contexts. To one degree or another, a person who is seriously addicted is using that addiction to avoid facing some painful reality. As we say in the psychological business, the addict is "acting out" his or her feelings instead of "talking out" those same feelings. As members of AA often say, alcohol is the perceived solution to the problem, but over time alcohol *becomes* the problem. The abuse of a substance or a particular activity does not in the long run meet the individual's emotional needs.

Psychotherapy is great. It is a process that helps people become more aware of their emotional needs and find and implement ways of constructively addressing those emotional needs. I have noticed that my addicted clients have been almost universally out of touch with their emotional needs and have had poor verbal and coping skills when it comes to personal and interpersonal emotional dynamics. Psychotherapy can be an effective means of helping them deal more effectively and maturely with their emotional needs, but not if they are locked into avoiding their emotional pain through the abuse of alcohol or drugs or through escaping into a compulsive activity.

What is true in general about the interplay between emotions and addiction can also be true in particular emotional settings. Some people, for example, start abusing drugs right after a traumatic event in their lives as a means of anaesthetizing the horrific memories that they are experiencing. It is commonly reported that at least 50 percent of people diagnosed with PTSD have a dual diagnosis; that is, they are diagnosed with both PTSD and some type of alcohol or drug addiction.[8] Others abuse alcohol as a means of coping with a failing marriage or a frustrating job. Drug abuse and sexual addictions are prevalent among military personnel, obviously serving as a means of coping with or escaping the stresses of war. Other people cannot deal with the inner pain or guilt they have over the death of a loved one and fall into an addiction as a way of masking or avoiding their necessary grief work. Addictions can start when there are both unresolved feelings and a lack of tools for processing those feelings.

---

8. Weaver and Koenig, *Pastoral Care of Alcohol Abusers*, 23. The National Center for Posttraumatic Stress Disorder (PTSD) is an excellent source of information about returning veterans. In the Center's 2009 Report on Consensus Conference, the participants noted that 22 percent of patients diagnosed with PTSD also received a Substance Use Disorder (SUD) diagnosis at the same time; the life-time prevalence of PTSD and SUD is 50 percent (National Center for Posttraumatic Stress Disorder, "Report").

The well-known phrase "Addicts mistake intensity for intimacy" speaks to another dimension of emotional avoidance. The thing that many addicts are avoiding is interpersonal intimacy or emotional vulnerability. In this view, addiction is really a type of over-attachment or misplaced attention and as such is actually a displacement of the normal desire for human attachment, i.e., genuine intimacy. Nowhere is this perspective truer than among sex addicts or romance addicts, who clearly use their addiction to actually avoid genuine intimacy even though the object of their addiction appears to be a loving human relationship. As their disease grows, the tendency of addicts to socially isolate themselves and further avoid emotional intimacy becomes more pronounced. In a sense, the addiction becomes a substitute for emotional intimacy.

If all addictions begin with a substance or activity that causes mood change, then one of the implications for recovery is that we all need to find and nourish the natural highs of life wherever we may find them—highs that are not addictive, but life-giving.

Habits Lead to Tolerance

We humans are really good at forming habits; we are habit-forming creatures. So the second step in the formation of addiction is habit formation, which we do naturally and automatically. It begins rather simply; if something feels good, we do it again. Over time, habits grow stronger the more often they are performed. Every time we reach for a particular substance or engage in a particular activity, the pattern is reinforced and strengthened. As this happens, the neuro-pathways are thickened and deepened with each subsequent repetition. Habits are low-grade addictions or, as the saying goes, "An addiction is a habit on steroids" (an interesting phrase). The language of habits provides some useful labels for understanding addictions. In dealing with nicotine addiction, for example, we still refer to the process of cessation as "kicking the smoking habit." Or, a drug addict may say that he needs to "feed his habit"!

Each repetition of a particular habit involves a repetitive mood change. Gradually, over time, we build tolerance. Tolerance occurs chemically as the brain becomes increasingly dependent on something external and artificial to change its mood. Over time, our brains manufacture less and less natural neurotransmitters. To the brain's way of thinking, we do not need as many neurotransmitters because we are getting more than we need

What Is Addiction?

through artificial means. A vacuum of neurotransmitters is thus created, a vacuum that is experienced by the individual as a craving, particularly when the artificially provided high wears off. Because the brain makes less of the natural neurotransmitters over time, it requires more of the artificial chemicals or stimulants to maintain the same level of mood alteration that was previously enjoyed. This is the mechanism of tolerance.

The result of tolerance is that it takes an increased amount of the addictive substance to generate the same mood change that was previously created by lower amounts of the substance. Whereas we once got a good buzz from just one drink, it now takes three of the same drinks to give us the same sensation. Whereas it once helped us to smoke one joint, now we need heroin to produce the same mood change. Whereas we once got excited by viewing pornography, it now takes a risky real sexual encounter to give us the same excitement. This is the beginning of the addictive process, when we pass from habit to addiction. Because of this, over time the process is inevitably progressive.

Addictions are progressive. After a while, one drink is not enough, one cigarette is not enough, a daily fix is not enough, and gambling once a month is not enough. Addicts often swear that they can control their behavior and keep it from getting any worse. They swear that they can limit their shopping. They say they are able to drink socially only. They know when to quit at the roulette table. They can cut down on the cigarettes. After all, they are not harming anyone. They say to themselves, "I will never become an addict."

I do believe that some people can in fact manage their addictive behaviors reasonably well, at least for a time. In the world of alcoholism, these people are called problem drinkers or alcohol-dependent people, not true alcoholics (yet). But, the boundary between the problem drinker and the alcoholic is thin. The path between the problem drinker and the alcoholic is a slippery slope because alcohol abuse, in fact all addictive disorders, tends to be progressive in nature. This is so because of tolerance. For most people it is just a matter of time.

Largely because of this progressive dynamic, which is particularly obvious in drug and alcohol addictions, clinicians and scholars alike have come to understand addiction as a disease. Addiction seems to progress naturally, often running through some fairly predictable stages, much like any physiological disease might. Addiction is described as a psycho-physical-social-spiritual disease. Surely it is more psycho-social in nature than most diseases, but nevertheless it is a still disease. Understanding addiction as a disease has benefits and drawbacks. Among the benefits, the disease model has allowed the treatment of addictions to be covered by various health insurance programs. Now many of the finest drug and alcohol treatment programs are located in medical facilities, and the disease of alcoholism or chemical addiction is handled financially and treated medically in much the same ways as any other disease. The liability of the disease model of addiction is that it de-emphasizes personal responsibility and the moral dimensions of the problem. I will speak more of this issue in later chapters.

As noted above, tolerance has generally been understood largely in terms of the mechanisms of brain functioning in relation to substance abuse, but in recent years some writers have suggested that the dynamic of tolerance can be seen in behavioral addictions as well as substance addictions. For example, consider the thrill that most people get from gambling. There is evidence now to suggest that intense gambling alters the mood-generating chemistry of the brain in a manner similar to a chemical upper, although the research is complex.[9] The highs come both in the occasional winning and in the adrenaline associated with the intensity of the game. It appears that some compulsive gamblers build a tolerance to the activity—in other words, over time they want a bigger thrill that can only come from a bigger risk. They raise the stakes, change the game, and/or gamble more often. In short, over time they take bigger risks in order to get the same high that they used to get at lower levels of risk. Gambling normally does not involve any direct ingestion of substances, and yet applying the dynamics of tolerance to gambling may offer insights similar to those related to tolerance to alcoholism or drug dependency.

The reverse side of tolerance is withdrawal; in other words, withdrawal is a sure sign that tolerance has occurred. Withdrawal refers to a collection of symptoms or problems that occur when a serious addict abstains for an extended period of time. The body/brain reacts, sending alarm signals that it is under stress. The cravings initially become more intense. Withdrawal symptoms are most pronounced among drug addicts and alcoholics, resulting in the necessity for some to receive medical care as the first step in their recovery process. Normally, withdrawal symptoms dissipate over time as the body/brain returns to more normal functioning. If the individual has been severely addicted for a long period of time, however, the damage to the brain's chemistry may be permanent and/or may result in a slower return to normalcy. In severe cases, prescribed medications can be used

---

9. Petry, *Pathological Gambling*, 117–34.

to substitute for the brain's damaged functioning.[10] Withdrawal indicates the presence of tolerance. As with tolerance, the concept of withdrawal can be applied in illuminating ways to the behavioral addictions, although admittedly the symptoms are more psychosocial than physiological in the behavioral addictions.

As I have said, we humans are habit-forming creatures. Habits can serve us well, of course, if our habits are healthy habits. Habits help us to avoid having to re-invent the wheel every time we have a problem. We just go to what worked before . . . without thinking. That is the key: without thinking. Habits must be re-evaluated and reassessed periodically to determine if they are healthy and life-affirming.

Obsessive Thinking

As we experience greater and greater levels of craving, our minds go into crisis mode, devoting more and more mental energy to finding, securing, and sustaining our next fix, whatever it may be. This mental component is described by psychologists as obsessive thinking.[11] Obsessive thinking simply means that we think about something over and over again. We cannot take our minds off the topic. Even when we try to get our minds onto something else, thoughts pertaining to our craving—savoring past episodes and strategizing how to get the next fix—return again and again. We are haunted and tortured by what an alcoholic friend of mine calls his "demons." The stronger the addiction, the stronger the obsessive thinking.

The typical addictive episode begins in the mind. One thinks about the substance or the activity, dwells on it, and relishes it, gradually building up mental steam until the restraints are loosened and one acts out again. The addictive cycle typically moves from the inside out. The addictive behavior—the sex act, the drinking binge, the gambling episode—is only the climactic stage of a larger cycle that begins in the mind. The behaviors are anticipated before they are enacted. In this sense, addictive episodes follow the typical obsessive-compulsive pattern, and this is why some scholars describe addiction as a variation of an obsessive-compulsive disorder.

---

10. Methadone, prescribed as a substitute for heroin, is one example of this approach. A nicotine patch is a less-invasive example of the same principle.

11. Everyday examples of an obsession include being unable to get an annoying jingle out of our minds or reviewing a perceived embarrassment over and over again in our minds. One of the defining characteristics of an obsession is that the obsession is involuntary, against our will or desire.

Ancient Sins... Modern Addictions

As the disease of addiction moves through its progressive stages, our mental energy and attention become increasingly diverted away from normal relationships and activities. We become more preoccupied, more mentally consumed with our addiction. Drug addicts are thinking about where they will get their next fix. Sex addicts are anticipating their next rendezvous. Workaholics are thinking about work, even when on vacation or relaxing at home. Loved ones become concerned as their addicted family members distance themselves, gradually isolating themselves more and more. Ashamed of our behavior, we begin to live a secret life. We hide our addictive behaviors and also try to hide how much we are thinking about our addiction even when we are not acting out.

Family members and friends become confused. They conclude that we—their family member or friend—do not love them any more or that we are in love with someone else. In a sense, we *are* in love with someone or something else. The addiction is all we think about, which is a lot like falling in love. Over time, we start to ignore our normal activities, eventually even our own self-care needs. As the addiction grows, the disease occupies more and more space in our minds, crowding out all other normal thoughts.

In my view, the mental aspects of addiction are the heart of the problem. It is the mind's obsessions that give addiction its fuel and that over time compound its intensity and severity. Thus, to be successful a recovery program must get at the mental processes; the program must be able to divert, calm down, or defuse the over-active mind that is at the heart of addiction. This is why meditation or a prayer practice is often a valuable component of recovery.

As the addiction disease process advances, not only does the addict's mind start to dwell on the addiction more and more, but the content of his or her thoughts starts to change, to become distorted. When we are addicted to a substance or behavior, our mental processes are more intense and also more distorted, more disconnected from reality. This occurs because our mind has become overly dependent on the addictive substance or activity. Our mind or psyche has started to feel at an existential level that this is a life-and-death issue. In the face of such urgency, our mind starts to distort reality in order to maintain the addiction or the illusion of freedom in the face of the addiction... and yet we do not recognize this distortion in ourselves. This is called denial.

Denial is the most dramatic and destructive of the defense mechanisms associated with addiction. It is always amazing to outsiders, to non-addicts, that addicts come up with more excuses, denials, justifications, and rationalizations than anyone else they know. Denial takes many forms and can function to varying degrees. Some denial is absolute, as in "I am not alcoholic." Some denial is more subtle, more illusory; we hold on to the illusion that we can stop, that we still have control and willpower. Sometimes the denial takes the form of pretending that there are no risks, no harmful effects to ourselves or our loved ones. The mind under the control of an addiction can rationalize away nearly any immoral or manipulative or destructive behavior in order to maintain the addiction.

Over time, loved ones experience the increasingly addicted individual as "no longer themselves." They are "not in their mind." It is as if something else, someone else has taken over their personality. Non-addicts are bewildered by the choices of their addicted family member. Morals, values, and ethical principles that normally defined this person are gradually undermined by the addict's distorted thinking process. When addicted persons choose lies over the truth, or steal to get money to support their habit, or spend the family's paycheck, their loved ones are baffled. How can he or she do this? This is not the father or wife or child we thought we knew! Indeed, it is often as if the addict has become someone else, or as if something demonic has taken over their mind. They are out of their ever-lovin' minds! And yet they are the last ones to know this because of the strength of their denial.

If addictions begin in the mind, then the capture of the mind by the addiction is the final and ultimate prize. The battle for recovery is fought out in the mind of the addicted person.

Loss of Control and of Willpower

The most obvious and easily observable trait of an addiction is repetitive or compulsive behavior. An addict repeats certain behaviors over and over again. The more frequent the behavior, the stronger the addiction. In the case of drug addiction, the repeated behavior is using the drug. In the case of an eating disorder, it may be binge eating. In the case of gambling, it is betting or playing the game. In the case of sex addiction, it is viewing or securing sexual tricks. The behavior is repetitive, compelling, and normally harmful. This is why the adjective "driven" is often used to describe addicted persons, as in "driven to drink" or "driven at work." This repetitive nature of addictions is often illustrated in the form of an addictive cycle or addiction wheel (see Figure 2).

Figure 2
The Addictive Cycle

As the addiction wheel illustrates, there are identifiable stages in the cycle: mental preoccupation, ritualized behaviors, consumption or behavioral addiction, and regret and despair. Each stage leads to the next, and the last stage only sets up the next cycle. With each repetition of the cycle, the addiction grows in strength and the individual loses more and more control or choice in the matter. However, the cycle can be interrupted at one of several stages.

Compulsive behaviors like those illustrated in the addiction cycle are habits gone bad—or perhaps it's more accurate to say habits gone *mad*. We all live with habits and use habits to our advantage to keep us on track, as in the case of healthy habits. Habits can be defined as behavioral patterns that we can choose to alter, to change, to modify if we need to. Compulsive behaviors are unchangeable, much more resistant to even slight modifications. We are compelled to perform the behavior, to behave the same way again and again. We lose freedom—the freedom to choose. The compulsive nature of these repetitive behaviors, even in the face of their destructive results, makes addiction dangerous and gives addiction the power to enslave.

As the behaviors become more compulsive, more driven, and more demanding, we increasingly lose willpower. We increasingly lose the ability to choose and thus alter or control our behaviors. If we are in the grip of an addiction, we deceive ourselves into thinking that we do still have willpower or self-control; this is part of the distorted thinking resulting from the addicted mind, but, in reality, we have less and less willpower as the disease advances. At this point, the imagery of bondage becomes an apt metaphor for the experience of being addicted. We feel like we are enslaved by some power outside of ourselves, some evil power that has possessed our mind and is wrapping us in chains. It is an experience of the loss of freedom. We have become the puppet and the addiction has become the puppet master, controlling our every move.

Sometimes the repetitive behaviors may not be displayed regularly but may instead occur episodically. Once the ritual starts again, however, the truly addicted person cannot stop. This is one of the most common definitions of addiction—that an addict does not know when or how to stop. Once true alcoholics take that first drink, for example, they are out of control. They may not have consumed alcohol in twenty years, but once they start again, they cannot stop. They have lost control. They must have another and another. So the advice often given to diagnosed alcoholics is, "Don't take that first drink." Conversely, if we can stop—stop after just one drink or after just one smoke or after our allotted money is gone or after one serving of dessert—that is a fairly good sign that we are not yet addicted. If we still have some choice, some ability to stop, then we are not (not yet, anyhow) enslaved.

So, one of the chief features of an addiction is the increasing lack of control we have over our own behavior. As the disease progresses, we lose willpower and the ability to choose, to change and/or to control our lives. One of the paradoxes of addiction is that when hooked we claim over and over again to have control of our lives, but clearly we are out of control. The addiction controls us, controls our every thought, behavior, and intention. Another paradox of addiction, or more precisely of the recovery process, is that we only regain control over our life by giving up control, by admitting complete and absolute surrender, as in the first step of the Twelve-Step Program.

Ancient Sins... Modern Addictions

It is generally agreed that all addicts by definition have poor impulse control. Addicted persons are typically poor at delayed gratification. They want what they want and they want it now. They need, want, and demand instant gratification. They want their drink or their pill or their reward... now. They have a low tolerance for frustration and anxiety.

Poor impulse control, the urge to fulfill our needs immediately, increases the sense that our behavior is out of control. Poor impulse control speeds up the uncontrollable aspects of addictive behaviors. Addicted persons just react. They act in the moment, driven by the demands of the present. They have a hard time anticipating the future consequences of their choices. This inability to think through the consequences of their behavior often leads to increasingly negative or destructive consequences of the addiction. By jumping in without thinking through the consequences, addicts get themselves into further trouble.

It is hard to know whether people who are prone to addictions had a low tolerance of frustration before they become addicted, thus making them vulnerable to the lure of an addiction, or whether the addiction process itself creates within the individual a greater and greater sense of urgency. Probably both statements are partly true. Teenagers typically have a harder time with impulse control compared to their adult counterparts. The tendencies among teens to act without thinking through the long-term consequences of their behavior makes adolescence the stage of life in which all kinds of addictions typically start. Much research has documented that the addictive process often begins in adolescence. Research also suggests that there is a great deal of overlap between impulse control problems and addictive disorders. More specifically, people with attention deficit problems are often at risk for developing various drug addictions. Children who have been diagnosed as ADD or ADHD have a much higher risk for the development of addiction problems as teens or adults than those without such a diagnosis, in part because the ADD condition is itself characterized by poor impulse control.[12]

Clearly, as an addiction progresses in intensity and severity, we become poorer and poorer at self-control of any kind, at what might simply be called patience. Addicts of whatever kind or variety often are impatient

---

12. This finding was confirmed recently in a study led by Timothy Wilens, MD, at Massachusetts General Hospital that followed 268 eleven-year-old children who had been diagnosed with ADHD. After ten years, "the children with ADHD had one-and-a-half times greater risk of developing substance abuse than the control group" (Petrochko, "ADHD Increases Risk").

people, and one of the warning signs of becoming addicted is not just the amount of the substance we may consume or the activity we engage in, but the impatience that characterizes the process. Food addicts eat fast. Nicotine addicts smoke rapidly. Alcoholics drink in a hurry. Workaholics are always in a hurry. Even gamblers gamble fast. It might be said that addicts do it faster and enjoy it less. As the disease progresses, there is both an increase in the quantity of the addiction and a decrease in the enjoyment of the substance or behavior.

Self-Destructive Behaviors

With increased lack of control, with increased impatience, with increased distorted thinking, and with an increased sense of urgency, the addictive process inevitably becomes more self-destructive. The fifth and final characteristic of an addiction, any kind of addiction, is self-destructive behaviors. Addicted persons know, at least at some level, that continuing to use, continuing to drink, continuing to play, or continuing to indulge is dangerous, even destructive, and yet they do it anyway. It is this self-destructive piece that is one of the hallmarks of addiction. It isn't just the inability to stop oneself; it is the compulsion to go ahead with the same behavior knowing full well how destructive it is to oneself and one's family.

The addict is the fellow who still smokes after the heart surgeon tells him it will kill him. The addict is the woman who still drinks after getting her third DUI. The addict is the father who continues to use speed even after his children have been removed from his custody by child protection officers. The addict is the clergyman who continues to act out sexually, even though he knows that it will cost him his ministry. Addicts are self-destructive. That is part of the definition of addiction. Addictions kill; it is death by suicide.

So, the last key element in any definition or understanding of addiction is this self-destruction dynamic. Surely, some behaviors can be addiction-like but not actually self-destructive. Some professional athletes are driven to succeed, consumed mentally by their sport, get a high from the competition, and, in a sense, are out of control, but addiction is not usually employed to describe such people. Other people can be devoted to a mission, even a religious mission, and are consumed with it mentally, driven in their behaviors, and even aware of the spiritual high they receive from this sense of purpose, but again we usually do not include them in the category of those who are enslaved to an addiction. We often admire such people. So, one of the essential aspects of the definition of addiction is that the dynamic is self-destructive. The addictive behavior is placing at risk one's own life or health or is placing at risk the life or well-being of others. The behavior is placing a job at risk or a marriage at risk. The behavior might be placing the addict at risk of criminal or ethical charges. Yet, in spite of all of these risks, the addicted person continues to behave in the same way. Addictions lead to death in one form or another.

Summary

In this opening chapter I have tried to provide a fairly concise summary of the current thinking about addictions, including their nature, variety, and treatment. Addictions have grown dramatically in the United States in the last seventy years, both in the number of people suffering from addictions, the severity of the addictions, and the variety of addictions. One of the most significant developments has been the identification of compulsive behaviors as a type of addiction, despite the fact that behavioral addicts do not ingest any physical substance. I have identified five essential characteristics of addiction: mood change, tolerance, obsessive thinking, loss of control and of willpower, and self-destructive behaviors. These features are present across all forms of addiction. All five of these features need to be present in order to earn the label "addiction."

I should note that most people who are not addicted to a substance or behavior have addictive traits in the form of one or several, but not all, of these criteria. In this sense, most of us struggle with addictive processes, even though our problems may not rise to the level of an identified addiction. Many of us are problem drinkers but not alcoholics. Many of us are pre-diabetic but not yet food addicts. In my view, then, the problem of addiction is far wider and more universal than we might suppose if we focus just on those who are severely addicted. It is a matter of degree, not type. Most of us struggle to manage our addictive dynamics and teeter on the edge of the abyss.

So, armed with this understanding of the dynamics of addiction, let's take a look in the next chapters at each of the Seven Deadly Sins. In what ways are these sins addictive? Do they meet the criteria for addiction?

QUESTIONS FOR SELF-REFLECTION

Through the questions in this concluding section, as in subsequent chapters, I invite you to reflect personally upon the material in each chapter. Do your own self-assessment.

1. What is my addiction of choice? Be honest. Everyone has addictions, large or small. Some we manage and some manage us.
2. What do I do or ingest to improve or change my mood on a regular basis?
3. List five of my most life-giving habits and five of my less desirable or unhealthy habits.
4. What do I find myself thinking about more than anything else, and for how much time, over the course of a day?
5. What destructive things do I feel compelled to do over and over again?
6. Do addictive dynamics run in my family?

2 Pride

Self-Absorption and Self-Deception

Rosalie: Why can't you say you're sorry? Is that so hard to do?
    [Dan does not respond.]

Rosalie: You really blew it. You promised the kids to be home to take them to the ball game and you weren't, and then when you did come home, you were cursing at me.

Dan: Fathers do not apologize to children. They should apologize to me.

Rosalie: For what?

Dan: For aggravating the hell out of me. If it wasn't for those damn teenagers, I wouldn't drink so much. I would not have to drink so much.

Rosalie: Well, then apologize to me. I am your wife.
    [Dan sits in silence.]

Rosalie: Is it such a hard thing to do . . . just say you're sorry?

YES, FOR DAN WILSON saying he's sorry *is* a hard thing to do. It is darn near impossible for him to admit he made a mistake, to acknowledge his faults, to recognize that he needs help. Dan Wilson is suffering from and with the sin of pride in the form of arrogance, defensiveness, and denial. His pride is fueling his growing alcoholism. It is a deadly sin. If it continues, it will result in the death of his family.

Nothing marks how much the Western world has changed in the last thousand years than the shift in the connotations that are attached to the word "pride." In the Christian world of the Middle Ages, pride was a four-letter world! Pride was considered to be the chief sin of the Seven Deadly Sins. The worst insult you could hurl at another was that he or she was prideful. This was thought to be a sin that demanded confession and pardon. In today's secular, post-Christian culture, the word "pride" is used mostly with positive connotations in phrases such as, "Take pride in yourself!" "Black pride," "gay pride," "I am proud to be an American," and "Take pride in your appearance." When a child graduates, we say, "I am so proud of you." When a co-worker gets a new position, we say, "You should be proud of yourself—you deserve the promotion."

There is widespread confusion in Western popular culture about pride. Part of us still associates pride with being conceited, selfish, or arrogant. Another part of us associates pride with honor, self-respect, and accomplishment. This confusion has arisen in part because of the unfortunate association of pride with self-esteem. We have come to think of pride as high self-worth and of humility, the traditional Christian virtue that mitigates pride, as low self-worth. We Americans live in a culture that emphasizes self-expression, self-glorification, self-assertion, and self-promotion. Such values stand in sharp contrast to the traditional meaning of humility as a characteristic of the self-effacing, modest, and submissive person. Today, humility and its synonyms meekness and timidity have become the new four-letter words. In today's Western cultural context, pride has become a good thing and humility a bad thing—just the opposite of traditional Christian teachings. There is certainly some scriptural evidence to support placing the dynamic of pride/humility into the context of self-esteem but, as I will suggest, the true meaning of pride in the Christian spiritual tradition is something far more important and complex than healthy self-esteem.

Pride as Narcissism

It is interesting to note that the concept of self-esteem does not appear anywhere in the Bible. In fact, it is a modern invention of our psychological age. Certainly, one could argue that the concept is implicit in scripture, as when Jesus says "Love your neighbor as yourself" (Luke 10:27) or when St. Paul says, "I can do all things in Christ who strengthens me" (Phil 4:13). Yet, for the most part, the biblical writers are not concerned with self-esteem as a psychological construct. The biblical perspective, as is true in most non-Westernized cultures today, is that self-esteem or self-worth, to the extent that it is acknowledged at all, is understood in a relational or systemic context as a function of right relationships with one's community and with God.

"Self-esteem" is a modern, individualistic term that is familiar in the popular culture of the West. Everyone in the United States wants to have good self-esteem. We have become consumed with self-esteem, taking our internal esteem temperature almost daily. We want our children to have good self-esteem. We tend to think of positive self-esteem as our birthright or as a panacea for what ails us. We tend to see low self-esteem as the root of all evil. We blame poor self-esteem for everything from addictions to business failures. One of the ironies of today's over-emphasis on self-esteem is that it is driven in large measure by an inner anxiety that actually reveals how little true self-esteem we really have. For example, some parents are so nervous about supporting their child's "fragile" self-esteem that their very anxiety communicates to their child how fragile the parent believes their child's self-esteem to be. Or, consider the man who acts boastfully in public settings, trying to appear important; by doing so he actually displays the opposite—how little self-esteem he really does have. In such circumstances, we might use the phrase "false pride" to describe these self-promoters. These examples illustrate my point, which is that because Western culture places such a strong emphasis upon self-esteem, it is easy to confuse self-esteem and pride.

Even though Westernized cultures have replaced the concept of pride with that of self-esteem and are thus confused about the difference between pride and self-esteem, it is interesting to note how often young Americans still refer to the dynamics of the sin of pride, often without using the term at all. Adolescents might say, for example, "She is on an ego trip," "He acts like he is better than everyone else," or "He is always tooting his own horn." Most of us dislike people who are conceited and self-absorbed. Similarly, we dislike heroes who take all of the credit. On the playing field, we are disgusted by the athlete who does not give his or her teammates any credit. We dislike people who think they are better than others, who are not team players. Is not our dislike of such people illustrative of our instinctive dislike of pride, of what I call the sin of pride?

The relationship between self-esteem and pride might best be understood as on a continuum, running from no self-worth to healthy self-esteem to inflated self-esteem or pride. Both ends of the continuum can be equally problematic. People with little or no self-esteem are self-devaluing and sometimes self-destructive. Conversely, people with over-inflated self-esteem can be conceited, defensive, and very hard to live with. Too much self-esteem can be as dysfunctional as too little self-esteem. What most of us want or should want is healthy self-esteem.[1]

It is difficult for many people to know where the boundaries are between low self-worth, healthy self-esteem, and too much self-esteem. Many times, these boundaries are determined by cultural and religious norms.

The normal, healthy valuing of one's self is not a sin. Sin lies in the distortion of this normal human need in either direction—as too little self-esteem or too much self-esteem. Perhaps another way to talk about the distinction between pride and self-esteem, then, is to introduce the concept of honesty or truth. A healthy self-esteem is rooted in an honest self-appraisal. In contrast, pride as an over-inflation of one's importance is rooted in dishonesty. In this sense, the sin of pride is inherently dishonest—no one is really that wonderful all the time. This is a denial of our human condition. The same argument can also be made from the other end of the continuum; extremely low self-esteem is also essentially dishonest because no one is that bad all the time. Low self-esteem is also a violation of our essential worth, both as naturally bestowed upon us in creation and as confirmed to us in divine revelation. In light of modern psychology, the sins of self-esteem are two-fold, a dishonesty in both directions: the sin of pride and the sin of low self-worth. If we use honesty as the measure of self-appraisal, one could be genuinely great or genuinely not so great. The sin lies in the inaccurate self-estimate. Indeed, the sin of pride, understood as an over-inflated view of oneself, does have this element of dishonesty or untruth. By definition, pride is essentially deceptive.

If too much self-esteem and too little self-esteem are both sins, how do we understand healthy self-esteem, especially from an informed theological perspective? For Christians, I would suggest that a healthy self-esteem lies in the biblical model of balance: love for God, love for others, and love for self. Jesus commands his disciples to love God and "to love others as yourself." There is an implicit assumption of self-love, not more than is appropriate but in balance with loving God and loving one's neighbors. The triangle of love—love of God, love of neighbor, and love of self—suggests a balance wherein each point of the triangle is both necessary and reinforcing of the two other points. The triangle is only as strong as its weakest link!

---

1. A Buddhist colleague of mine notes that Buddhist teachings focus a lot on pride. He says that one aspect of pride is being overly self-critical and the other aspect of pride is being overly boastful. Both are signs of pride.

Ancient Sins . . . Modern Addictions

The love of God helps keep our love of self in check. The love of neighbor reminds us that we are always in community, never in isolation. And the love of self helps us avoid co-dependency and fanaticism. The key is balance. A healthy self-esteem is not found in isolation, as our individualist Western culture often implies, but in balance with and ultimately reinforced and strengthened by our love of God and neighbor. This view of what constitutes a healthy self-esteem takes into account both the sin of too much self-esteem and the sin of too little self-esteem. Although the sin of pride is generally associated with too much self-esteem, addiction is rooted in and sustained by errors in both directions.

Narcissistic Personalities

During family negotiations, my adult children frequently tease me with the refrain that they heard as children, ". . . 'cause we are special." Indeed, my wife and I are guilty of trying too hard to infuse our children with positive self-esteem. We overemphasized their specialness. Now, as adults, we can laughingly put it in perspective. Yet, our misplaced efforts speak to a larger issue. Western culture has increasingly emphasized the values of self-expression, self-indulgence, and self-importance. These values are communicated through the mass media, largely as a means of selling a service or a product. Many a commercial ends with the slogan "because you deserve it." The work of Jean Twenge of San Diego State University, who administered the Narcissistic Personality Inventory to young people in 1982 and again in 2006, suggests that the younger generations are become more self-absorbed, if not outright narcissistic.[2] Yet, young people are but the canary in the coal mine for the larger culture.

It is interesting to note, too, that in this cultural atmosphere of specialness we have seen the rise of a new kind of psychiatric disorder, a mental illness, if you will, called narcissistic personality disorder (NPD). Narcissistic personality disorder was officially recognized and defined by the American Psychiatric Association in the most recent edition of the *Diagnostic and Statistical Manual of Mental Disorders, Fourth Edition* (DSM-IV), which was formulated in the early 1990s.[3] People with NPD have grandiose

---

2. Twenge, *Generation Me*, 69.
3. American Psychiatric Association, DSM-IV-TR. The lifetime prevalence of NPD is estimated at 1 percent of the population, but Jean M. Twenge and W. Keith Campbell suggest that the incidence of NPD has more than doubled in the United States in the first

self-images. They think that they are very important and are often the center of attention. They believe they can do no wrong or that they do not need the advice or comfort of others, and they frequently react defensively to any criticism or challenge to their infallibility. They are blind to their own shortcomings and faults. In short, they suffer from too much self-esteem.[4] Their patron saint is the Greek mythological figure Narcissus, who was in love with himself. He was consumed by vanity, another old-fashioned but still apt word.

Two observations are important here. First, as Western culture moves us all further along in the direction of self-indulgence, self-branding, and self-gratification, it is inevitable that a greater portion of us will become dysfunctional on this issue because of our upbringing, the influence of our careers (particularly careers that encourage self-expression), or just because of our good (or bad) fortune. Such people often are in the spotlight and draw attention to themselves; unfortunately, they are often in positions of power and influence. They can thus cause havoc and harm out of proportion to their numbers. Mental health professionals typically refer to NPD as ego-syntonic, meaning that individuals with this disorder do not see any problem in themselves or with their behavior. They think of themselves as perfectly normal or, shall we say, perfectly entitled. The negative impact of this disorder is on others, those who must live with or work with narcissists. In short, people with a narcissistic personality disorder are a problem to others, but not to themselves.

Famous people, actors, politicians, and sports figures tend to be narcissistic personalities, more so than the general population.[5] When such people are caught in addictions—and addictions and narcissism tend to go hand in hand—their true character is revealed. From time to time, famous people appear in the news for their sex addictions or problems with greed (which can be a type of addiction) and/or their drug addictions. Often, their public statements only reveal how self-absorbed, shallow, and insensitive they really are, thus shattering our idealized image of them. They often appear quite full of themselves, sure that the rules do not apply to them,

---

decade of the twenty-first century (*Narcissism Epidemic*, 2).

4. Even though narcissistic personality disorder was not recognized until the 1990s, the awareness of this cultural problem dates back to Christopher Lasch's *The Culture of Narcissism*, first published in 1979.

5. People who are narcissistic tend to be attracted to vocations that meet their narcissistic needs, and, in turn, those particular careers tend to shape and reinforce narcissistic traits even in "ordinary" people.

and insensitive to those whom they have disappointed or harmed. Most of the time, their addiction or moral failure is only the outward manifestation of sin. The underlying problem is the narcissistic personality, or what I call the sin of pride.

Second, our instinctual dislike of narcissists and, in fact, our decision as a culture to label such people as mentally disturbed (as having narcissistic personality disorder) only illustrates my contention that the sin of pride is still alive and well. The sin of pride is not just defined by culture and thus changeable from generation to generation, but it also is reflective of a deeper, universal human value. Narcissism is precisely what our spiritual ancestors meant by the sin of pride: too much self-esteem, self-esteem that is not only too strong, but is based on dishonesty. Narcissism is false self-esteem.

Addictions and Self-Absorption

The interface of self-esteem issues and the dynamics of addiction is complex. Most alcoholics and drug addicts are characterized by what appears to be low self-esteem. People in twelve-step recovery programs frequently cite self-criticism as one of their chief faults that needs to be addressed. It is a truism among addiction treatment professionals that alcoholics drink in order to avoid feelings associated with criticism—criticism by themselves and by others. However, it is not clear whether addicted persons have low self-esteem issues before they become addicted or whether their low self-esteem is a product of their addiction. Is the issue really self-esteem, or is it self-absorption?

Joseph W. Ciarrocchi, in *Addiction and Spirituality*, argues that pathological gamblers have as many problems with egotism as they do with low self-esteem.[6] Egotism, which encourages an over-confidence in oneself, leads the compulsive gambler to misjudge the inherent risks in gambling. Egotism is the psychological dynamic that creates and sustains the gambler in his or her addiction. Indeed, even at a typical Alcoholics Anonymous (AA) meeting, where alcoholics complain about their low self-esteem, it is interesting to observe that in the very act of repeatedly complaining about their low self-esteem, they are demonstrating a high degree of self-absorption that is characteristic of too much self-esteem, or what I call the sin of pride. While it appears that low self-esteem is one of the typical

---

6. Ciarrocchi, "Spirituality for High and Low Rollers," 173–92.

psychological factors in addiction, if we look a bit closer we see that addicted persons have as much trouble with too much self-esteem, egotism, or narcissism as they do with too little self-esteem. In the Christian tradition, the sin of pride does not precisely equate to self-esteem issues. The spiritual meaning of pride is probably closer to self-absorption than to self-esteem.

Flora Jackson had a background as an entertainer before she went into full-time motivational speaking. She was indeed a powerful, charismatic, and popular speaker. As she said, "It's a gift," a gift that she saw as her way of helping others, helping them believe in themselves and achieve the success that God desired for them. Flora's outward success disguised considerable personal unhappiness. She had had three marriages and numerous boyfriends. Twice she had admitted herself to recovery programs for alcohol abuse. Alcohol was not her primary addiction, however. As she put it, she "craved being on stage, the applause, and adrenaline rush . . . and then to see that you are having a positive impact on people's lives. . . . It's just such a high! I love it."

Flora's narcissistic traits certainly fit her career. She really could not do what she did without having a dynamic personality. Yet, at the same time, the underside of her psyche was her inability to see negativity—in herself or others. This was reflected in her limited ability to form and sustain intimate love relationships. It also manifested itself in a scandal that erupted when it was discovered that her accountant and publicist had colluded to embezzle close to $300,000 from her accounts. At the trial, Flora kept saying that she could not believe that these people whom she loved, whom she gave jobs when they needed work, who were children of God's blessings, could do this. It must be a mistake. Depressed and now fifty-eight years old, Flora was washed up. Pride is not just self-absorption; it goes hand-in-hand with arrogance and denial.

Pride as Arrogance

While pride is characterized by too much self-esteem or self-absorption, there is another meaning to pride in the Christian spiritual tradition; pride is portrayed as defensiveness, arrogance, or being closed. The sin of pride is the sin of thinking that we know everything, that we have no sin and thus have nothing to learn or improve upon. The more we are full of ourselves—self-absorbed—the more we tend to think that we have no weaknesses. Yet, the sin of pride is also and more precisely refusing to admit shortcomings and being closed to feedback.

When considering pride, many Christians think first of the biblical story in which Jesus's disciples argued over who was going to be the greatest in the coming kingdom (see Luke 22:24ff.) or the related parable in which Jesus wants his followers not to sit at the head of the table, but rather to take the lowest seat, from which he extracts the principle, "Everyone who exalts himself will be humbled, and he who humbles himself will be exalted" (Luke 14:11). In short, it is better to be humble and modest than it is to think of yourself as more important than you are. This lesson in humility was reinforced by Jesus's own example, of course, as one who came not to be served but to serve and to suffer on behalf of others.

In terms of biblical writings, I think that the concept hard-hearted accurately describes the sin of pride. Throughout both the Hebrew and Christian scriptures, hard-hearted people were people who were self-consumed, but they were also individuals who were closed off, defensive, not open to feedback, afraid of change, lacking mercy, and, in all of these ways, not open to the influence of the divine. Within the Christian tradition, I think that the definitive passage regarding the sin of pride is 1 John 1:8, which reads, "If we say that we have no sin, we deceive ourselves and the truth is not in us. If we confess our sins, he is faithful and just and will forgive our sins and cleanse us from all unrighteousness. If we say we have not sinned, we make him a liar and his word is not in us." This is the true sin of pride—saying that we have no sin, no weaknesses, no shortcomings, nothing to learn, nothing to be sorry about, no need for confession or apology, no areas that need growth—in short, no need for God at all.

I am told that the Roman Catholic sacrament of Holy Confession is not as popular today as in former times, at least among Western congregations. Indeed, many Protestants do not see the value of the weekly confession, either. Confession was designed to be an antidote for the sin of pride. It keeps one humble, broken open before God. Is the decline in the use of confession in Christian churches of the West due to our not being as religious as our ancestors, or is it because the sin of pride has so thoroughly crept into our lives and culture?

This meaning of pride as arrogance is captured by the term "hubris" and by the phrase, "Pride goes before the fall." For centuries, and across many cultures, people have spoken of this typically human dynamic: when we think that we can make no errors, we set ourselves up for inevitable failure! Sometimes the higher up we go, the farther down we fall. There are hundreds of stories, myths, and legends that illustrate this truism. But why is this so? Simply, pride blinds us to our own faults. Pride has a self-deceptive dynamic. We think we can do anything. We think we know everything. We become over-confident and foolishly bold. Remember the fairy tale about the emperor's new clothes? The emperor was blinded by his vanity from seeing the truth that he was wearing nothing at all. He imagined himself in beautiful garments. This is the sin of pride at work. Pride is not just being full of ourselves; it is a failure to see our sins, and it is thinking that we have no sin.

In the 1993 blockbuster movie *Jurassic Park*, director Steven Spielberg tells a story of arrogance and its downfall. The movie is about a paleontologist who finds a way to isolate the DNA of extinct dinosaurs and rewrite it to bring the dinosaurs back to life in an island-park. A mathematician played by Jeff Goldbum raises ethical questions at the celebratory dinner, calling it arrogance to think that we humans can ultimately control nature in this way. "You have been so preoccupied with whether or not you could do it, you didn't think to ask yourself *if* you should do it." He warns that when we think we know everything, when we think we can control everything, we set ourselves up for disaster. We should have some "humility before nature," he argues. His warning proves correct, as the now-living dinosaurs adapt to and defy human control, rising up to destroy the park and its creator. Many environmentalists have pointed to similar dynamics or spoken similar words of warning about the collective pride of humanity in reference to nature. Interestingly, they often couch their warnings in terms of pride, saying that humans foolishly think that the earth is ours to alter, rape, and destroy.

Spiritual Pride or Self-Righteousness

People who have special knowledge are often most vulnerable to the sin of pride in the form of arrogance. Doctors, who have tremendous medical knowledge and expertise, often have a hard time admitting errors or apologizing. Fervent politicians on either the left or the right of the political spectrum, who are devoted to a particular ideology, are often impatient with and condescending to those whom they consider less enlightened. Even computer nerds can be impatient with those who are less comfortable navigating the pathways of the Internet. Some of the greatest scientists of our time, winners of the Nobel Prize, have not always been the best teachers, in part because they have had little patience for students who asked basic questions or were seemingly not as advanced as they were. It is a rare professional indeed who does not let his or her special knowledge go to his or her head and who can set aside the temptation to arrogance and learn to communicate knowledge in clear language with both enthusiasm and patience.[7]

People of faith from all religions are susceptible to spiritual pride or self-righteousness. Often the more fervent the believer, the more he or she is susceptible to this holier-than-thou attitude. It is not an endearing trait, and the irony is that believers who are self-righteous often do not recognize it in themselves. People become self-righteous in part because their spiritual leaders teach them that they or their religion or their version of a particular religion is better than others. Their view is true and authentic, and they are the truly saved, more pure and more knowledgeable than other people. There is a certain appeal to this self-righteousness, as there is a certain appeal to pride itself. Many people long for the moral certainty and psychological rigidity that the self-righteous exhibit. Yet, self-righteous believers probably turn away as many people as they attract.

It is really quite difficult to be an earnest Christian and not be self-righteous. It is especially difficult to be a Christian evangelist and not be self-righteous. Christian theologians teach that their faith is unique among the world's religions. In the footsteps of our Jewish ancestors, Christians are God's chosen people. Yet at the same time, Christian teachings emphasize that the true measures of faith are love, a servant's attitude, and humility. Therein lies a paradox—Christians are special, but their specialness lies not in being superior, but in being the servant of all, even of the unbelievers. Like I said, it is really hard to be an earnest Christian and not be self-righteous.

It is interesting to recall that in the traditional ordering of the Seven Deadly Sins, each sin was associated with a certain day of the week, a day when it was thought that people were most vulnerable to that sin. In this traditional ordering, on what day of the week are we most tempted by pride? Sundays! Our spiritual ancestors sensed that, fresh from Sunday services, we might become a bit self-righteous, a bit tempted to think we are better than others or that we know it all. Self-righteousness is not supposed to

---

7. It also seems to me that many a malpractice dispute or political scandal could be easily resolved if the offending party would just tell the truth and apologize, instead of clinging to pride as arrogance and denial.

be the result of Sunday worship services, but the temptation to distort the truth of the gospel is part of our sinful nature.

Self-righteousness was particularly distasteful to Jesus, as it has been to most authentic spiritual leaders. Nothing seemed to make Jesus angrier than the self-righteous attitude of the Pharisees. The parable of the Pharisee and the tax collector (Luke 18:9–14) puts into a teaching format Jesus's disgust with spiritual pride. Both parties—the Pharisee and the tax collector—come to the altar. The Pharisee, illustrating the sin of pride, prays, "I'm glad that I am not like other men . . . not like that tax collector." The tax collector, illustrating the virtue of humility, prays, "Have mercy on me, a sinner." From this parable, Jesus draws the familiar conclusion, "Everyone who is exalted will be humbled, and everyone who humbles himself will be exalted" (v. 14). I would suggest that this lesson is not just about self-esteem, but about defensiveness and openness. In being humble, the tax collector was being open to God's mercy, to God's direction, and to God's teaching. In being prideful, the Pharisee was being defensive, closed off to God, to himself, and to "that sinner" in the next prayer stall.

The same principle might be applied to all of the -isms that plague human relationships around the world. Do not racism, classism, nationalism, sexism, and various ideologies of the left and right have at their root the sin of pride, the assumption that one's own race, class, nation, or gender is better than all others? We are quick to cite the faults of the other group, but we fail to acknowledge the shortcomings of our own group. We are quick to think we have nothing more to learn from them, whoever "they" may be. In short, we are self-righteous. We usually consider these deadly sins within an individualistic frame of reference, but clearly each deadly sin has its corresponding social manifestation or social sin.[8]

My own philosophy is that life is a journey. We strive to arrive, but we never really arrive in this life. There is always something more to learn, some new way to grow, some new issue to wrestle with in each and every stage of life. Life is a process, not an event. If we ever think that we have arrived, then we surely have not arrived. If we ever come to think that we have it all figured out, or that we have been made perfect, or that we are truly whole, then surely that is the moment when we are not! Pride always

---

8. One of the insights of twentieth-century Protestant liberal theology is the realization that sin must be understood in a systemic way as well as in an individualistic frame of reference. This theme of the interplay between individual sin and the social/systemic manifestations that reflect and reinforce each sin is addressed throughout this book.

tempts us into thinking that we have arrived, but humility keeps us ever open to the process of being saved.

The Scottish dramatist Sir James M. Barrie is quoted as saying, "Life is a long lesson in humility."[9] Indeed it is! Just when we think we have arrived, God has a way of reminding us that we have not arrived. Just when we think we have all the answers, God has a way of pointing out to us that we know nothing. Just when we think we have no sin, God allows us to stumble in some dramatic way. The voice of God is often heard in the children, the innocent, and the honest among us who are not afraid to tell the emperor that he has no clothes on. God seems to be regularly breaking down our pride, breaking us open so the Spirit can work within us and among us once again. Like the Hebrews of old, we too have a tendency to drift away from God, to chase false gods (see Isa 2:11–12). So, God speaks—sometimes through prophets of all sorts—to challenge our pride and, if necessary, to humble us or allow us to fall on our faces, not because God desires to hurt us, but because God desires us to be open, to grow, and to be truly alive in faith.

Pride as Denial

We learned in our review of addiction studies that as the disease of addiction progresses, our thinking becomes distorted because our mind seeks to protect and sustain what it perceives it needs to survive. Our minds work very hard and sometimes quite creatively to find rationalizations, justifications, and arguments to sustain our addiction of choice, whether it is gambling, food, sex, or alcohol. Collectively, this pattern of distorted thinking is commonly referred to as denial. It leads us to ignore or minimize the risks associated with our drug of choice.

A similar pattern is present in the sin of pride. As discussed earlier, pride is essentially dishonesty, a distorted estimate of reality. We mistakenly believe that we are better or more important than we really are. A person afflicted with the sin of pride believes that he or she has no sin and no weaknesses and has made no mistakes. Pride reinforces and contributes to denial and in turn leads to lying, a distortion of reality. Denial is a form of lying. Denial is grounded in a lie.[10]

---

9. James M. Barrie (1860–1937) is perhaps better known as the author of *Peter Pan*.

10. Donald Capps, in his book *Deadly Sins and Saving Virtues*, argues that the sin of pride is most tempting during the adolescent years when youths typically struggle with identity issues. This dynamic may account for the fact that most people with drug

Often when people are caught in their addiction, perhaps by being arrested, exposed, or confronted by a spouse, the first response out of their mouth is a lie. "I did not do that!" "You are mistaken!" "Your facts are not correct." "How dare you!" In time, as more and more information is revealed, these denials give way to an honest or semi-honest (denial dies hard) acknowledgment. Most of the time, loved ones or the public at large (if the addicted person is a public figure) just want the truth, whatever it is. "Just tell the truth." Unfortunately, the addicted person is often the last to recognize the truth.

In his popular book *The Road Less Traveled*, published in 1978, psychiatrist Scott Peck made a coherent and persuasive presentation of the principles that underlie sound mental health. In an increasingly permissive age, he made a case for discipline as a core feature of good psychological health, saying, "Discipline is the basic set of tools we require to solve life's problems. . . . What makes life difficult is that the process of confronting and solving problems is a painful one."[11] The third tool of discipline that he cited was a "dedication to the truth" or to reality. Sound mental and spiritual health lies in being a person who is committed to the truth, discovering the truth about oneself, and following the path to truth. In the softer language of positive psychology, I would say that it is a matter of being curious, curious about oneself. Denial is the opposite of curiosity. Denial disrupts this dedication to truth and to seeking the truth. As people become increasingly addicted, the addiction process robs us of truth. We might say, as we sometimes say about war, that truth is the first casualty. In turn, the path to recovery lies in confronting the truth, breaking through the denial and distortions.

We do not have to be addicted to something or to some activity to have a pride problem, but if we are addicted, then we surely have a problem with pride, too. The very presence of denial in the addicted person is evidence that pride is also a problem. But which comes first, you might ask? Does the problem with pride make us vulnerable to addictive processes, or does the addictive process create the sin of pride? The answer is: some of both. Certainly, people who are prideful in the sense of arrogant, narcissistic, and

---

and alcohol problems started down the road of addiction in their youthful years when pride in the form of self-absorption, arrogance, and denial is most acute. See pp. 46–52 in Capps' book.

11. Peck, *Road Less Traveled*, 15–16. Peck went on to make the astounding statement, "This tendency to avoid problems and the emotional suffering inherent in them is the primary basis for all human mental illness" (p. 17).

defensive are vulnerable to falling prey to addictions. Certainly, too, some people can become addicted without having a moral or spiritual predisposition to addiction. But, in all cases, the addictive process, the progression of the disease itself, creates greater and greater levels of narcissism, arrogance, and denial—the chief features of the sin of pride.

It is interesting how the concept of denial is used in psychological literature. In addition to its use in addiction literature and programs, denial is also a common term in the literature on loss and grief recovery. Denial is understood as the first stage in the grief recovery process. When a loss is sudden, dramatic, and painful, our first emotional response is often denial. We are in shock. We do not believe it emotionally. We deny it happened. We search for evidence to the contrary. We grasp for rationalizations and justifications for why the loss is not as bad as it seems. Denial in grief recovery functions much like denial in addictions recovery; denial prevents grief work. In addictions, denial blocks recovery. Sometimes the two parallel processes actually intertwine. The denial associated with addiction recovery can include a denial of the various losses associated with the addiction: the loss of family, health, control, happiness, relationships, jobs, and numerous other positive aspects of life.

Finally, let me note that denial has a relational or systemic aspect. Addiction treatment programs tell us that a family can become dysfunctional as a result of the addiction of one of its members. Families and co-addicts[12] can participate in the denial by enabling and sustaining the addict's justifications, impaired thinking, and rationalizations about the disease. In short, denial can be a group phenomenon. By participating in the family secret, we maintain the denial and in a sense participate in a lie. When family members are co-conspirators in the denial, the pattern of denial is that much harder to break, often requiring some person or some objective reality outside of the family system to function as an intervention.

Pride as the Gatekeeper to Recovery

In traditional Christian spirituality, pride was considered to be the chief sin of the Seven Deadly Sins, because pride was at the root of all of the other sins. Indeed, when pride is defined as self-absorption, one can see where all of the sins, almost by their very definition, have at their base a self-centeredness, a choosing of self-interest over the interest of others or

---

12. This term was first used by Patrick Carnes (*Out of the Shadows*, 113).

of God. Yet, there is another meaning to the concept of pride as the chief sin. This meaning is grounded in the definition of pride, noted above, as defensiveness or arrogance. Pride is the chief sin because pride involves a defensiveness, a blindness to seeing one's faults. The breaking down of denial, the creation of an openness to authentic self-confrontation, is the beginning of all recovery work, regardless of the nature of the sin. So, in this sense, pride is the chief sin, the key dynamic that blocks or facilitates growth in reference to all of the remaining six sins or addictions.

In this understanding, pride is the gatekeeper to personal growth and, more specifically, to recovery. If we can get past pride, we can be open to growth, but if we stay stuck in pride, recovery is impossible. No therapy is possible, no change is possible. Every therapist knows this truth. Unless a client is open to change, psychotherapy is largely useless. A client must begin with a simple declaration that there is a problem and that he or she does not have all of the answers. With this simple awareness, therapy can proceed. Humility is the open door, the path to growth. Until the door is opened, there is no possibility of spiritual growth, much less recovery, whether the needed recovery is from an addiction or a tragic loss.

Over my forty years of professional work, I have conducted hundreds and hundreds of psychological evaluations in which I use various psychological tests to determine the psychological fitness of a person for a particular career or job. One of the most common standardized tests is the MMPI-2, which has various scales that measure everything from depression to cynicism. Yet, before the assessor can examine the various clinical scales, he or she must study the validity scales that are designed to measure how open or defensive the test-taker was in approaching the assessment process. When the validity scales are elevated, the candidate probably approached the test with a defensive attitude. They tended to minimize their faults, the negative aspects of themselves and their weaknesses. They tried to present themselves as having "no sin." They tried to put their best foot forward. As a result, the test data do not reflect an accurate portrait of the individual. The sin of pride is similar to this—if there is basic defensiveness, nothing else is valid, nothing else can be accomplished in therapy or recovery. One must begin with humility—an openness to new revelations.

The sin of pride, as the chief sin, is like a validity test on a spiritual assessment. If the validity test is off, the rest of the assessment is invalid. Until one adopts a basic humility, a basic openness to truth, the recovery from any of the six other deadly sins is blocked. Every spiritual growth process begins with humility.

How Is Pride Deadly?

The Seven Deadly Sins are referred to as deadly. How might the sin of pride be considered deadly? In what ways is it deadly?

I first met Dan Wilson in the context of marital therapy wherein he and his wife were trying to improve their argumentative, volatile, and blame-based relationship. The brief verbal exchange that opened this chapter is typical of the dynamics between them during that period. I noticed then that they both had a significant drinking problem, which often made their arguments more intense, but I did not see then what I saw clearly later—the dynamics of pride and addiction. They both had a great deal of difficulty swallowing their pride and making the first gesture toward reconciliation.

After they separated and divorced, I kept in touch with Dan through occasional counseling sessions. In his loneliness, his drinking and drug use grew. He got one, then two DUIs. I urged him several times to try AA. He resisted. He denied the problem was that serious. "After all, AA is for losers," he would proclaim. But then, in a serious moment, he revealed how embarrassed and humiliated he felt by the DUIs when he murmured, "If it ever happened again, I would just kill myself rather than go to jail." Well, several months later, it did happen again. I had not heard from Dan for months. The first I knew of the third arrest was when my eye caught the brief notice in the local newspaper that "Dan Wilson, recently arrested for a DUI, died in the county jail last Friday. Circumstances related to his death are unclear. Funeral arrangements pending." My heart sank to my stomach. I was sickened. If ever I am tempted to think that the sin of pride is not deadly, I remember Dan Wilson . . . and there are thousands more like him.

Dan Wilson's story also reminds me that there are many forms of death. We can die literally. We can also die relationally. Pride is destructive to relationships. The person suffering from the sin of pride is, by definition, incapable of or limited in his or her ability to show empathy. Prideful people are not good listeners. They are not open to others, just as they are not open to themselves or to God. They have a certain psychological rigidity; they know what is right and often feel compelled to impose it on others. They need others to reinforce the lie, to adore them, to agree with them, to give them lots of attention. Most mature people know that marriage and family life are built on compromise, love, mutuality, and honest feedback. Such traits are difficult for persons caught in an addictive cycle of pride. Many love relationships have crashed on the rocks of pride.

The Christian spiritual tradition also argues that there is a particular type of spiritual death that pride induces. In pride, we make ourselves the center of our existence instead of God. We close ourselves off. We become defensive. In doing so, we cut ourselves off from the source of life, of meaning, and of salvation. In the imagery of Genesis, we imagine ourselves to be God; after all, we know everything, have no sin, and do not need any help. Certainly, the sin of pride kills one's spiritual life. "Pride is the cancer of spirituality," C. S. Lewis wrote, because it "eats up the very possibility of love."[13] Thus, the only real solution to this cancer is a full, fresh surrender of ourselves to God in Jesus Christ. Yet, surrender is never a one-time event. Like some cancers, pride can be arrested but never cured. Pride may creep back into our lives, little by little, until again, unbeknownst to us, we come to think once again that we have no sin.

The Virtue of Humility

The traditional virtue that prevents or blocks the sin of pride is humility. If we practice humility, we insulate ourselves from the sin of pride and thus also insulate ourselves from the snares of addictions.

In this self-indulgent age, the term "humility" has come to suggest a deflation of one's self-esteem—being and acting less than we are. Instead, I argue that humility is better understood as openness:

- Openness to God—realization that one does not have all the answers
- Openness to one's self—awareness that one has faults as well as strengths
- Openness to others—empathy for the needs of others

What exactly is humility as openness? To be open might be best described as a willingness to be vulnerable—vulnerable to ourselves, to others, and to God. It is hard for all of us to be vulnerable some of the time. It is hard for some people to be vulnerable at any time. It is risky. We are afraid of being hurt, rejected, overwhelmed, and/or abandoned. So, in response to our perceived fear, we close down, build walls, become rigid, act defensively, and justify it all with prideful and deceptive statements.

During my years as a counselor, I have occasionally intervened in congregations where members were in conflict with or unhappy with their

---

13. Lewis, *Mere Christianity*, 97.

pastor. I have noticed that, almost universally in such circumstances, the congregation had not done a job performance review of the pastor's work in years. I found this to be true across Christian denominations. It makes sense! The normal mechanism whereby complaints about the pastor might be aired and resolved was not operational, thus allowing such complaints to bubble and boil in the congregation until they finally erupted into open conflict. It is true that pastors are often very sensitive types and congregations are generally not very skilled at evaluating their minister's work in a professional manner, but even so, we must view these unfortunate situations as another illustration of the dynamic of pride and humility or, if you will, of defensiveness and openness. Pastors must be willing to be open, to welcome feedback, and to model for their flock the humility that Christ taught. In a spirit of openness, congregational issues can be resolved, the pastor's work can be improved, and their common ministry will thrive. In an atmosphere of defensiveness, some otherwise loving communities of faith degenerate into blaming, negativity, and divisiveness.

We can practice the virtue of humility by doing the following:

- realizing that life is a process, a journey, and that we are works in progress and that every stage of life has its lessons and growth opportunities
- realizing that we need the help of others and that loved ones can see our emerging sin of pride long before we do
- praying regularly for openness; seriously asking God to open up our hearts
- asking for feedback on a regular basis from loved ones, from friends, from employers, and from God
- reflecting, after we receive feedback, upon questions such as, What are my faults? How might I improve myself? What are my blind spots?
- confessing our faults, shortcomings, and sins regularly; making confession a regular part of our prayer life; reaching deeply in confession
- overcoming our reluctance to apologize and saying humbly and authentically, "I'm sorry"
- creating self-improvement plans and showing steady progress
- relating to people who are different from us culturally, racially, religiously, and even politically; being open to what we can learn from and through these encounters

- holding all of our beliefs or doctrines in what Gordon Allport termed a "heuristic" way by treating them as working hypotheses until further information, experience, or evidence comes along;[14] being open to God's continuing revelation in our lives
- practicing careful, attentive, and active listening, putting aside our biases and preconceived ideas; if need be, taking a workshop to improve our listening skills
- learning to listen not only to others, but to God as well, who is always speaking to us, trying to teach us, guide us, and correct us; hearing the voice of God, whether it be in the voice of others, in "the still small voice" within, or in the message of coincidental events; learning to listen with a third ear

The spiritual path of cultivating humility in all of its forms, but especially in the form of openness, is preventive behavioral health. By reducing the sin of pride within us, we are simultaneously reducing our risk of becoming another victim of the modern plague that today we call addiction.

Summary

In this chapter, I have explored the sin of pride. I have argued that pride is indeed the chief sin of the traditional Seven Deadly Sins because pride as narcissism and arrogance is central to all addictions and because pride as denial blocks us from seeing the truth that we need help. But is pride addictive? Not directly, because it does not have a behavioral component, which is one of the key features of the definition of addiction we discussed in chapter 1. Like all of the Seven Deadly Sins, pride is a mental sin. It is primarily an attitude, a characteristic trait, a pattern of thinking. Pride is the soil in which addictions grow. While it is related to all of the addictions, alcoholism, perfectionism, and gambling seem to be especially rooted in the soil of pride.

Once an addiction gets established, pride works to prevent addicted persons from seeing their bondage and beginning the recovery process. Until pride is broken, recovery is stalled. Dealing with one's pride is at the center of the Twelve-Step Program. For Bill W., one of the founders of AA, there is no recovery until pride is dealt with. He writes:

---

14. Allport, *The Individual and His Religion*, 72–74.

> We perceive that only through utter defeat are we able to take our first steps toward liberation and strength. Our admissions of personal powerlessness finally turn out to be firm bedrock upon which happy and purposeful lives may be built. . . . Indeed, the attainment of greater humility is the foundation principle of each of AA's Twelve Steps. For without some degree of humility, no alcoholic can stay sober at all.[15]

Questions for Self-Reflection

1. Is it difficult for me to admit mistakes? How often do I say I'm sorry?
2. Once I make up my mind, am I very stubborn? Have I been called pig-headed or stubborn or narrow-minded?
3. Do I like giving people answers? Do I have a difficult time considering other points of view?
4. Do I welcome criticism and feedback?
5. How well do I know myself? Is my social persona different from my true self? Do I have secrets that I hide?
6. Do I honestly think that I am better than most people? Am I a gift to most organizations?
7. Do I like being the center of attention?
8. Do I secretly wish God would put me in charge of the world for a day?

Biblical passages related to pride: Gen 3:1–7; Num 12:3; Prov 16:18; Matt 5:5; Mark 10:35–45; 12:38–40; Luke 14:7–11; 18:9–14; 20:45–47; John 3:30; Rom 12:3; 2 Cor 11:21b–30; Titus 1:1; Jas 4:6, 10

---

15. Alcoholics Anonymous World Services, *Twelve Steps and Twelve Traditions*, 21, 70.

3 Envy

A Problem in Community

Scott: You have been mildly depressed for years now. . . . Can you recall when and where you first remember being depressed?

Alice: I was thirteen years old or so . . . overweight, skin problems, and plain looking. I spent hours upon hours in my room thumbing through teen magazines, admiring the pretty, popular, thin girls in all of the featured stories and ads.

Scott: Would you say you were envious?

Alice: Oh, green with envy! Why couldn't I be like them, be shapely and popular? I wanted what they had . . . whatever it was. If it was a new hair style, a new kind of shoes, or even a new kind of cigarettes, I had to have it. And, of course, boys. I dreamed of having Ricky Lake as my boyfriend, just like Heather.

Scott: Were you able to get those things for yourself? I mean, did all that thumbing through magazines motivate you?

Alice: No, mostly I just spent hours in my room dwelling on what I did not have, how I was inadequate in one way or another.

Scott: It does sound depressing.

Alice: Yeah, that's my first memory of being depressed.

THIS CONVERSATION WAS HELD in my therapy office. Alice, a thirty-four-year-old divorced mother, was referred to me by the local hospital. She had made an attempt on her life. She had also struggled with bulimia most of her adult life. Her compulsive eating disorder began in her teen years, then appeared and reappeared throughout her adult years. Upon her release from the hospital, because she had limited resources, Alice landed in the community counseling center where I worked. Within a few sessions we mapped the extent and depth of her depression and her addictive behaviors. When she managed her eating and felt that she looked good, she felt good about herself. She felt attractive and confident. Yet, if she had one—just one—minor slip in her eating regime, she fell back into her black hole of despair. This cyclic pattern had been going on in one form or another for most of her adult life. In the above conversation, we were trying to trace the roots of this depressive-compulsive pattern.

In Alice's case, envy was one of the dynamics in the origin of her depression. By comparing herself to her peers, there was always an implied inadequacy. "I am not pretty enough. I am not popular enough. I do not belong." Dwelling on thoughts like these day after day will make anyone depressed! Comparing herself to others motivated her to try to look perfect like those she admired, creating internal pressure to control her eating. Several other issues complicated her life, including a failed marriage and some medical concerns, but always in the recesses of her psyche, even as an accomplished professional teacher in a private school, there was this dynamic of comparison, of comparing herself with her peers. This is the basic dynamic in envy.

Let's define envy. Envy is the desire to have what another person has—some possession, some advantage or blessing, something that we do not have. If envy lasts awhile, it becomes an attitude of resentment or antagonism toward the other(s) because he or she has (or they have) something that we do not. Envy is built on a dynamic of comparison, comparing our status to that of another. Correspondingly, then, envy is a discounting of the self, an assumption that we are not as good as nor as worthy as the other who has been blessed, who has good fortune, or who is privileged in comparison to ourselves.

At first glance, envy appears to be the weak sister in the list of the Seven Deadly Sins. Envy is not that bad compared to anger, lust, or greed. Envy is a lightweight sin. After all, envy is the driving force in capitalism. Motivated by envy, we all strive to improve our lot in life—purchase a new car, compete for a new girlfriend or boyfriend, earn a promotion, improve our appearance. We do all these things because we want what we see others have. Envy is a great motivator. How can envy be a sin—and a deadly sin, at that?

In the Hebrew Bible, envy is called covetousness.[1] The tenth commandment reads, "You shall not covet your neighbor's house, wife, servants, livestock or anything that belongs to your neighbor" (Exod 20:17). Strong language! God thought this was a very important subject—so important as to be included in this divine human code of conduct. God considered this to be a moral issue, right up there with murder, lying, adultery, and stealing (the sixth, seventh, eighth, and ninth commandments). We might ask ourselves, "Why?" To our modern minds, envy does not seem like a serious sin compared to murder, stealing, adultery, or lying, but in the Creator's mind it is a serious problem. Maybe we should explore envy a bit further.

Envy Is Everywhere

When we stop and think about it, envy shows up in many places and in varied ways. It is woven into the fabric of our common social and economic life, particularly in capitalistic economies. It is so common, so *normal*, that we fail to think of it as a problem. Indeed, I would argue that envy is pretty ordinary and therefore inevitable. Here are some everyday examples:

- A recently widowed woman who is having great difficulty getting through her bereavement sheepishly admits how envious and bitter she feels watching couples walk hand-in-hand down the street. "My heart aches with loneliness. Why can't I be married? Why couldn't my Charlie have lived?"
- A plain-looking nerdy fellow talks endlessly about how "cool" his work peers are. They know so much about cars. "Me? I just drive this tin can."
- Two adjunct instructors are fuming about how the tenured faculty have all the privileges, like no administrative duties, regular sabbaticals, and getting to walk in the rear of the line at graduation and have the seats of honor. "Yet, most of them couldn't teach their way out of a paper bag!"
- "Cheery people bug me," says Karen. "I find them so annoying. What do they have to be so damn happy about? Not everyone is as lucky as they are."

---

1. Sometimes greed is also cited as the sin behind the verb to covet.

- Robert complains that if he hears one more story about his neighbor's wonderful European vacation, he will vomit. After all, the farthest vacation he ever took was to Idaho.
- Susie, Kara, and Heather are hotly engaged in a good old-fashioned gossip session. Their neighbor Liz had left town for a few days, and speculation is running high that Liz and Tom are having troubles, maybe even that Liz is cheating on Tom. Liz had gotten a new car and new wardrobe last year and seemed to be showing off at every turn in the neighborhood. It feels good to bring her down, even if only in words.
- "My father always seemed to favor my older brother, like he could do no wrong in Dad's eyes," says David. "He was showered with favors and privileges."

Feelings of envy are more common than we might imagine. They can emerge not just in reference to the material advantages of others, but in reference to any perceived advantage, blessing, or favor. Envy is a pretty normal human emotion. Yet, how we use these feelings shapes our well-being. If we use our feelings of envy to motivate ourselves to work harder to achieve what we see our neighbor has, then we might say envy works for us. But if we allow envy to become strong, chronic, and/or bitter, it will destroy us as surely as will its cousin, jealousy.

Envy and Jealousy

Envy and jealousy are both sins of the mind, sins that are rooted in a dynamic of comparison. They are the sins that consume us mentally, make us crazy, make us obsessive and possessive. The daytime soap operas are filled with stories of the perils of jealousy, and many times the perils include death. Jealousy, if unchecked, can lead to such sins as adultery, murder, and lying. Chronic jealousy almost always destroys relationships because it eats away at the trust that is foundational in a healthy relationship. Jealousy can have obsessive—if not addictive—qualities. Certainly, jealousy could have been a candidate for an eighth deadly sin or maybe even a replacement for envy.

Envy is similar to jealousy, but it is slightly different. Jealousy is more fear-based than envy. We feel jealous when we fear that we might lose something that we already have or think we have. Jealousy can easily move into anger, even rage, as we fight to protect what we possess. It can be pretty primal in its intensity. In contrast, envy is a desire for something we do not yet have. Envy can also create resentment, if we are chronically blocked from securing what we desire, which creates anger-like emotions.

Both envy and jealousy are built on the dynamic of comparison. We are comparing and contrasting our status with that of other people, and in one way or another, in our minds, we come up short. Both envy and jealousy have an implied diminution of the self: "I am not worth much because I don't measure up in some way."

Envy and jealousy are both associated with forms of anger. Anger that is hot, intense, and reactive is often associated with jealousy (like the color red). Anger that is slow, chronic, and bitter is associated with envy (like the color green). In both cases, anger is a secondary reaction to the primary feeling of either jealousy or envy. Because envy and jealousy are linked to anger, envy and jealousy can be deadly—deadly to our relationships, deadly to our health, and deadly to our souls. Dynamically, envy and jealousy are more similar than different, and in the context of the modern world, the two could easily be lumped together as the same deadly sin. Both of them destroy community as well as individuals.[2]

Envy as a Community Problem

Human beings are social animals. We live in communities, whether large or small. Our place in our community is important to our sense of being safe, our sense of belonging and being worthy. Envy or covetousness undermines community. Envy divides people. In subtle ways it turns neighbor against neighbor. It can create antagonism, hostility, and resentment between people. Envy is really not about things, like greed is; it is about community. It erodes community because instead of standing in solidarity with our neighbor, we are now competing with our neighbor. We are resentful of our neighbor's status. In short, envy destroys genuine community. Even though envy as a sin is lodged in the individual, it is really about relationships.

---

2. Let me say a word about envy and greed. Prior to 590 CE, when Gregory the Great gave envy its own place in the list of the Seven Deadly Sins, envy had been a subset of greed. Envy and greed do seem to be similar. They both involve distortions of appetite. However, greed focuses more narrowly on material possessions, whereas envy is more generally applied to the whole range of human advantages and disadvantages. Furthermore, envy in its full-blown form seeks not just to acquire things, but also to do so at the expense of one's neighbor. Envy is really a social sin.

The traditional saving virtue for envy is love, which supports my contention that envy is about community. The saving virtue is not inner peace, which might be appropriate if envy were just an appetite problem. Rather, the virtue is love—love of others instead of envy of others. Due to its characteristic lack of love, envy contributes to many a family dispute and to various conflicts between social classes, races, and nationalities. In its full-blown form, envy not only pushes us to want to succeed, to have what our neighbor has, but also to want our neighbor to fail. Envy leads us to secretly smile when we see a once-blessed neighbor crash and burn. Momentarily, we feel better because the neighbor has come down to our level! In its most intense form, envy rejoices at the misfortunes of others.

In modern terminology, envy assumes that life is what is called a zero-sum game. When we feel chronically envious, we are assuming that there really aren't enough good things for everyone in the community. Envy assumes that every blessing another person, family, or group gets is one less blessing we will receive. Conversely, the more possessions we have, the fewer possessions our neighbor can have. Life is competition, not community, when we are consumed with envy. Envy destroys community by turning neighbors into competitors.[3]

This perspective suggests why God (or Moses) considered envy such an important problem that it needed to be addressed in the Ten Commandments. God is very concerned about human communities, not just individual humans. This was especially true in the social context of the ancient Hebrews, who needed to be a supportive, united, non-competitive community if they were to survive the trials of the wilderness and the wars of conquest and grow to become a prosperous nation in the promised land. Yet, God is pro-community across all human times and places. God is concerned for and works to promote authentic human community as an essential piece of the larger moral, spiritual, and psychological health of humanity. God knows that envy, if left unchecked, can destroy community. This truth is still as valid today as it was in ancient Israel. Humanity will continue or will self destruct, depending in large part on how we form and sustain authentic communities, including the global community. In the Decalogue, God is saying that envy can destroy community, communities as small as families and as large as whole races or classes of people. By

---

3. I asked an Asian doctoral student of mine how envy is understood in the more collectivist cultures of Asia. He said, "Oh, yes, envy is what we call the 'crab mentality.' Watch freshly caught crabs in a bucket climb all over one another trying to get up the sides of the bucket. That is envy." This is a powerful image.

implication, God prefers a human community characterized by cooperation, mutual support, and the inherent dignity of each individual. This is what Christians have come to call koinonia (see Acts 2:44–47).

A Systemic Sin

All of the seven deadly sins have a social element and social implications. Yet envy, more than the other six, seems to be a relational sin, a sin that is systemic in nature. Envy cannot exist in isolation. It is part of a system.

While driving to work the other day, I was listening to a radio commercial for a new office building that was opening. This building has all of the modern technological conveniences that allow a person to work from literally anywhere—their office or a nearby café or their car as they drive to Las Vegas. The announcer concluded his appeal for new tenants with these words: "Don't be like those poor devils chained to their desks all day. Come, rent at Novel Towers, a cut above the rest." As I listened to this commercial repeatedly for days on end (I commute a lot), it occurred to me that this is the other side of envy. If envy truly is systemic in nature, a sin that grows out of a social context, then a condescending attitude is the other side of envy. Superiority and envy are two sides of the same coin, the same dynamic! The more people display an attitude of superiority, the more they invite others to envy them . . . and the more we display envy toward our neighbors, the more we invite them to see themselves as superior to us. There cannot be a top dog without a bottom dog, to use the phrase coined by Gestalt therapy founder Fritz Pearls, and every bottom dog has to have a top dog. Envy grows in a circular, self-reinforcing pattern.

There are many examples of the systemic nature of envy. The one that comes first to my mind is the role of entertainment stars in our media-saturated society. These include movie stars, famous musicians, professional athletes, the stars of fashion, and, in a generalized way, some politicians and leaders of industry. Many entertainment stars, but not all of them, have publicists and media companies that cultivate a carefully crafted image of the star as a person to be admired and even envied. There is a whole industry built around reporting on the rich and famous—where they live, where they travel, who they love or don't love, how they look, what they eat, and sometimes how they die. Books, magazines, and television shows provide up-to-the-minute information about the lives of movie stars. This industry feeds both the curiosity and envy of average Americans who can only dream of such privilege. The industry also feeds the other side of the dynamic by fostering the impression of superiority, of the celebrity as a shining star in the midst of us ordinary, dull humans. Sometimes the fame and fortune of certain movie stars are earned. Other times, it seems that actors with just average acting skills are sold to the public as examples of people to be envied. Of course, the real motive here is to sell tickets, or shoes, or cologne, not just magazines. The stars of entertainment (or, more precisely, their fame) are commodities to be bought and sold based on their star appeal. By hooking our natural envy, the industry pushes us to become vulnerable to the sales pitch, whatever it may be.

My point here is that envy is a systemic sin. Envy does not exist in isolation, but exists in partnership with an attitude of superiority or entitlement. In my view, it is no accident that as envy grows in our culture so too does the attitude of entitlement.[4] These are two sides of the same dynamic. The sins of envy and superiority can affect all people—rich and poor. We are all vulnerable.

Envy in Capitalistic Cultures

The Seven Deadly Sins framework is a product of Western European culture. It was fashioned in the fourth and fifth centuries as Western civilization was just emerging from antiquity. Cooperative communities in the form of extended family systems, neighborhoods, congregations, villages, towns, and guilds were vital to the welfare and commerce of society in this period. Yet, there was something about the character of early Europeans—maybe it was the rising materialism—that led our spiritual forebears to issue a warning. The warning was this: "Watch out for envy. Envy will destroy community, turning us all into competitors instead of neighbors." Their warning proved prophetic. With the rise of capitalism, envy was transformed from a sin into an economic motivator.

Capitalistic economies, as most Westernized nations are to one degree or another, encourage envy. Envy is the psychological fuel of capitalism. Every night on television, hour after hour, commercials play to our envy

---

4. Included in the criteria for Narcissistic Personality Disorder is this phrase: "is often envious of others or believes that others are envious of him or her" (American Psychiatric Association, *DSM–IV-TR*), 717. The growing incidence of narcissism in our society, which I spoke about in the previous chapter, parallels this understanding of envy as a systemic sin and suggests that the sins of both pride and of envy are increasing in tandem in our world.

by showing us people with new cars, beautiful faces, money to spend, new clothes, bigger houses, many friends—all freely enjoying the good life that comes with consumption. Each commercial invites us to compare ourselves to these fictional people, and the implication is always that we are lacking in comparison. In fact, 99 percent of us are indeed lacking in comparison to such unrealistic ideals. Many commercials imply or end with the phrase, "Wouldn't you like to be the envy of your neighbors?" We are invited to envy and to strive to be envied. The suggested solution to our envy problem is to go buy, buy, buy some more in an effort to keep up with the Joneses. This is the psychology of the capitalistic culture in which most Western Christians live. Capitalism, with its emphasis on envy, makes the formation and sustaining of genuine community difficult, whether the community is at the level of families, towns, or nations.

In the heat of his 2012 campaign for the Republican nomination for president of the United States, Mitt Romney said, "This country already has a leader who divides us with the bitter politics of envy. We must offer an alternative vision . . . where we are lifted up by our desire to succeed, not dragged down by a resentment of success."[5] The next day, Romney returned to the theme: "I think it is about envy. I think it's about class warfare." In addition to criticizing President Obama, Romney was implicitly criticizing the views of the Occupy Movement that was sweeping America about this same time. The central theme of the Occupy Movement is that there is a growing inequity of wealth in this country, creating a large concentration of wealth in the top 1 percent of the population, a shrinking middle class, and an ever-larger lower class. Romney's comment points to larger questions, such as: What is the role of envy in class consciousness? Is the cry for greater economic fairness just a form of misplaced envy?

For eons we humans have differentiated ourselves by socioeconomic classes. In today's lingo, commentators use the generalized terms of the haves and the have-nots. Classifying humans is also done by race, ethnicity, family, religion, and gender, and in each classification one group is perceived or deems itself to be the haves and the other group is perceived or deems itself to be the have-nots. I cringe just writing these words in this way. It is such an insensitive way to treat one another, and so un-American. Americans have envisioned their nation as one that has done away with the class system of Europe. Yet have we really? Divisions by social class, race, economic status, and religion are just as present in twenty-first-century

---

5. Goodman, "Romney's 1 Percent Nation."

America as in any other society, in spite of our Constitutional premise of the equality of all. Perhaps these divisions are more subtle in American society, but they are just as present and, in some ways, more pronounced in the first decade of this century than at any other time in our history. So, envy is inevitably present and operative. Is that a good thing or a bad thing? It depends in part on how we think about the social inequities we observe.

Attribution theory is a concept in social psychology that studies how people explain behaviors or events. When we compare ourselves to others in our perceived reference group and we notice that the other has more or better things than we do (they may be richer, more privileged, prettier, or more fortunate in some way or another), we must explain this observation by answering the question, How and why is this so? To what do we attribute this fact? Is it because they are just luckier, or is it because they worked harder, or is it because they cheated, or is it because they are blessed by God? Similarly, we must explain why we are in this circumstance. Is it because we are not as good, not as smart, not as lucky, not as blessed by God, not as fortunate, not as hard a worker? The conclusions we draw from this attribution process then shape our feelings of envy. If we conclude that our sibling is smarter than we are because she worked harder at it, then our envy may motivate us to work harder in order to keep up with our older sister. If we conclude that this same sister is smarter than we are because she got all of the "good genes" and we got none of them, then our envy may well turn into resentment.

On a broader plane, how do Americans attribute or explain the economic inequity of a nation built on equal opportunity for all? We Americans tolerate a good deal of economic inequity because we believe that through hard work every poor person can become wealthy.[6] We generally attribute the inequities among us to hard work or lack thereof. By drawing that conclusion, our envy is motivational, motivating us to work harder to earn what we envy that others have. Suppose, however, that we attributed the inequity among us to other causes, such as discrimination or lack of opportunities or inherited wealth. Drawing such conclusions, our envy might turn bitter or at least call forth from us cries for justice. Indeed, as the inequities of wealth become more pronounced, the dynamics of envy become more crucial. Will Americans continue to use envy to motivate themselves

---

6. This observation about the American character was noted as early as the 1830s by French sociologist Alexis de Tocqueville. Because of this belief and the fundamental equality of American society, he argued that social revolutions were less likely in America (*Democracy in America*, 2:252–63).

to work harder or will Americans become increasingly bitter, resentful, and primed for social revolution?

Let's return to the other question raised by Mitt Romney's comment: Are the cries for economic justice just misplaced envy? The implication is that the poor are inevitably envious of the rich and that their envy, instead of fueling hard work, has turned bitter and resentful and will lead us all toward class warfare. Are the cries for justice that arise from those who perceive themselves to be the have-nots really pleas for justice, or are they just disguised envy? It is too easy for the wealthy to dismiss the complaints of the have-nots by saying they are just envious. Of course, envy is present. That is not the issue. We would all like to have some of the advantages we see others having in abundance. The cries for justice are not just about getting our fair share; they are also a protest against a system that is broken, unfair, and rigged against equal opportunity for all. At the same time, the litmus test for any social revolution is what happens when the have-nots become the haves. If the issue really is the unjust system, the former have-nots will implement just reforms so that injustice is vanquished, but if it is just misplaced envy, the haves and the have-nots will just change places and class warfare will continue in a different form. In that case, we will never reach authentic community, where cooperation overrides competition and where we see ourselves as all part of God's family.

In the long view of things, humans have survived on this planet through a combination of competition and cooperation. Early humans were successful in the evolutionary process because they were both effective competitors and effective cooperators. Sports, business, and military enterprises function successfully when they balance the cooperative and competitive impulses. But knowing when to cooperate and when to compete is a tricky social and personal issue in our culture. One wonders whether unregulated capitalism encourages too much competition at the expense of cooperation. Religion has traditionally balanced this over-emphasis upon competition by encouraging cooperation. Yet, organized religion is steadily losing influence in an increasingly secularized Western world. The net effect may be that comparison and competition is becoming more pervasive at all levels of society. We can only wonder what are or will be the long-term effects of such an imbalance upon humanity's efforts to build an inclusive global community.

The Psychology of Envy

We humans are social creatures. We live in communities. We thrive best in communities where we feel physically and psychologically safe. When our psychological make-up was formed millions of years ago, we traveled in small family groups that were our primary communities. We organized ourselves into various roles in order to survive and function as a family unit or tribe. We tended to give status to those roles. We formed pecking orders based on power, wealth, age, appearance, etc. Social status helped the group to function and helped each member to know his or her place. Knowing our place was essential in order to negotiate issues like food and sex without violence and in order to ensure safety from outside threats.

In modern times, we humans still carry around the same psychological need to belong, which is expressed in part as a need to identify our place or status in our social group. Today, our safety and our next meal rarely depend on our neighbor or even our next of kin. Yet, we are still concerned with identifying and clarifying our status in reference to our neighbor or family member. So we do what we have done for thousands of years; we compare and contrast ourselves with others.

Envy is rooted in this basic need to clarify, secure, and advance our social status. Envy is rooted in a natural, normal human need. So we might say that we humans are programmed to feel envious or, more accurately, that we have a natural capacity for envy. If placed in the right situation, we all can get our envy button pushed. Of course, if our buttons are pushed too often or too intensely because we live in an envy-saturated environment, exaggerated or excessive envy can be destructive to both community and our personal well-being. Let's explore how envy can destroy individuals.

Envy begins with comparison—comparing ourselves with our peers or people we perceive to be our peers. We do it all the time. It is inherent to the human species, social creatures that we are. How many of us run through the alumni news from our college or university with a critical eye toward what our peers have accomplished in comparison to ourselves? With painful pangs of envy, we read of their accomplishments and note their appearance. Or, with a sense of superiority we note how much we have accomplished compared to those who were popular students.[7] In

---

7. Evolutionary psychologists suggest that men tend to compare themselves to other men along the lines of wealth and power, whereas women tend to compare themselves to other women on the basis of children and appearance. My experience is that we modern humans can compare ourselves across a wide variety of domains and standards. There are no truly universal gender differences.

short, we have a basic inclination to compare ourselves to others. How do we stack up? What is our status in the tribe?

In modern societies, the threat underlying status anxiety is not so much safety or death, as it was for our primitive forebears, but self-esteem. We compare ourselves with others as a means of gaining or losing self-esteem. If we have more possessions than our neighbor, or our kids are more outwardly successful, or we have a larger home, a newer car, or more vacations, then we feel greater self-worth. "I am better than my neighbor!" But, if we determine that we do not measure up to our neighbor in whatever domain, there is an implied minimization of the self. I am a loser compared to my successful neighbor, who is clearly a winner. One of envy's toxic influences arises from this implied devaluation of self. Chronic envy can undermine our self-esteem. By being envious, we are discounting ourselves. In the modern age, materialism has become the domain in which self-esteem rises or falls. Things, or similar externals, translate into greater self-esteem, first and foremost in our own eyes, but certainly also in the eyes of others.

We tend to compare ourselves with our peers, with those in our reference groups, those groups that we belong to or identify with. This is a fairly simple observation. Yet, modern urbanized societies have scrambled our sense of reference groups. We no longer live in a single family or tribal unit. Modern people may be a member of several communities at once—e.g., a congregation, an extended family, a neighborhood, acquaintances at the gym, business co-workers, and a professional group. Our sense of community is fragmented, and many of our communities are temporal in nature. They take up only a piece of our lives, not the totality of our lives. So which group is our primary reference group, the group that we identify with, the community we long to belong to? It varies.

In this media-dominated culture, advertisers study and try to identify reference groups. They want to create commercials that place their sales pitch in the context of the viewer's reference group because they know that we are more likely to compare ourselves with those whom we perceive as our peers. Envy then motivates us to keep up with our peers. So advertisers spend a lot of time and money studying the demographics of various groups and subgroups in our society. If a good-looking, "cool" African American teenager appears on television making a pitch for McDonalds, it is an obvious appeal to all of the African Americans or teens among the viewers: "Be like me—eat at McDonalds." If a young rock star makes a pitch for a deodorant, this message will not affect a sixty-year-old widowed woman who does not see herself in the rock star's group.

Television has also had the effect of leveling the playing field, so to speak, making all of us feel we are part of the same reference group—modern Americans. Television invites us to compare ourselves to people who are clearly in a higher socioeconomic class than ourselves. This is the essence of the American dream, that each of us can strive beyond our original social class. This dream is still very appealing. It is interesting how advertisements try to make us think we are in community when we are actually not in community. Television commercials try to treat us all as members of the same peer group, electronically connected. We share in the joys, agonies, and hardships of fellow Americans many thousands of miles away. Commercials play on our need for community, trying to make us feel like every movie star pitching a product is a member of our reference group.

People who are insecure seem especially vulnerable to the appeal to envy. Teenagers are more sensitive to media than most age groups, in part because of the search for identity and self-worth that characterizes adolescence. Teens seem to be consumed with trying to look like, be like, dress like, and have a life like their peers—or those who appear to be their peers on television, in popular music, or in movies. Thus, I would suggest that teenagers are more vulnerable to envy as a dynamic in their efforts to organize their identity, status in the group, and/or self-esteem. Adolescents are more concerned with their social status and place and role among their peers than are adults.[8]

Finally, envy can be good or bad. It is a natural enough emotion, based as it is in our deeply rooted need for social status. Mild doses of envy can energize us to work harder. As noted in a recent *Psychology Today* article, "The Measuring Game," envy can be a good thing if it energizes us to put our nose to the grindstone and earn more money to secure the things that we desire.[9] In short, let envy motivate you, not paralyze you.

Capitalism thrives on this kind of envy. But, envy that is exaggerated, intense, or prolonged keeps us at odds with our neighbors and blocks cooperation within families and communities. Furthermore, envy, shaped by negative attributions or based on unrealistic comparisons, can paralyze us

---

8. This observation raises the question of whether there is a connection between the prevalence of envy during the adolescent years and the fact that most drug and alcohol addictions begin in this same time period.

9. Flora, "Measuring Game," 42–50.

with depression or cause resentment. It is the soil in which one or several addictions can grow.

Addictions Associated with Envy: Are They Deadly?

Envy is a sin that operates within small systems such as families and large systems such as classes of people and even societies. Envy is probably most intense, and therefore the most dangerous, in families. In fact, I would argue that envy is learned, for better or worse, in the social laboratory called the family of origin. Interestingly, one of the foundational stories in the Hebrew Bible is a story about the destructive power of envy. In the Genesis story of Cain and Abel, Cain's envy toward Abel's perceived advantage leads to revenge and murder (Gen 4:1–7). In verse 7, God says to Cain,

> "Sin is crouching at the door,
> Its desire is for you,
> But you must master it."

What a powerful and compelling image—envy crouching at the door like a wild animal bent on consuming us! Cain's envy was inevitable, maybe even natural, but it did not motivate him to try harder. Rather, it became consuming and obsessive, a lingering resentment that drove Cain to murder his brother whom he perceived to be unjustly favored. In this case, envy was not a flash in the pan. It sustained itself long enough for Cain to plot and execute a murder. The verb "to covet" similarly implies a process, a dwelling upon sinful thoughts, not a single thought. One can covet or be envious in passing, as with a fleeting thought, but when one allows envy to abide in the mind, envy begins to do harm.[10] So the sin of envy is not the sin of a passing envious thought, but an envious brooding hour after hour and day after day that results in a resentful attitude and sometimes a sinful deed. This kind of prolonged envy can be a breeding ground for various addictions. First among them is violence fueled by resentment, as the biblical account so graphically illustrates.

In the opening vignette of this chapter we briefly met Alice, who struggled with an eating disorder and depression. Bulimia and anorexia nervosa are two of the most common types of eating disorders that have

---

10. As I will discuss elsewhere, all of the Seven Deadly Sins are really sinful attitudes rather than occasional sinful deeds. Envy is thus the soil in which sin grows or, to be more precise, the soil in which addictions grow.

exploded upon the scene in Western cultures in the last thirty years.[11] In both disorders an individual, usually a female, is obsessively striving to maintain a certain body image by either not eating or by eating and purging. It is estimated that there are about eight million persons in the United States with one of these two conditions, most of them not receiving treatment.[12] It should also be noted that anorexia nervosa, one of these eating disorders, is the most fatal of all the mental health disorders.[13] My view is that these disorders are best understood as a type of behavioral addiction, which I described in chapter 1. These disorders are not addictions to *food* or to the behavior of *eating*. Rather, they are addictions to *a certain image*. These disorders reflect an obsession with an image, a look, a size, and/or a psychological/physiological sensation. In short, it is a kind of perfectionism. Perfectionism can be both an obsession and a behavioral addiction.

It seems clear that one of the dynamics in perfectionism is comparison. Young people—these disorders typically start in adolescence—are constantly comparing themselves to an idealized image, an image shaped by the media, an image often very unrealistic for 95 percent of the population. I would suggest that envy is at work here, too. Teens like Alice who spent years in chronic envy are ripe for both an eating disorder and depression. Statistics suggest that up to 50 percent of those who are diagnosed with an eating disorder also have diagnosable depression.[14]

Why has this type of addictive disorder surfaced in recent decades in Westernized cultures? For 99 percent of our history we humans have been obsessed with getting food and avoiding starvation. Now, in this rare and troubling development, some of us are obsessed with not eating. I believe that these new forms of addiction are the product of a culture that has become envy-driven and envy-promoting. The more this media-driven capitalistic culture creates envy, the more people will become victim to these kinds of eating disorders.

---

11. Overeating is also increasingly being classified as an eating disorder, but this discussion is limited to those disorders that reduce or eliminate food intake, which are primarily these three disorders: anorexia nervosa, bulimia nervosa, and binge eating disorder.

12. This is sometimes reported as 4 to 7 percent of the population, depending on the specific diagnosis (Insel, "Spotlight on Eating Disorders").

13. The mortality rate for anorexia nervosa is about 10 percent (ibid.).

14. Sometimes depression can lead to an eating disorder, and sometimes an eating disorder can trigger depression. See Devlin and Walsh, "Eating Disorders and Depression," 473–76.

Let me offer another example. In the last twenty years or so, compulsive shopping has become a recognized problem, even an addiction. The term "shopaholic" has surfaced in the popular culture to describe this problem. Indeed, there are now twelve-step groups for compulsive shoppers. Shopaholism, or compulsive buying disorder (CBD), is described as occurring in people, again mostly females, who spend beyond their means and/or spend an extreme amount of time and energy shopping to the point where the behavior has negative consequences. The negative consequences include consumer debt and/or disturbed family relationships. By some estimates there may be as many as ten million people with this condition, particularly when it is defined not just behaviorally but also mentally as the presence of obsessions or preoccupation.[15] The bewildering array of consumer choices and the constant urgency underlying sales pitches make us all a little nuts. Certainly compulsive shopping has not risen to the level of deadliness associated with alcoholism and drug addiction, but it can still be categorized as a destroyer of persons. Compulsive shopping can ruin the emotional, family, and spiritual lives of its participants.[16]

Again, I would pose the question of why and how it is that this addictive disorder has surfaced in the latter half of the twentieth century in Westernized cultures. As with the addictive eating disorders, I would argue that the common psychological dynamic is comparison and the fuel is envy. Westernized capitalistic and media-oriented cultures are envy-promoting and envy-encouraging cultures. What is the impact of this upon our psyches and the psyches of our children? How can we teach our children to value themselves and be content in life, in such an atmosphere?

Lest we think such problems exist only in women, let me offer one more example. I recall an occasion when Jamison, one of my counseling clients who was also a friend from church, dropped in on my therapy office one week before Christmas. His opening exclamation was, "If I hear one more diamond commercial on television I am going to kill myself." He was complaining about the constant commercials, clearly aimed at affluent white males, urging men to buy their spouse or girlfriend diamond jewelry for the holiday. "My wife deserves diamonds as much as anyone. She has

---

15. According to a recent Stanford University survey, 5.8 percent of the U.S. population qualifies as having compulsive buying disorder. Of these, 80 percent are female (Black, "Review of Compulsive Buying Disorder," 14–18).

16. Compulsive buying disorder may be understood as an addiction related to greed, but I think that it can also be understood as an addiction growing out of the seedbed of envy.

put up with me for thirty years... but I cannot afford that stuff. Not in these economic times." Jamison is a self-made man, a real estate entrepreneur. He is as hard-driving as the next guy—actually, he is more hard-driving than the next guy. He is what most therapists might call a Type A personality.

"I am sure Holly does not expect diamonds, Jamie," I said.

"No, I guess I do."

"How is it that you make those expectations of yourself?"

We talked for a while. What emerged in our conversation was a story of a life filled with envy. From an early age, Jamison had had his eye on what the big boys had—running in the fast crowd and being the most successful in his class. From my perspective, I would say that a dynamic of envy was just built into his personality and colored everything he did. At his present age of forty-eight and under the stress of an economic slowdown, some cracks were beginning to show themselves in his stance toward life, but as he himself said, "It's hard to let go of my lifestyle. It is a bit addictive, this competitive drive I have."

The holiday season, with its focus on cheerfulness and the acquisition of material goods, leads many people to compare their lives to the lives of others, past or present. Envy seems to be intensified. Based on my forty years of work as a therapist, I believe that much of the depression that surrounds the holiday season arises from comparison and from a dynamic of envy, an envy that turns into a low-grade resentment that in turn translates into a low-grade depression. There are many reasons for depression, some of them biological and idiosyncratic to the individual, and it may even be related to the increased hours of darkness during the winter holiday. Yet there is also something about Christmas that actually seems to intensify this connection between envy and depression. It is really about expectations, isn't it? The holiday season carries a whole host of expectations and, for many people, those expectations are burdensome.

The hidden death in envy, when it becomes addictive in nature, is resentment. There is a hidden anger in envy, anger at the neighbor's advantage, and if that envy is sustained over time, due to personal and/or societal limitations, resentment grows and grows. As I said earlier, envy in its full-blown form is not just wanting what the neighbor has, but also wanting the neighbor to be robbed of his or her advantage. There is a hidden hostility in chronic and excessive envy. Researchers over the last twenty years have documented that prolonged anger is a risk factor for heart disease, hypertension, and death.[17] Anger that is talked out and released is less of a risk factor, but prolonged, bitter resentment is risky, and this is the kind of anger associated with the sin of envy. I will say more about anger, of course, in a later chapter.

So, in many ways and forms, envy can be a deadly sin, deadly to communities, deadly to family relationships, and deadly to individuals on a variety of levels. It is deadly in its own right, if unchecked, because it creates obsessive resentment, and it is also deadly because it provides the rich soil in which several possible addictive disorders can grow. How can we use our spiritual resources to block or prevent envy from becoming addictive?

Envy's Antidote: Learning to Love Others

Traditionally, the virtue that is considered to be the antidote for envy is love. If you are a Christian, you probably know that in the New Testament a particular kind of love is advocated that is called *agape*. Agape, which is sometimes translated as charity, is selfless love, love that puts the interests of the other above one's own interests. This is the kind of love that God has for humanity and the kind of love we are to strive for in our interactions with family members and neighbors in need.

Agape, or altruistic love, wants what is best for another. A person with this kind of love is happy for another's good fortune rather than resenting it. Love empathizes with the other. Love walks in the other's shoes. Love unites people and brings people together. Love builds community. So, the more we can practice love, fill our hearts with love, and promote love, the less we will feel envious. Love is the preventive medicine for envy. The best description of love as agape is found in 1 Corinthians 13, a passage often read at wedding ceremonies. Interestingly, in this passage Paul contrasts true love with envy. He says directly that "love is not envious . . . it is not resentful. It does not rejoice in wrongdoing but rejoices in truth" (vv. 4–6). Envy breeds resentment. Envy, in its intense forms, rejoices in the misfortune of others—a truly unloving attitude—whereas love rejoices in the good fortune of others. Love rejoices in truth.

We can practice the virtue of love by doing the following:

---

17. See Miller et al., "Hostility and Physical Health," 322–48.

- getting to know our neighbors as persons by understanding and empathizing with their struggles; going out of our way to get to know people; avoiding judging others until we get to know them
- letting envy motivate us, not paralyze us; channeling our envy
- counting our blessings; practicing gratitude; focusing on what we do have, not on what we do not have
- teaching our children to share; practicing sharing
- finding and building genuine community where everyone works for the common good, possessions are shared, and the operating principle is that "I get ahead only when everyone in the community gets ahead"; soaking up the healing ethos of this kind of community
- attending on regular basis a twelve-step program, where recovery is achieved and sustained by participating in a community that is non-competitive, non-judgmental, and supportive
- affirming our own unique measures of success; reminding ourselves how far we have come; remembering that each of us is on our own path in life
- defining success in broader terms than material possessions or achievements, including success in family, success in health, success in spirituality, success in the arts, and success in intellectual development
- minimizing our exposure to commercial advertising on television and in other media
- examining and challenging our hidden assumptions about ourselves and our expectations about life; understanding that we are valuable in our own right, that it is futile to compare, and that there is more than enough love to go around

Summary

In this chapter on envy, I have argued that envy is essentially a problem in community, a problem that communities need to learn how to manage to avoid being destroyed by prolonged and excessive envy. A little envy here or there is not a bad thing, if it motivates us to work harder, but prolonged and excessive envy is destructive. Furthermore, envy is the breeding ground for all addictions, particularly for perfectionism (eating disorders), compulsive shopping, hoarding, workaholism, and anger in the form of resentment, and occasionally envy even results in violence. The path of love and the way of cooperation are the antidote and remedy for envy.

Questions for Self-Reflection

1. What makes me envious? Do I get envious over a neighbor's house, car, vacation, job, children, or spouse? Do I get envious over someone else's good fortune, popularity, skill, success, or appearance?
2. Do I like watching stories of the rich and famous? If so, how does that help me?
3. Do I consider myself to be a highly envious person? Am I a possessive person? Am I a jealous person by nature?
4. Am I primarily competitive or cooperative with others?
5. What do I do with my envy? Do I allow it to make me resentful and depressed or do I let it energize me to work harder to achieve what I perceive that I lack?
6. Have I ever been a member of a community in which comparisons, status, and possessions truly did not matter? When and where do I find genuine community in my life?

Biblical passages related to envy: Gen 4:1–7, 37:1–4; Exod 20:17; Prov 23:17; Matt 7:1-5; Mark 15:10; Luke 15:28; Rom 1:29b; 1 Cor 13:4; 2 Cor 10:12; Gal 5:21

4 Anger

A Cycle of Resentment, Rage, and Violence

Judge Lawrence: I see here, Mr. Rodriguez, that this is not your first appearance before this court: two prior arrests for assault and one for disturbing the peace. Now we have what the court considers the gravest offense yet, a conviction of child abuse upon your ten-year-old son. Before I sentence you, do you have anything to say for yourself?

Mr. Rodriguez: I am sorry, your Honor. I really do not mean to hurt my family. I have prayed to our Lady of Guadalupe that may wife may forgive me. . . . Please don't take my family from me. [Mr. Rodriguez cries.]

Judge Lawrence: In the past, the court ordered you into counseling and an AA program. These programs did not seem to help you much.

Mr. Rodriguez: They did help me, your Honor. I learned a lot, but people make me mad, like when my son disobeys me or someone insults me or my family. I cannot help myself. I get a little loco . . . out of control. Diablo takes me over.

Judge Lawrence: Well then, the court will have to control your temper for you. I sentence you to ninety days in the county jail, and when you are released you must attend a court-approved anger management program. Visits with your children will be monitored by the Department of Children's Services until such time as they are convinced you have been rehabilitated. Case closed.

INCREASINGLY, PEOPLE WITH CHRONIC anger problems are ending up in the courts charged with offenses such as domestic violence, child abuse, road rage, assault and battery, and even murder. Juan Rodriguez, age thirty-four, is a husband and father of three children. He has a long history of anger problems dating back to his involvement with a neighborhood gang as a teenager. His one brother was killed in a gang-related shooting. His father was in and out of jail when Juan was younger, and by the time Juan was a teen, his father was absent. Juan's anger difficulties have been compounded by his abuse of alcohol and drugs. He has lost a couple of jobs due to his temper, and he is now about to lose his family as well. He is paying a high price for his intense and quick temper.

The statistics about anger-related violence are grim. One source suggests that every nine seconds in America a woman is assaulted or beaten.[1] Road rage or aggressive driving accounts for 56 percent of the fatal auto accidents in the United States.[2] In 2010, an average of over four children died every day in America due to child abuse.[3] The National Institute of Mental Health reports that sixteen million Americans have been diagnosed as having Intermittent Explosive Disorder.[4] Yet, out-of-control anger is only the more obvious face of anger. Chronic low-grade anger contributes to depression, sexual impotence, heart disease, family conflict, and various addictive problems—just to name a few of the less immediately obvious problems. Even a casual survey of the world around us tells us that Juan Rodriguez is not alone. Anger in one form or another is a problem for many Americans. Among the traditional Seven Deadly Sins, anger seems to be the sin of our times. Anger is everywhere these days, from the crime dramas that fill our television screens to afternoon talk shows that disclose the personal and tragic results of violence to the hallowed halls of Congress.

Where does this kind of anger come from? Why can't Juan stop himself? He attended counseling for a time and explored his feelings, the various issues that upset him, and his family's stresses. He tried a few of the techniques that the therapist suggested. However, his continuing over-use of alcohol did not help; alcohol reduced his ability to think before he acted. And Juan's various financial and work problems only added stress and tension to his life. The forces outside him and the forces within him often overpowered his limited resources. He wants to control his temper, but he

---

1. See Domestic Violence Statistics, "Domestic Violence Statistics."

2. The survey was conducted by the AAA Foundation for Traffic Safety over a five-year period from 2003–2007 ("Aggressive Driving," 1).

3. Administration for Children and Families, "Child Maltreatment 2010."

4. Kessler et al., "Intermittent Explosive Disorder," 675.

cannot. Perhaps if he understands himself as having an addiction, he might change how he approaches this problem.

A Brief History of Anger Treatment

The history of anger research and the treatment of anger problems in the United States are illustrative of contrasting views on anger. In contrast to the moralistic view of anger held by previous generations, modern psychologists argue that anger is a feeling, nothing more and nothing less. It is not right or wrong. Anger is not a sin.[5] We cannot help feeling angry. Feeling angry is a normal part of life. It is a normal reaction to situations in which we feel hurt, rejected, or attacked. What we do with our angry feelings, however, is important and has consequences. Anger can fuel aggression and violence, or anger can fuel constructive action, as when righteous anger helps us stand up for justice.[6]

In accordance with this view of anger, psychotherapists in the 1950s and 1960s thought that if expressed in appropriate ways, anger usually dissipated without harm. The image of a simmering teapot was often employed to illustrate that anger is best handled by blowing off steam on a regular basis. Thus, the emphasis in the treatment of anger problems was upon venting, expressing yourself—assuming that if you get it off your chest, you will feel better. I recall participating in many a therapy group in those days when the participants were encouraged to beat a pillow and exchange blows with sponged bats. The biggest "sin" in those days was the repression or holding in of anger because it was thought you might give yourself an ulcer or a stroke by doing so.

From the 1970s through the 1990s, scholars and clinicians rethought the subject of anger in light of the growing number of people with anger problems, especially in the context of research that suggested that people who "get it off their chests" do not always get over their anger problem. Psychologists have documented that some people, even after venting their anger over and over again, do not get much relief. They can be just as angry

---

5. The Bible even supports this view. For example, St. Paul says, "Be angry but do not sin" (Eph 4:26). The implication is that angry feelings are not sins—they are only feelings; only the subsequent actions are potentially sinful.

6. Righteous anger is anger on behalf of another, usually a victim or an unjust situation. There are lots of people in the Bible—Hebrew prophets, Jesus, even God—who display righteous anger. Righteous anger empowers us and motivates us to take corrective action. Anger if channeled correctly can serve many constructive purposes.

as before treatment! Venting angry feelings does not bring peace, or at least not for everyone. Sometimes—or for some people—venting angry feelings only adds fuel to the fire. The prevailing motto, "the more one gets angry the better one will feel," began to be replaced with the truism that "the more one gets angry, the more one gets angry!"

So, increasingly, therapists have begun to place anger problems in an addiction model, not a therapy model. They see anger as having an addictive lure. They use terms like "rage-aholic" to describe this different perspective on anger. This view of the dynamics of anger as having addictive elements is supported by cognitive therapy, which takes the view that anger tends to reinforce itself through distorted thinking. Further, the new field of neuroscience has suggested that the brain forms neuropathways ("anger pathways") that deepen with each expression of anger, thus making angry explosions habitual if not inevitable. So, for some people, or for all of us some of the time, anger does not go away when expressed but actually gets worse. Some people seem to have a bottomless pit of resentment—once it is tapped, it just keeps coming and coming.

Nowhere has this change in the prevailing understanding of anger been more striking than in how therapists do couple therapy. In the earlier view, a couple's difficulties were often understood as due to pent-up anger or the inability to talk frankly to one another. So, the therapist tried to help them express themselves to each other. If this happened, the air would be cleared and a positive atmosphere created in which problems could be resolved. Now, in light of the addictive understanding of anger and of the fact that some people have a chronic anger problem, therapists are encouraged not to do couple therapy if there is a history of spousal battering or physical conflict. Venting in the therapist's office may only give license to the batterer to go home and be even more violent. The current treatment of choice is to first get the partner with a chronic anger problem into an anger management program; after that, couple therapy may be effective.

This change in how anger is understood also has resulted in a new approach to the treatment of individuals with chronic anger problems. The treatment of choice is no longer emotive therapy, but cognitive-behavioral work. The treatment of anger problems now centers on anger *management*, not anger expression. Participants in anger management programs are taught to recognize their distorted thoughts, to practice self-control and relaxation techniques, and, in short, to manage their anger rather than vent their anger.

In a sense, then, modern psychology has moved 180 degrees in relation to anger. Yes, anger is largely a morally neutral feeling. It is what we do with our anger that is morally good or evil. I heartily concur. Yet, anger also has great addictive power, the power to reinforce and embellish itself, thus consuming and poisoning our minds, our hearts, and our relationships. In a sense, then, the sinfulness of anger does at times begin long before any sinful deed.

In earlier versions of the Seven Deadly Sins, the sin of anger was termed wrath. The modern translation might be rage. This sin of anger is not about anger as a feeling, but about excessive anger, violent anger ("violent" here is understood as both verbal and physical violence). In a sense, the wisdom of the Seven Deadly Sins was ahead of its time—pointing to the addictive qualities of anger as rage or wrath.

Rage/Violence as an Addiction

Recent research in neuropsychology suggests that our anger style is wired into our brains. So when we get inappropriately angry, especially intensely angry, we create or reinforce a neuro-pathway in our brain that then predisposes us to fall into that pathway again and again when presented with similar social cues. This pathway is like a rut in a muddy country road, and each time we get angry we make the rut deeper and deeper. In everyday language, we say that we are "programmed" like a computer. All someone has to do is "push our button" and off goes our programmed angry reaction.

With this information, we have a physiological model to explain how rage can be addictive, seemingly reinforcing itself over and over again. If someone has a problem with a quick temper, for example, he or she has a corresponding well-developed neuro-pathway in his or her brain, in a manner not too dissimilar from the drug addict who has also altered his or her brain chemistry and pathways in such ways as to drive the addiction. So when something even remotely similar happens again, our preprogrammed brain reacts automatically, quickly, intensely, and impulsively—because our brain is literally wired to do so.

If rage is addictive, then what is the high? When people become filled with rage and violence, their brain chemistry does change. Rage has a cleansing effect—it cleans out the emotions. That's one high. Physical violence also provides a high in the sense of relief from or release of pent-up tension and frustration.[7] Still another high is that we can feel empowered when we are angry. The sense of power, arising out of violent acts, can be a tempting lure, particularly so if it is felt in the context of a mob or gang of similarly violent peers. Group violence adds to the sense of power by reinforcing it with group solidarity. Finally, rage is reinforced by our cognitions (our justifications, rationalizations, or explanations) about why we exploded. For all of these reasons, professionals who work with anger management programs and domestic violence programs have come to embrace the understanding of violence as having addictive elements, at least for some people. They have adopted "rage addiction" as a working concept.

Anger is the mental component or mental sin that leads to the addictive behavior of rage. Rage is both verbal violence and physical violence. Violence is the behavioral component of rage. Perhaps, then, we may also describe the problem here as "violence addiction," although that term is seldom used by professionals in the field. Professionals who work in domestic violence programs do refer to the cycle of violence as an addiction cycle, however. Anger management and domestic violence programs have various versions of the wheel of rage. Figure 3 presents a composite version of this cycle.

Note that the cycle of violence looks suspiciously like the addiction cycle that I described in chapter 1. The cycle begins with unmet emotional needs, moves to obsessive thinking and the build-up of tension and frustration, and then eventually the rage erupts into verbal or physical violence. In the aftermath of this out-of-control behavior, there is release, shame, and apologies. Then the cycle begins again. Just like with drug and alcohol addictions, this cycle also becomes regularized and predictable over time. With each turn of the wheel of addictive rage, the neuro-pathways and social habits become deeper and deeper. Caught in this cycle, the addict feels like Sisyphus, condemned to push a boulder up a hill over and over again for eternity. There is a sense of doom and of slavery in this cycle of violence, just as there is in all addiction cycles.

---

7. This is why regular physical exercise is prescribed for anger and stress reduction. Physical exertion releases the pent-up energy associated with stress, anger, and frustration. There is obviously a huge moral difference between regular physical exercise and domestic violence, but the physiological function is similar.

Ancient Sins . . . Modern Addictions

Figure 3
Cycle of Rage/Violence

How does one break the cycle? At what point along the wheel can interventions succeed in interrupting the addictive cycle? Before I answer these questions, let me re-emphasize several points. First, rage and violence are bad enough and rarely justified, but the problem I am focusing on here is repetitive rage and violence, not single incidents. Not everyone who gets angry and even violent on occasion will become a rage-aholic, just as not everyone who drinks will become an alcoholic. Some people, by virtue of their personality, environment, upbringing, and/or genes are vulnerable to an addiction to violence. Yet, we all struggle with anger problems, and even if we do not become a full-blown rage-aholic, we all must learn to deal effectively with our angry impulses.[8]

8. Although we all struggle with managing our angry feelings, current statistics and even a casual review of human history suggest that men have more trouble with rage and violence than women. More often than not, women have been the victims of violence, not the perpetrators of violence. It may also be that women experience anger differently than men; due to cultural norms, women certainly express anger differently than men. Men have a lot to learn from women on this subject, but my view is that anger in the

Second, rage and violence as an addiction can capture groups as well as individuals. It may not be appropriate to apply the concept of addiction to a group, but group dynamics certainly can reinforce and intensify the addictive process. And when groups become enslaved to rage and violence, when these behaviors become built into their culture and history, the whole process takes on an eerie, even satanic tone.

Third, let me also note that what we have discussed about anger, rage, and violence also applies, although in less intense ways, to vicarious participation. Some people get a charge from the violence associated with certain professional sports, war video games, media violence, or urban gang violence. It is exciting, dramatic, and tribal. Even if we are never or rarely physically violent ourselves, the mental aspects of violence can become addictive along the lines we have discussed above.

Anger as Reaction: The First Steps

There are many varieties and shapes of anger.[9] The type of anger that the Seven Deadly Sins point to is excessive anger, anger that is over the top, anger that is out of control, anger that becomes violent—in short, wrath! It is also quick anger, the anger we refer to when we say that someone has "lost her temper." It is anger that sneaks up on us, catches us with our guard down, and, before we can bite our tongue, leads us to say or do something we regret. Thus, the traditional virtue that corresponds with the sin of anger is patience. Most of us had a grandparent whose advice for temper problems was to count to ten. Indeed, timing is everything. Rage feeds on immediacy and a sense of urgency.

Many anger management programs use the term "reactive anger" to describe the anger we feel when someone has hurt us. We are reacting.

---

form of reaction and resentment is a universal struggle and potentially addictive for both genders.

9. The various types and expressions of anger have been classified in different ways. In this book I am emphasizing the distinction the tri-part distinction between anger as reaction, anger as resentment, and anger as frustration, although I am not giving much attention to the latter. Another common way of classifying anger is by its expression: internalization, assertion, or aggression. These three anger expression styles are placed on a continuum from the one extreme of internalization (swallowing angry feelings, submitting in order to avoid conflict) to the other extreme of aggression (expressing angry feelings by attacking another person or invading his or her space). This view sees extreme internalization as just as bad as extreme aggression and presents assertion as a healthy approach to channeling one's anger.

We are being defensive. Perhaps someone has attacked us, hurt us, cheated us, scared us, threatened us, rejected us, abused us, or insulted us. And so we react . . . but sometimes we over-react. So it is that the first step in many anger management programs is to help participants identify their triggers—those persons, situations, words, or hidden messages that spark their anger. Often these triggers have histories—we have been reacting to these same triggers for years upon years. So, all of us who struggle with anger problems need to know our triggers, avoid our triggers as much as we can, and, if we cannot avoid a trigger, escape the situation altogether (i.e., give yourself a time-out). This is one way to interrupt the addictive cycle: avoid your triggers.

Anger management programs also teach that reactive anger can be thought of as a secondary emotion. In other words, we feel some other primary emotion before we feel the anger. We feel hurt . . . *then* we feel angry. We feel jealous, or frightened, or threatened . . . *then* we feel angry. A useful intervention then for this kind of anger is to pause—do not react—take time to identify the primary feeling, and begin by expressing not the anger, but the primary feeling.

Instead of saying, "You s.o.b.," say, "You really scared me."

Instead of saying, "I'm going to get even with you for that," say, "That really hurt my feelings."

Anger management counselors point out that there is an element of helplessness or powerlessness in reactive anger. Reactive anger happens when we have been acted *upon* rather than being actors. Anger born of powerlessness can be intense. It is anger that lashes out. It is anger that is mean, anger that wants to hurt someone else as we have been hurt. Revenge has its roots in powerlessness and can be understood as a mistaken attempt to regain personal power. Victims, whether they are individuals or groups of people, want and need to take back their power. As I will discuss again in a moment, revenge seldom works, in part because of its addictive elements. So a positive step to take in the management of reactive anger is to find constructive ways to assert our power, i.e., to set boundaries, take action, verbalize our needs, and stand up for injustice. In anger management programs, all this is grouped under the label of assertiveness training.

MANAGING ANGER THROUGH PATIENCE

The traditional Christian virtue that is the antidote for anger is patience. Patience can slow down anger's impulsiveness, allowing calm, rational, and moral responses to kick in. Patience stops the automatic reactions, giving us time for our brain to get engaged in a new way. Patience gives us time to make constructive behavioral choices like those described above.

Reactive anger or anger as revenge is associated with the more primitive parts of the human brain.[10] It tends to be quite irrational, illogical, and intense. It dates back in human history to our more primitive tribal instincts and loyalties. It is the kind of anger involved in ethnic strife. It is the kind of anger involved in gang warfare. It is the kind of anger that seeks revenge and is not satisfied or appeased until revenge is exacted from the offending party. This is the anger that feeds the cycles of revenge that we are so familiar with on the evening news. Violence begets revenge and revenge begets more violence, which in turn only leads to another round of revenge. In fact, we could say that revenge is an addiction, an addiction that grows out of the soil of reactive anger. The Middle East, among many other places, is the most dramatic example of such cycles of revenge. But revenge-filled anger is not limited to nations outside of the United States. Many a divorce and child custody battle in the courts of modern America has been fueled by the desire to exact "a pound of flesh" from the offending party. In such circumstances, as we all know so well, those who suffer the most are the children. Revenge as a desire to hurt when we have been hurt is a universal, but often regrettable, human impulse.

If we can find a way to be patient, even by simply counting to ten, we give our brains time to engage the cerebral cortex, which examines evidence, thinks through consequences, and then makes decisions. Patience gives our brains time to engage the higher faculties. Patience gives us time to make choices, not react.

---

10. In fact, several if not all of these Seven Deadly Sins may be understood as originating in the more primitive parts of the human brain, which are the brain stem and limbic system. Impulses or behaviors originating from the primitive brain are often intense, reactive, automatic, and not subject to the executive functions of the cerebral cortex.

WHAT MAKES US ANGRY?

Another useful insight from the world of anger management programs has to do with the role of cognitions (thoughts) in making and keeping us angry. It is not situations or people that make us angry, but what we think about those situations or people. We usually think of anger as an emotion, as a strong and even primitive emotion, but cognitive therapists argue that we are "made" angry by what we think. It is not an event by itself that makes us angry, but what we think about that event. It is not being fired from a job that makes us angry, for example, but the conclusions we draw from that experience, conclusions like "It was unfair," "The boss was picking on me," or "I'll never find another job." Yet, from the same experience—losing one's job—we could just as easily conclude, "I'll find a better job," "I didn't like that boss anyhow," or "I deserved it and I'll do better next time." One set of thoughts about the loss of our job makes us mad, whereas another set of thoughts about the same event does not make us mad. Clearly, what we think about events in our lives is a variable in the anger dynamic.

Juan Rodriguez, whom we met in the opening vignette of this chapter, stated, "People make me mad." If we had the opportunity to talk further with Juan, the cognitive approach might go something like this:

Juan: My supervisor made me mad. He does not pay us jack, and we have to put up with his shit.

Counselor: So your boss is a trigger; he triggers your anger. What about him exactly triggers you?

Juan: Lots of things, but when he gives me shit. When I am late, 'cause the bus is running late or something, he is on my case. Like his old lady was on him that morning, and he is taking it out on us.

Counselor: So criticism, especially what seems like unmerited criticism, triggers your anger. We cannot avoid criticism entirely in the work setting. Supervisors are supposed to be critical of employees from time to time. What are you thinking when you experience his criticism?

Juan: I think that he is insulting me, treating me like I am low class or something, not as good as he is.

Counselor: Let's examine that assumption that his criticisms are insulting. What evidence do we have to support that conclusion? Could there be other explanations for his criticism? You mentioned, for example, that you thought maybe his wife had given him a hard time and that now he was taking it out on you. Have you shared your perceptions with your peers?

Juan: Yeah, we have talked about him a lot at lunch time. Everyone agrees that he is a real ass.

Counselor: So what you are telling me is that your boss criticizes everybody, not just you. They also think that he is being unfair or overly harsh?

Juan: Yeah, they all agree.

Counselor: So it is not personal with you. He is a jerk with everyone on the assembly line. Does that help you not take it like a personal insult?

Juan: Yeah, it kinda does. When we talk over lunch, I do feel better for a while, like maybe it is not an insult to me and my family.

Counselor: I am wondering what other evidence you might find to help you draw different conclusions.

As this conversation continues, Juan realizes that there is some truth to his supervisor's criticism—after all, Juan was in fact late. Maybe his supervisor is just doing his job. "He could have written me up. Instead, he gave me a warning," Juan realizes. "I suppose it could have been worse." These ideas will help Juan calm down and not react with anger in the future, and this ultimately will help him keep his job. Later, the conversation goes in another direction.

Juan: He is white, you know. And all of my people are Latino.

Counselor: So you are thinking that maybe there is a racial issue here? Suppose for the sake of argument that there is some evidence to support the conclusion that your supervisor is treating you with prejudice—so what? What conclusions do you draw?

Juan: Well, that makes me mad.

Counselor: Why, exactly?

Juan: Because it is a put down. He is treating my family like we are trash or something.

Counselor: And are they?

Juan: Hell no. We are a proud family, filled with hard workers from the migrant camps.

Counselor: So, you are proud of your family. You have a high esteem of your worth, of your family's value. So, tell me again what you are thinking when you are so angry.

Juan: I am thinking that we are trash or something.

Counselor: So in that moment, when you are angry, you are agreeing with your supervisor? You are acting like it's the truth. "We are just trash."

Juan: I don't want to do that.

Counselor: What does it mean to you to be a Rodriguez?

Juan: I guess, it is something better than this.

Juan's partially fictionalized case is more complex than this simple exchange would suggest, but this conversation is illustrative of the larger point that our angry feelings are shaped by our thoughts, assumptions, and conclusions, and those thoughts, assumptions, and conclusions are in turn shaped by our personal, family, and cultural histories. Therefore, an effective approach to chronic anger problems is to examine and re-examine our cognitions. This is another place where the addictive cycle of rage can be interrupted, if we pause long enough to identify our self-talk and examine and reformulate our internal messages. Yet, our cognitions are both "descriptive" and "prescriptive." They not only explain and justify our anger, but work to keep us resentful year after year.

Anger as Resentment

We have been discussing the problem of excessive anger and the deadly consequences of rage and violence. Here, I want to touch on the other adjective I used earlier to describe the deadly sin called anger: prolonged. I believe that prolonged anger is implied in the traditional word "wrath." Anger that is quick can be deadly. So too, can be anger that is prolonged. These two kinds of anger are interrelated; they are two aspects or stages of the same addictive cycle. Chronic anger, anger that is largely mental, turns us into time bombs waiting for the event that triggers an explosion into rage. Yet, each explosion, along with its subsequent shame and apologies, reinforces the anger pathway and restarts the cycle of building resentment all over again. But even if we never explode in a rage, chronic anger can be deadly in its own right.

Current research on the links between anger and coronary heart disease focuses on what is called "trait anger," or anger as a personality trait. Trait anger, or what I more precisely call chronic resentment, is considered a risk factor for heart disease by many health organizations.[11] It is not the occasional flash of anger, but the chronic, simmering anger—anger as a personality trait—that is damaging to our health.[12] This observation gives new meaning to the scriptural verse, "The wages of sin is death" (Rom 6:23). Do you know people who were angry most of their lives and seemed to have put themselves into an early grave? Well, now we know that, at least for some people, chronic anger is a health risk.

After I spoke at a conference on ministry and aging, I met George, a seventy-eight-year-old talkative and delightful human being. After a long conversation that covered everything from history to politics, I commented on his apparent contentment in life. To my surprise, he noted that he had not always been so peaceful. In fact, for most of his life George was what he called a "hellion," one of those for whom anger was a problem. He lost a couple of jobs due to his temper. He alienated at least one son, who still does not speak with him. His anger was a factor in his marital unhappiness and eventual divorce. As he described it, he was always offended by something or someone. "My trouble," he said, "was that I would brood about it day after day, month after month. Over the years, I developed a good case of hypertension, and then a stroke almost killed me."

"There I lay in the hospital," he continued, "and suddenly it become graphically obvious to me that the only person my anger has hurt over the years was me. . . . The people that I was so mad at were not in the hospital—*I* was. The people with whom I wanted to get even were not near death—*I* was." He noted, "Revenge does its greatest harm to the one who hoards it

---

11. There has been a wealth of research on the link between "trait anger" and the development of coronary heart disease. For example, see Williams et al., "Anger Proneness." An abstract of this article is available at www.circ.ahajournals.org/content/101/17/2034. This study identifies "proneness to anger" as an independent risk factor for middle-aged men and women with otherwise normal blood pressure.

12. This research goes back to the work of physician Redford Williams, whose books *The Trusting Heart* and *Anger Kills* laid the foundation for the link between resentment as a risk factor for heart disease as well as an assortment of other medical problems. More recently, Fred Luskin, a researcher with Stanford University School of Medicine, has studied resentment in the context of forgiveness. He understands the destructive kind of anger as having an element of revenge. See Luskin, *Forgive for Good*, 78.

and nurses it. It eats away at your heart. So I began that very day to let go of it and to save a life . . . mine."

Chronic anger, or anger as resentment, is a stage in the wheel of addiction but is also deadly in its own right. The obsession with taking revenge consumes some people for years and years and some groups for generations upon generations. Such people secretly plot revenge against an offending party, a party who might have long since forgotten what they did to offend the revenge seeker. In the world of literature, there is no more graphic example of the addictive nature of prolonged anger than Melville's classic story of Moby Dick. In this epic tale of man vs. beast, Captain Ahab is consumed with the desire for revenge, searching the seas for the mysterious and elusive white whale that once robbed him of his limb. Over time he becomes more and more obsessed with his quest for revenge, more and more irrational and oblivious of the needs of others, his ship, or even himself. In the climatic scenes, Captain Ahab exacts his revenge, but he does so at the loss of his own life. Trapped in the ropes, tied to the whale's side, Ahab is bound eternally to the whale and is thus destroyed. Anger as resentment is like that, ultimately at least as destructive to the person seeking revenge as it is to the original offending party.

Prolonged anger or anger as resentment can actually nurture a variety of addictions. If you scratch the surface of an alcoholic or a workaholic or even a sex addict, unresolved chronic anger problems will bubble up. Chronic anger not only nurtures various addictions, but it also sustains those addictions once they become established. Even so, the addiction that is most typically associated with prolonged anger is clearly rage and revenge. Prolonged anger sets up excessive anger. And excessive anger, if not resolved, falls back into resentment where it simmers like spoiled milk, waiting for the next eruption. Prolonged anger and excessive anger reinforce one another. Anger as resentment and anger as reaction are both part of the same continuum, the same addictive cycle. This view of anger as resentment and as linked to immoral behaviors has some biblical support. In the Sermon on the Mount, Jesus says that it is not enough that we do not murder; we must also eliminate the anger of the mind that leads to murder (Matt 5:21–22). In Jesus's perspective, anger as resentment is connected to reactive anger and thus to murder. They are part of the same continuum—both immoral, different only in degree.

Resentment and Forgiveness

Although the traditional antidote for anger is patience, anger as resentment, with its undercurrent of revenge, can be best addressed and prevented through the spiritual practice of forgiveness. In recent years, there has been renewed interest in both religious and secular circles in the health-giving value of forgiveness. Forgiveness is not just about letting offenders off the hook; more importantly, it is about letting go of the resentment within us, the anger that is ultimately eating away at our health. Forgiveness is often not as easy or simple as some religious people may think. It often takes some work, some intentionality. Yet, it is a spiritual practice that bolsters us against anger as resentment and thoughts of revenge.

Confession and Release

Another traditional spiritual resource for anger management is confession. I employ the term "confession" in the general sense of the word, as in talking out your anger. Angry feelings demand to be expressed. There is a natural impulse, when we feel angry, to want to express it, to tell someone. We want to let it out!

We have language for a variety of reasons, but one of the functions of language is to help us verbalize our strong emotions and thus manage them. The primary God-given way that we are to express our angry feelings is through speaking. We are to use our words, not our fists, our guns, or our bombs. We are to talk it out, not act it out. When we were young and did not have much language, all we could do when we were mad was to show our anger through our behavior. Our parents told us over and over again, during those years, "Use your words." The maturing process includes the acquisition of a greater and greater command of language, which gives us the tools for managing our feelings of anger.

It has been my professional experience that the people who have the worst trouble with temper and violence problems are generally people who also have poor verbal skills. They either do not talk much or do not have a full array of words with which to express themselves. The more such people can learn to verbalize, the more tools they will have at their disposal to manage their anger—in fact, all of their strong emotions. There is a great deal of truth in the phrase "Confession is good for the soul."

Patience in an Impatient World

It is hard to practice patience in this media-driven, high-tech world that surrounds us with a pervasive sense of urgency. In our large urban areas, everyone seems to be in a hurry. The modern world emphasizes speed, instant results, and limitless consumption. "Buy it now." "Instant credit." "Faster Internet speed." "Fast food." "The quick fix." "Speed dating." This is not a patient world. We are not a patient people. We want quick answers to complex problems. Many of our difficulties with interpersonal relationships and even financial matters may have much to do with our need for quick results.

In chapter 2, which is about pride, I noted the interface between individual psychopathology and cultural trends and described the recent recognition of the personality disorder known as narcissistic personality disorder. I suggested that our society, with its increasing emphasis on self-gratification and self-promotion, is in a sense creating more and more narcissists. Similarly, in the last fifty years or so psychologists have labeled a cluster of traits the Type A personality. The Type A personality is characterized by a sense of time urgency, free-floating hostility, impatience, and competitiveness. Such people are ripe for coronary heart disease.[13] They are also prone to behavioral problems related to issues of anger, rage, and violence. And these people, like narcissists, are becoming increasingly common in our fast-paced and stressful world. Again, I would suggest that what shows up in the extreme among a few of us actually shapes all of us, all of the time, in lesser but more pervasive ways. We—and particularly our children—are being conditioned every day by the media to be impatient. In this atmosphere, it is little wonder that more and more of us are having difficulty with anger.

On the other hand, patience can be learned. We are not victims of our brains' faulty wiring. We can rewire ourselves through the formation of new neuro-pathways, new habits. Our brains are wonderfully plastic, as today's scientists tell us, and thus can be shaped by our behavior, much as our behavior is shaped by our brains. Patience is like a weak muscle that, with practice, can be strengthened to become stronger. A stronger patience muscle will help us manage whatever addiction we are struggling with.

---

13. The identification of Type A personality as a risk factor in heart disease dates back to the 1950s, when Meyer Friedman and Ray Rosenman first documented this finding ("Association of Specific Overt Behavior Pattern"). Later studies have suggested that the mechanism of this correlation is stress and/or chronic hostility.

Addictions of all kinds feed on impatience or what psychologists call "poor impulse control." When drug addicts want a fix, they want it now. When I've got to have a smoke, I've got to have it now. We see another new dress, and advertisers urge us to buy it now. Workaholics operate in a perpetual state of urgency. Road rage is fueled by drivers who cannot wait. Overeaters tend to eat fast. Sex addicts tend to rush to orgasms. And so on, and so on. Addictions of all kinds are fueled and sustained by an atmosphere of urgency and impatience. Cravings—to drink, to over-eat, to strike out in anger—are often experienced by most people as coming in waves. If we can just wait before acting, sometimes as little as five minutes, the craving will simmer down or even pass. Don't think about abstaining the whole day, just five minutes. Diverting our attention onto something else, even just for a little while, might be just long enough to give us the resources to manage our addiction one more day. That is what we do in addiction work; we do not cure the addiction, we just try to manage the cravings one day at a time.

So, any efforts we make to strengthen our patience muscle will help us manage our anger and prevent it from become rage or resentment. It is also true that strengthening our patience muscle in any area of life will have a spill-over effect, helping us with our ability to manage an addiction. For example, if we learn to be more patient with our children or more patient as a driver, we are indirectly helping ourselves develop better tools for managing our addictions. A little patience helps us shift out of our primitive, impulse-driven brain into our frontal lobes, where a calmer, more rational decision can be made.

We can practice the virtue of patience by doing the following:

- slowing down; taking regular time each day to meditate, pray, and "be" rather than "do"; practicing releasing prayers—releasing our anger to God; creating a peaceful imaginary place where we can go in our mind to center ourselves in times of stress or anger
- taking time every day to do physical exercise
- following my grandmother's advice, which was, "If you do not have something nice to say, say nothing"
- learning to take our anger temperature, even recording it in a daily log
- learning to give ourselves a time-out when our anger temperature reaches mid-range on the scale; finding a regular place where we can calm down, away from others; going for a walk

- enrolling in an anger management class where we will be held accountable for implementing what we have learned and will receive support from class members
- learning to identify the primary feelings that underlie reactive anger; practicing pausing long enough to identify and be with our primary feeling and then sharing that feeling instead of our anger ("I was really hurt when you . . .")
- learning to wait; trusting that we do not have to seek revenge because we know that God is a God of justice
- identifying our triggers, the situations that trigger our anger; avoiding these triggers as much as possible and having a plan for what we will do when our anger temperature rises

We Have Choices

People caught in the addiction of rage or violence often feel as if they have lost agency, lost the ability to choose and control their behavior. This sensation is also typical of all the addictions associated with gluttony: drug addiction, alcoholism, and over-eating. The development in recent years of neuroscientific explanations of addiction adds greatly to our information about addictions, but it also contributes to our sense of powerlessness. There is a subtle biological determinism at work in the various explanations of addiction involving brain chemistry. For example, after six weeks of domestic violence class, and thus armed with a little information, a rage-aholic announced: "I am a victim of my brain chemistry. I cannot help myself. It's the way I am wired." A deterministic view of addiction can lead to a lack of personal accountability for our actions.

The Christian spiritual tradition teaches that we are free, responsible, and ethical beings who know right from wrong and who must be accountable for our choices in this life. In the case of anger, we cannot always choose whether or not to feel angry, but a little patience can help us choose our behaviors. Ultimately, we are moral agents. We have choices. We need not be victims of our anger. Instead, we need to be masters or managers of our anger, because if we do not manage our anger, it will manage us and lead us into the deadly grip of an addiction. One of the greatest assets of a spiritual approach to recovery work is the reclaiming and building up of our ability to choose.

Summary

A little anger is not a bad thing. In fact, it is pretty normal and even inevitable, although its intensity and expression will vary by gender, personality, family background, and cultural influences. Anger can be helpful and lead to appropriate self-assertive and self-protective behaviors. But anger that is chronic (resentment) and excessive (rage) moves easily into an addiction, as is reflected in the cyclic nature of rage/violence. Resentment, rage, and violence can reinforce each other and recycle over and over again in repeated rounds of destruction. In this way, rage meets all of the criteria for a behavioral addiction, and a very destructive one at that. Patience and forgiveness are the two traditional virtues that, if practiced, can strengthen our ability to choose a behavior other than acting out our anger.

Questions for Self-Reflection

1. Do I lose my temper easily? Do I over-react to situations? Am I tense, uptight? Do I have health problems in which anger might be a factor?
2. Do other people irritate me a lot? Do I tend to blame others for my problems? Do I think that other people "make" me mad?
3. What makes me angry? What are my anger triggers? What have I learned about my anger and how to manage it?
4. What is my anger history like? What style of anger did I learn as a child? What events or relationships have influenced my storehouse of anger?
5. When and where is it hard for me to be patient? What helps me be patient?
6. Think of a situation when I was wronged. When and how did I forgive? What process did I go through or should have gone through?

Biblical passages related to anger: Ps 103:8–9; Prov 15:1; Matt 5:21–26; 23; Mark 11:15–19; Rom 12:17–21; Gal 5:20; Eph 4:26–32; 6:4

5 Sloth

Apathy and Lack of Motivation

Cindy: We have been drifting apart for years. We don't do anything together any more. We don't go out or go to movies. Our sex life is dull. We don't talk about much of anything other than who paid the bills or what the price of gasoline is this week. We are not excited with each other like we were when we were younger. Our marriage is dying here, Harry.

Harry: I guess you are right. We don't have much in common any more. . . .

Therapist: Sometimes this happens with couples who get very comfortable with each other over the years. You have to work at relationships these days.

Cindy (after a silence): I don't want to live this way. It is boring. You are boring. We are boring. We're boring, Harry! Like two old stick-in-the-mud middle-aged people.

Harry: I suppose we could take a trip or something.

Therapist: I think what Cindy is asking for is emotional, intellectual engagement. I would suggest you read a book together. Any subject would do—something to discuss and engage around.

Harry: I really don't like reading.

Cindy: You certainly like watching TV often enough. [Silence.]

Cindy: (now calmer): The real problem here is motivation. I think we have gotten a little sick of each other over the years, the same old arguments over and over again. We are stuck in a rut.

Therapist: I am wondering if you guys are stuck in other ways too. Career, health, spirituality?

Harry: I am not sure I have the energy for all this.

Cindy: I am not sure I have enough energy for both of us.

THE CONTEXT OF THIS conversation is the office of a couple therapist with whom Harry and Cindy are reviewing and evaluating their thirty-eight-year marriage. The younger of their two children is in college, and in this empty nest period they are discovering that they have lost each other along the way. In this excerpt from their conversation, Cindy is confronting and pushing her husband to engage with her—any response will do, she just wants a response. Harry is tired, indifferent, and apathetic, and Cindy is too, in her own way. Not only are they tired of each other, but they are tired of *trying*, of trying to resolve several chronic conflicts that surface over and over again. Their inability to resolve some of these perpetual disputes has led them to retreat to their respective corners and cease communicating except about the most mundane topics. The therapist is right, too. The "stuckness" they are experiencing is not just in their relationship. Harry talks later about how his career has plateaued, and Cindy reveals her secret despair over her lack of fulfillment as a mother and wife. They have a lot of work to do. Yet, as I see it, the primary challenge here is for them to overcome their apathy. They have run out of gas. They have misplaced their motivation, their desire to grow, learn, and become more than they are. They have fallen into the thicket of sloth—mental, emotional, and spiritual apathy. And clearly the sin of sloth is very deadly . . . maybe even addictive.

The Latin word for the sin of sloth is *acedia*. Acedia means more than laziness. Acedia also means a laziness of mind and spirit—indifference or apathy. If we think of sloth as physical laziness, we see images of slow-moving animals, welfare recipients, lazy teenagers, or your cousin Vinny who hasn't worked a day in his life. Then we start lecturing about how this country was built on a foundation of hard work and how idle hands are a playground for the devil, about the need to be early to bed and early to rise, and so on. Slow down! Like I said, sloth is not primarily about physical laziness. Physical laziness is one of the manifestations of sloth, but there are others, too, like mental laziness, spiritual laziness, or even relationship laziness, as illustrated by Cindy and Harry.

The term "sloth" in the English language implies a laziness or apathy over time. Being slothful does not refer to a weekly rest day or a vacation or even a season of life, but a pattern of laziness or apathy over time. Sloth is primarily an attitude, a sin of the mind, what psychologists call a personality trait that is present day after day, month after month, and even year after year. People caught in the sin of sloth are bored, indifferent, unmotivated—not just occasionally, as we all are, but as a style of life. Slothful people are apathetic people, both across time and across the spectrum of human behaviors.

Sloth, Apathy, and Depression

Reading the standard list of symptoms of clinical depression, one notices a couple of symptoms that sound a lot like sloth or apathy. Typically, clinical depression includes symptoms like lack of interest or pleasure in activities, chronic fatigue or lack of energy, and little motivation. So, one wonders what the connection is between depression and sloth. Medieval Christendom did not have a word for what we now know as depression. Perhaps "depression" was called melancholy, despair, or mourning . . . or sloth. Two of the meanings of the word acedia are discouragement and indifference. And one of the earliest lists of the deadly sins listed an eighth sin that was called melancholy or *tristitia* (sorrow). Later, this eighth sin was merged with sloth.[1] Maybe the sin of sloth was our spiritual ancestors' way of talking about depression or an aspect of depression. Maybe, as we have moved from a religious culture to a secular culture, we have moved from sloth to depression. We have moved from a moral model to a disease model.

In modern times, depression has become very common. It is the most frequent of all of the psychological illnesses. It is sometimes called the "common cold" of mental illnesses. At any given time about 10 percent of Americans have been diagnosed with one of several depressive disorders.[2] Depression comes in mild and severe forms, sometimes single and sometimes alternating with periods of mania. Depression has roots in our brain chemistry, in our situational stressors, in our self-talk, and sometimes even

---

1. See Capps, *Deadly Sins*, 12.
2. The National Institute of Mental Health ("Any Mood Disorder") reports that in any given year, 9.5 percent of U.S. adults are significantly depressed, including the diagnostic categories of major depressive disorder, dysthymic disorder, and bipolar disorder. Lifetime prevalence is 20.8 percent of the U.S. adult population.

in our stage of life. Depression is usually treated with a combination of psychotherapy and medications.

Sloth as apathy and sloth as clinical depression are not quite the same thing, yet they are close. I wonder if some of the many people who are diagnosed with mild, chronic depression these days might be better served if they understood their condition as apathy. The overlap of sloth and depression leads me to suggest that sloth may also be habit-forming in terms of brain chemistry, like depression is now understood to be. Once we get caught in the sin of sloth, we tend to stay there. Sloth creates sloth. Apathy breeds apathy because, at a chemical level and the level of cognition, apathy is being reinforced.

Human Needs and Sin

Throughout this book, I have suggested that each of the Seven Deadly Sins is actually a distortion of a basic human need, a need that is natural, ordinary, and healthy. A sinful state arises when these basic human needs are distorted, twisted through the addictive process to become more intense and/or more prolonged than normal. The descriptive phrase I have employed is "excessive and prolonged."

The sin of gluttony, which I will write about later, is the most obvious example of this dynamic. Gluttony is a distortion of a natural human need—eating. We must eat to survive. The sin of gluttony uses our natural need against us, so to speak. What is a normal, healthy need is now distorted and twisted into an addiction. What starts out as a good part of God's creation becomes a part of our destruction.

Similarly, the sin of pride is rooted in the natural need for self-worth. The sin of envy is rooted in the ordinary need for social status. Figure 4 outlines all seven basic human needs and their corresponding sinful distortions. We might say that each of these addictions becomes rooted in our psyche by using the natural reinforcers of these needs to transform these normal desires into addictive cravings.

Ancient Sins... Modern Addictions

Figure 4
Human Needs and their Distortions

Natural Human Need for:	*Distorted into the Sin of:*
Self Esteem	PRIDE
Social Status	ENVY
Assertion	RAGE
Security	GREED
Rest or Ease	SLOTH
Food	GLUTTONY
Sex	LUST

Our spiritual ancestors said that Satan assigned to each of us at our birth a demon specially programmed to attack our particular inherent weakness, be it pride, envy, anger, or some other vulnerability. This schema presents that truth in a little different frame of reference. I would say that our vulnerabilities have more to do with the strength of our needs. People with a strong need for or a high sensitivity to food are vulnerable to gluttony. People with a strong need for or a high sensitivity to security issues are vulnerable to the sin of greed. People who have a high need for or a sensitivity to rest or ease are vulnerable to the sin of sloth. Do you get the picture?

In a capitalistic culture, built on the Protestant work ethic that equates worth with work, being labeled slothful or lazy is as serious as being called a pervert or traitor. So many of us over-work, afraid to take legitimate holidays or vacations lest we be viewed as lazy. Yet, sloth is not the same as rest. Rest is an important part of the life cycle. We embrace this cycle every day of our lives—rest and work, work and rest. We embrace it on a weekly basis, too—it is written into the Ten Commandments—that one day a week we rest from work. Rest makes work possible. So, in a sense, a little bit of sloth is a good thing. Rest becomes sloth when it becomes prolonged and excessive. Sloth is a distortion of our need for rest or ease. It is rest on steroids.

How Widespread Is Sloth?

On first impression, sloth might seem to be a "light" sin compared to anger, greed, and lust. If we see sloth as apathy or lack of motivation, and if we know that such a condition can affect the whole of our lives, however, then our eyes can be opened to the presence of sloth everywhere and even to its occasional deadly effects.

When I shop at my favorite grocery store, I often take note of the number of shopping carts that are left throughout the parking lot. Most of the time shopping carts are abandoned all over the place, even down the street or around the corner in the alley, sometimes in very unsightly places. Even though we know that it would be good for us to walk a few more steps every day, the few more steps that it would take to return a cart to its proper resting place, many of us don't do it. Yes, we are often in a hurry, or have babies in tow, or it is raining. But, the issue is not about whether we return a shopping cart to its proper place or not; it is about our lack of motivation to do so. It is about not caring enough to do the right thing. Similarly, think about how hard it is to get all of us to recycle bottles, cans, and plastic containers; clean our yard weekly; iron our clothes each morning; or send a sympathy card to a grieving neighbor. Sloth is about an attitude, a lack of care, a lack of motivation, a lack of pride in what we do.

Each election year, pollsters tell us that only 50 percent of Americans bother to vote, even in hotly contested elections. This is called voter apathy. It is widespread. We justify our apathy by saying "My vote does not matter much" or "Politics are corrupt anyhow" or "My non-vote is a protest vote." Does our impersonal, urbanized society breed apathy? Certainly. Are many people so overwhelmed with their personal and family lives that they simply do not have time to study the issues and vote? Definitely. Yet, is it not also possible that apathy is more widespread than we realize?

I respect people who go to the gym after work. They come in all sizes and degrees of ability. They are all working up a sweat. They are all fighting inertia (which is the physicist's version of sloth). They are sloth fighters. Yet, even in the gym, filled as it is with seemingly motivated individuals,

I am surprised by the soiled towels left lying around the locker room. It would take very little extra effort to pick up a towel after using it and drop it in a bin while exiting out the door. Some of you are smiling as you read this, saying to yourself, "That's a gender issue. . . . Men are naturally slobs, leaving their clothes everywhere." Maybe so, but I think that sloth comes in all shapes and sizes and in both genders.

For that matter, I am surprised too by how often people walk right past litter in front of their own church or home without picking it up. What little effort it would take to pick up the litter, and yet many of us don't make the effort. I hope that I am not sounding judgmental. We all, including myself, are guilty of sloth. My point is only that apathy is everywhere, in small and large forms, in overtly lazy people and in hard-working people, in the poor and rich alike. Apathy directly or indirectly contributes to so many of the sins that plague modern life.

How many different kinds of human-made disasters or scandals have been proved by investigations to have been caused by simple human error, such as the mechanic who did not do a thorough repair job, the FBI agent who did not make the extra effort to double-check her information, the CEO who took the easy way out at the cost of millions, the engineer who did not double-check her blueprints, and so on? How many can you think of? Might these simple errors be part of a larger pattern of sloth?

Most of us have lived long enough to notice that we Americans run hot and cold on social ills. We tend to ignore the plight of the poor until there is an urban riot. We tend to ignore the problems of the mentally ill until one of them turns a gun on innocent people. We tend to ignore the presence of immigrants until one of them moves in next door. We ignore the difficulties of a far-away nation until it is threatened by communists or becomes a staging area for terrorists. We ignore the problems of our schools until test scores show that we have fallen behind the rest of the world. Americans have very short attention spans! The media gets us all excited for the moment. Promises are made for relief funds, for rebuilding, for alliances, for new programs, but the promises fade away like yesterday's news. Or, we throw some money at the problem and hope it goes away. We then tend to be apathetic until the next crisis. You see, sloth operates not just on an individual level, but also on a collective level. Sloth tends to breed sloth, not just across time, but also across social relationships, resulting in our becoming a slothful people, even in a nation that so prizes hard work in its collective myths.

Sloth

In Christian prayers of confession we sometimes use the phrase "sins of commission and sins of omission." The latter category of sin encompasses the sin of sloth. Sloth is being apathetic and not doing the things we know that we ought to have done. It is not doing the right thing, choosing instead to do nothing or to avoid any and all action. Someone once defined evil as what happens when good people have done nothing.[3] Sloth leads us to not take a stand when we should, not stand up for justice or peace—not just in big ways but in the hundreds of little ways where we could have or should have done the right thing. So often we let missed opportunities go by without noticing them. Our minds, lulled into indifference by sloth's lure, have a way of not even noticing what we should have done or conveniently forgetting the missed opportunities to do the right thing. One of sloth's cousins is ignorance. Another is denial.

Sloth as a Lack of Motivation

Jason was a twenty-year-old young man, an only child who was raised by his single mother. He was still living at home with mom and her new boyfriend in an over-crowded apartment near my counseling center. Since barely finishing high school, he had drifted from menial job to menial job, with long periods of doing nothing in between. He tended to spend hours on computer games, slept late, and had to be reminded to clean his room, even to take a daily shower. His mother brought him to counseling because she was worried that Jason was not taking responsibility for his life, not moving forward (and meanwhile, she wanted to move forward with her new marriage). More exactly, mother had busted him again "for the tenth time" for smoking pot in his room. Her complaint, interestingly enough, was about the risk of fire, not his obvious addiction that had been ongoing for years.

Yes, Jason was mildly depressed, but the diagnosis that I found to be more insightful was that Jason had a motivation problem. Most of his life his mother had done things for him—reminded him to do his homework, gotten him up in the morning for school, selected his clothes, nagged him to do chores, etc. Now Mom was frustrated because Jason would not get off the dime. He lacked motivation. He was apathetic. His favorite response, especially when nagged, was, "Whatever." What does "whatever" actually

---

3. This saying is a paraphrase of Edmund Burke's famous dictum: "All that is necessary for the triumph of evil is that good men do nothing."

mean? "Whatever you want to do is fine with me.... I do not care." As I saw it, for most of Jason's life motivation was supplied by his mother. For most of his life, Jason was motivated by externals—mom's nagging, mom's bribes, or mom's threats of punishment. He got used to it. He never internalized those external motivations to the point where he could regularly motivate himself.

I would submit that Jason's motivation problem could also be framed as a problem with apathy; he was a person who was caught in the sin of sloth. Yes, Jason's sloth is partly due to his family dynamics, partly due to his depression. Sloth isn't always something we choose. Like Jason, sometimes we fall into sloth.

According to research in psychology, the concept of learned helplessness offers some interesting insights into the problem of sloth.[4] The concept of learned helplessness was born of research in which rats were randomly shocked. It was discovered that if the rats had some measure of control over the frequency and intensity of the shocks, the animals handled the trauma relatively well. But, if the rats had no control over the shocks' frequency or intensity, the animals became apathetic, and later, even when the circumstances had changed and the rats now had the ability to alleviate the situation, the animals remained in a state of "learned helplessness." In effect, the rats had learned to be helpless. They learned that effort and motivation did not work, so they gave up.

This concept has been applied broadly to help understand persons in poverty who are repeatedly unable to help themselves, people experiencing repeated losses who are unable to bring closure to their sorrow, or people in prison who fall into apathy as a survival mechanism. I do not think that most people who are apathetic choose to be that way. Perhaps they have learned to be apathetic. Jason had, in fact, learned to be apathetic. His efforts had gone unrewarded, and so he took the stance, "Why try?" And over time, apathy bred apathy in the sense that when Jason made an apathetic or half-hearted effort, that very attitude often created negative results, which in turn only reinforced his apathetic stance. Apathy reinforces apathy, becoming a way of life.

The good news about learned helplessness is that because it is learned, it can be unlearned. Jason has moral choices to make, hundreds of them every day, between sloth and work, between caring and apathy. It's a habit that can be broken one choice at a time.

4. See Peterson et al., *Learned Helplessness*.

Apart from the concept of learned helplessness, which is largely a descriptive concept, motivation has been studied quite extensively by students of the human personality. Clearly, some people are highly motivated while others have low motivation. Some are self-motivated; others have to be motivated by others. Our motivation style is a product of various factors and our personal histories. How do you motivate someone? How do you motivate yourself? In a great over-simplification, psychology has argued that human motivation comes in two categories:

1. *Motivation by pleasure to fulfill bodily or social needs.* Freud first coined the term "pleasure principle," arguing that the seeking out of pleasure in whatever form is a universal human motivation. When we are children, we are typically motivated primarily by the gratification of our various needs, and then as we are socialized we learn the value of delayed gratification. This is part of what is implied in the term "mature." As adults, we have also learned the value of indirect pleasure or gratification fulfillment. We work, for example, to secure money that then indirectly leads to the securing of material purchases, social status, and bodily needs. We groom ourselves in order to make ourselves attractive to our potential or actual lovers, and in this way we indirectly secure sex, intimacy, bonding, and family. Persons with addiction problems often have trouble with the delayed and indirect nature of pleasure motivation. They have been programmed to want their gratification now and directly, and as their addiction grows, the immediacy and directness of their demands for gratification become more and more pronounced.

2. *Motivation by the avoidance of pain, rejection, discomfort, or possible harm.* This basic category of human motivation is about avoiding or escaping pain. Pain can come in many forms. There is physical pain, so we strive to avoid dangerous or threatening situations, sickness, conflict, medical procedures, even the dentist. There is social pain, so we strive to be liked and to avoid rejection and shame/guilt. There is interpersonal pain, so we strive to deny and avoid talking about painful subjects. People who struggle with addictive behaviors are programmed to avoid pain. Their addiction can be an escape from pain—sometimes physical pain, but more often interpersonal or intra-psychic pain. Rather than face the painful feelings associated with certain relationships or life situations, they cover over their pain with alcohol, drugs, or addictive behavior.

Another aspect of the sin of sloth is the lack of motivation to face pain in whatever form it surfaces. Sloth is a lack of effort or motivation to work through the pain, preferring instead instant gratification. Sloth is the foundational dynamic for instant gratification. Addictive behavior, in whatever form, is a form of taking the easy way out, going for the quick fix to feel better in the moment and avoiding the long-term or more profound pain that needs to be dealt with ultimately. Sloth is a lack of motivation to deal with pain and thus is the soil in which addictions grow and the dynamic that sustains addictions.

Taking the easy way out is not always a bad thing. The pleasure and pain avoidance principles have served us well as a species. Rather than carry rocks, we invented the wheel and a wagon to carry rocks. Rather than wash clothes in the local river, we invented a washing machine to do the wash. Rather than spend months traveling across the nation, we invented trains and airplanes so we can get there sooner. Our predisposition to take the easy way out has motivated us to come up with most of the great labor-saving technological inventions of civilization. Looking for ways to avoid work has its benefits. Similarly, rest has served humanity well, too. As I said earlier, rest has made work and sometimes invention possible. When rest or ease goes on chronically, becoming a pattern and a habit, and when it is applied universally across all human endeavors, we call it sloth. And then sloth becomes a garden bed in which addictions grow.

Abraham Maslow, the father of humanistic psychology, argued that both of the above motivations—seeking pleasure and avoiding pain—are really deficit motivations.[5] We are motivated to do something because of an experienced deficit. We are hungry (deficit), so we are motivated to find food. We are lonely (deficit), so we are motivated to find friends. We are ignorant (deficit), so we are motivated to find knowledge. While these motivations may be very strong, Maslow argued that we humans at our best can also be motivated by B-motives, which he defined as the desire to grow, expand, and improve ourselves. Growth motives push us to endure some pain or delay some gratification for a grander goal down the road. Deficit motives tend to motivate us just enough to satisfy our need, and then the motivation stops. We do just enough to get by, to get our need met this time. "Growth" people are motivated by the desire to seek out new experiences and meet new challenges. They have a passion to learn and grow, to "be all they can be." This is the kind of motivation that people in

5. See Maslow, *Motivation and Personality*.

recovery are struggling to claim for themselves . . . to endure the difficult work of recovery knowing that down the road they will enjoy the experience of freedom, new life, and personal growth. In some ways, recovery from addiction is a process of shifting from being motivated by deficit to being motivated by growth.

In a joint session with Jason and his mother (of the case illustration outlined above), we explored the various ways that Jason's mother tried to motivate him to do better in school, to find a job, to cut his hair. We agreed that all of these external or deficit motivations had been partial or temporary at best. It was not until Jason found something that he was passionate about—computer games—and visited a graphic arts college in a neighboring city that he began to experience and claim for himself some growth motivation. About the same time, he also began to deal with his inner pain regarding loneliness, peer rejection, and a sense of being emasculated by his mother. It was not easy, but his motivation began to shift. He began to overcome his sloth little by little. He attended the graphic arts college. And, in time, he found no need for marijuana, which he later proclaimed had been a "waste of time."

Grief Work

Years ago, I was involved with an organization that supported adults through the process of conjugal bereavement. Most of the members of To Live Again (TLA) had been widowed during the middle adult years of life and faced the challenges of raising their children, supporting the family, and maintaining their sanity as a single parent. The TLA folks had a motto that I have always found helpful: "The only way out is through."

Grief feelings are very painful and are often changeable, intense, and confusing. Like any pain, most of us want to avoid the pain of sorrow if we can. Most of us would rather not cry at all—as if that were possible. Indeed, many of the ways people cope with bereavement involve avoiding pain, like overusing alcohol, over-working, and rushing into a new relationship. Yet, the natural drive of the human psyche in times of loss is to move toward closure. We want and need to find acceptance and thereby begin to move on. New life lies on the other side of a long tunnel, and the only way out is through the tunnel. Going through the tunnel requires a willingness to do the emotional work of expressing our pain, talking it through, crying it through, and remembering it through.

Bereavement writers like to refer to American culture as a death-denying culture since we over-emphasize youth and hide death. I would add that it is also a grief-avoiding culture. In keeping with the general cultural emphasis on instant gratification and taking the easy way out, American culture does not encourage the full and complete expression of grief. Many an addiction originates in the context of bereavement when we use a substance or an addictive activity as a way of avoiding the pain of sorrow. And it works . . . and works so well that we keep it up, and the longer we keep it up, the more addictive it becomes. In my counseling work, I have noticed again and again that when some people get clean and sober, they often have to deal with the unresolved and delayed grief that their addiction covered up for years. More importantly, they must in recovery find new ways to deal with life's pains apart from addiction.

Spiritual Sloth

Sloth is not just about physical or even emotional laziness, but also about spiritual laziness. This meaning of sloth as spiritual laziness is probably not unique to our times, but it seems so when we consider the rise of secularism and the over-emphasis upon freedom over discipline. Fewer and fewer people appear to view the regular practice of spiritual disciplines as an important feature of their lives. This makes me wonder whether the rise in the incidence of addiction in our times is related to this societal trend away from the regular discipline of spiritual practices.

In general, slothful people—we are all slothful people some of the time, and some of us are slothful people all of the time—are not motivated to improve themselves. Mentally, slothful people do not want to learn anything new. They have learned it once, and that is enough for them. They are not curious. Yet, we live in a time when education is increasingly being thought of as a life-long process. Most professions now have continuing education programs that help its members stay current in their field. In the fields of medicine, science, and many of the helping professions, sloth is countered by professional standards and by requirements such as those for regular continuing education.

When they do think, slothful people don't like to work too hard. They tend toward simplistic thinking because complex thinking or complicated ideas require more work than they usually want to muster. They do not want to be bothered with the facts or with contradictory information or a spirited debate—anything that might require them to make some mental effort. "I know what I know and my mind is made up," or, as a bumper sticker puts it, "God said it. . . . I believe it and that's final." Does this sound like denial?

Many people like their religion spoon-fed to them. They want their spiritual leaders to give them the answers—give them five easy steps, four spiritual laws, six principles for positive living—because they do not want to work on their spiritual lives themselves. They do not want to work at faith. The spiritual practices, like daily prayer, scripture reading, fasting, authentic confession, and even worship all take effort and motivation. We know that the more effort we put into our spiritual life, the more we are going to get out of it. Yet, many of us are not motivated, not just on occasion but as a generalized approach to religion. We seldom work on our spiritual life but then, when a crisis arises, we are quick to demand a miracle.

Over the years I have listened to the frustrations of many a priest or pastor regarding how to motivate his or her parishioners in matters of the spirit. Believers today often approach religion with the same consumer mentality that infects all of modern life. Most parishioners just want to sit in worship as passive consumers, rather than truly participate in worship or the weekly activities of their congregation. Some of the newer, contemporary, Spirit-filled styles of worship seem to be trying to involve people more in worship—get them up, excited, singing and even dancing. This trend seems especially strong among the larger evangelical or charismatic congregations. Some people are critical of these forms of worship, arguing that they are actually drifting toward entertainment and away from a more reverent style of worship. Indeed, some worship centers look like movie theaters, with a stage, lights, and big screens. Yet, overall, the newer, contemporary, and experimental forms of worship and church seem to be efforts to overcome spiritual sloth.

Based on my experience as a pastor and therapist, I have come to understand this issue in a developmental framework. Many believers have had very powerful spiritual or religious experiences at a particular time in their lives. It may have been when they came to faith initially, were born again, were baptized by the Holy Spirit, were healed from a life-threatening illness, or were truly forgiven after a horrible sin. Yet, for one reason or another, sloth then sets in. They have ceased growing much after that defining moment in their lives. Years have passed. Much of the remainder of their lives has been spent trying to recreate that experience, perhaps by traveling from congregation to congregation or even religion to religion. In a sense, they have remained stuck in the past. They do not see life as a journey. They do not realize that the faith of a sixteen-year-old should not be the faith of a thirty-five-year-old or of a sixty-five-year-old. They do not want to put out the effort that it takes to move on and find a new, more current faith stance. I believe that God is always trying to do "a new thing" (Isa 43:19) in our lives, but we, because of our sloth, often fail to see it.

From the perspective of the Christian tradition, we could argue that God hates sloth. God hates apathy (see Rev 3:14) even more than those who do evil. God is love, and the opposite of love is not hate, but apathy . . . so God hates apathy. We are meant for so much more. We are meant to have passion in life. We are meant to have energy and enthusiasm. The literal meaning of "enthusiasm" is "filled with God." A life without passion, without commitment, is a wasted life. It is an insult to the Creator. I have always loved the quote that is attributed to St. Irenaeus, who had it right when he said, "The glory of God is man fully alive." Man or woman, are you fully alive? Sloth tempts us into apathy, but God invites us again and again to joyfully participate in the journey.

The Gift of Being Challenged

We humans universally admire individuals who overcome great odds to live life to the fullest. Stories fill the media of handicapped people who do not give up on life but work and work and work to overcome their handicaps. The handicap may be a war injury, a developmental disability, a physical disability, or even a mental disability. We admire such people. In their honor, we have even changed our language. We no longer call such people "handicapped." Instead, we call them "challenged"—physically challenged, mentally challenged, educationally challenged, visually challenged. We want to respect and honor their positive attitude, their message that there are no handicaps, only challenges to overcome.

One of the things that the disabled teach us again and again is that the victory is not in overcoming their disability, which may or may not happen; the victory is in their trying. The very fact that they try is victory enough. Why? Because the real battle is not in the disability per se, but in our attitude. The mental battle is between sloth and work, between apathy and motivation, between inertia and effort, between learned helplessness and a can-do attitude. If the handicapped person can win this battle, the rest is easy—or, the rest does not matter so much. Everything is attitude.

Christopher Reeves was one such person who was the focus of media attention for years until his recent death. We watched Reeves and his family struggle with the terrible disability of a spinal chord injury that paralyzed him from the neck down. A good many of us would have given up early on, and I am sure that Reeves had many a day when he felt that he would have liked to have given up, too, rolled up in the corner and let life pass him by . . . but he did not. He put out tremendous effort to rehabilitate himself as much as he could, to renew and deepen his spiritual, mental, and interpersonal life. And in the end, there was very little that he was able to do physically to improve his condition, but wouldn't we still term him a victor, a hero, one of the most admired persons in our culture? Why? Because the he won the battle of the mind, the battle with sloth.

Each time the Olympics come around, we witness several inspiring stories of challenges. In 2006, there was the story of the Chinese ice skater who tore his Achilles tendon just six months before the games. He worked and worked to repair his damaged leg, rebuild his strength and stamina, refine his routines, and develop his timing all over again. He only started skating again six weeks before the Olympics and only started doing jumps four weeks prior. The narrators were clear that he and his partner had no chance of winning a medal, but they skated reasonably well and when they finished, the crowd—the entire arena—gave him a standing ovation! As the commentators noted, "Just getting here, just skating in these Olympics, was victory enough."

I ask you, why do we admire such people who overcome their disabilities or show great courage in the face of insurmountable odds? Why are these tales of courage called feel-good stories? Do not these stories touch something deep within us, perhaps a universal struggle? There is a bit of sloth in all of us. Each of us battles sloth or apathy every day of our lives. Some of us are better at it than others, but it is a universal battle. Seeing a disabled person win the battle inspires us to work harder to overcome our challenges, to overcome our sloth.

Can Sloth Be Deadly?

I have already suggested several ways in which sloth or apathy might directly or indirectly be deadly to either ourselves or others. Apathy can contribute to literal death when mechanics or engineers or pilots or police officers do not do their jobs with effort and attention to detail. Sloth can be emotionally deadly, too, since it is a component of depression, and we know that depression is linked to suicide attempts. Sloth can make us lazy enough not to do the necessary grief work to respond to a major loss. In addition, I have suggested that sloth contributes to spiritual death by making us unwilling to seek the divine. Spiritually slothful people live their lives without passion, without mental and spiritual growth. They are unwilling or unable to put out the effort needed to engage life, to live life to the fullest, and to grow in their faith. So yes, sloth can lead to spiritual death, too.

Sloth can also be deadly to family relationships, as implied in the vignette that opened this chapter. Almost everyone who has been married a long time knows that being married requires work. Healthy families require work. It takes work to communicate, to solve problem, to clarify issues again and again, to confront when necessary, to be dependable, to put aside one's own needs to meet the needs of one's spouse or child, to keep promises, to make the extra effort to be thoughtful, kind, and forgiving . . . all this and more takes work. As a banner I recently saw read, "Marriage is hard work . . . and you are worth it."

In recent decades there has been a rising interest in preventive health care. Health administrators and researchers know that a disease is easier and cheaper to cure if caught early than if the patient waits until the disease is full-blown to seek treatment. Medical leaders have tried to emphasize to the public the importance of preventive health in the forms of physical exercise, a balanced diet, and regular check-ups. We know that "an ounce of prevention is worth a pound of cure." Two decades ago, Health Maintenance Organizations (HMOs) were created as a way of trying to restructure health plans to encourage preventive health care and maintenance of good health. Yet, for the most part, all of these efforts have been a hard sell. Preventive health measures require more effort, more work than waiting until something hurts enough. When it comes to health issues, motivation is essential and sloth can be deadly.

For those who do put out the effort, whether it is in terms of their health, their spiritual life, or their relationships, the rewards include a fuller and richer life, a healthier body, a deeper understanding of themselves, a more satisfying family life, and a greater degree of personal freedom over sin in whatever forms it takes.

Culture, Children, and the Value of Work

On the surface, it would seem that our work-valuing culture discourages sloth. We expect everyone in this society to work, to carry their own weight. We glorify the hard work of athletes who prevail against odds to find victory on the field of competition. Where possible, we even try to outlaw sloth through measures such as requiring welfare recipients to work. Yet, there are several ways in which modern culture encourages apathy.

First, the growing urbanization of our society fosters apathy. There are too many people. Everything and everyone is impersonal. We barely know our neighbors, living as we do inside our insulated walls and behind our locked doors. Fewer and fewer of us are invested in or care about the common good. There is an apathy or indifference that seems to come with modern, urban civilization.

Second, the world of mass communication inundates us with stories about tragedies and violence and the suffering of others. Over time, many people become so overwhelmed by these stories that they become insensitive, apathetic. Many psychologists call this condition compassion fatigue. Others describe an emotional numbing that occurs after viewing hour after hour of suffering and violence. We start insulating ourselves from life, withdrawing, even protecting ourselves from caring too much by becoming apathetic. Apathy can be a kind of defense mechanism.

Another theme of modern culture that encourages sloth is the increasing emphasis upon instant gratification. In the commercial world, there is great appeal to instant results, quick fixes, easy success. In recent years, I have noted with some interest the arrival of TV commercials and print advertisements for medications for various medical conditions. Although the ads do list disclaimers, I am concerned about how these commercials reinforce the growing trend of expecting instant and/or easy cures, cures without any corresponding and necessary behavioral, emotional, and lifestyle changes. Sometimes, in life, a real cure or pain relief requires sustained effort, not a short-lived quick fix.

This trend toward instant gratification is especially noticeable among the younger generations. Children in particular have a hard time learning the value of patience in this cultural climate. They crave excitement, novelty, and adventure. They expect to be entertained day and night, and they find it increasingly difficult to entertain themselves. How often have we heard the complaint, "It's boring"? It seems that children (and adults) are developing shorter and shorter attention spans. They expect work to be easy and to yield quick results. When work does not produce instant results, they become bored or frustrated and move on to the next area of attention. This cultural atmosphere undermines the value of sustained effort and sustained motivation.

How can we raise our children to be caring, responsible, and hardworking adults? The best thing we can do for our children is to model hard work, motivation, and high energy. The worst thing we can do for our children is to wait on them, to require nothing of them, to spoil them and give them whatever they want. Such behavior only encourages sloth, an inertia of mind, body, and spirit. The next best thing we can do for our children is to provide them with structure, routine, and healthy habits. Structure is especially good for people who are vulnerable to sloth. Slothful teenagers or young adults, for example, may find it helpful to join the military, enroll in a boarding school, or join a church that demands a lot of them, because such structured programs often provide an atmosphere in which they can finally get motivated.

At a recent social gathering, I asked a group of college administrators and faculty, How are college students today different than college students of our generation? The term "entitlement" came up again and again. Students these days feel a sense of entitlement, reported these teachers. They often act as if they are entitled to grades of A, entitled to financial aid, entitled to be waited on and catered to. Most of these educators worked in a private college or graduate school. I wonder if students that attend a state university or students that attend college on work-study programs display the same sense of entitlement these educators reported.

Our spiritual ancestors were correct: work is good for us.[6] Work teaches us to value what we earn, to appreciate life, and to avoid the pitfalls of sloth. Work teaches us to engage life. Parents need to remember another truth about human nature, which is that it is our challenges that make us strong. Humans need challenges as much as we need food and water. Our children also need challenges, challenges tailored to their age and skill level, but challenges nonetheless. For this reason, many parents encourage their children to participate in some form of sports or the arts or other structured programs. Most wise parents instinctively know that in such endeavors children, if they apply themselves, will learn to be motivated and

---

6. What I mean here by work is not just physical labor, but also emotional work, mental work, relationship work, and even spiritual work. Maybe a better way to say this is: motivation is good for us.

to embrace a motivated lifestyle. We know that our kids need this kind of experience, especially in modern society where hard work is not always required to survive.

Helping Ourselves and Others

The traditional virtue that is the antidote for sloth is fortitude, which is defined as endurance or strength, especially in the face of pain, hardship, or suffering. Fortitude is an old word. We do not hear it used much in modern times. Persistence might be a synonym. Persistence does imply sustained effort, which fits with the definition of sloth I have used in this chapter.

We can practice the virtue of persistence by doing the following:

- celebrating heroes who display the virtues of hard work, discipline, and motivation; finding people to be around who live passionate, concerned, and involved lives
- living a disciplined or structured life
- becoming a goal-setter, setting reasonable goals for each week, month, and year in all of the major domains of life (work, family, health, and spirituality)
- becoming more aware of sins of omission, the moral choices we make by default; paying attention to moral choices that go unrecognized all around us
- becoming well-informed, well-educated, and well-read
- valuing legitimate rest (spiritual rest as well as physical rest)
- valuing suffering, which is part of life; not spending our lives trying to avoid pain
- welcoming challenges; seeing problems as challenges; seeing every misfortune as an opportunity to learn, grow a stronger character, and prove our fortitude
- being a doer of the Word, not just a hearer; investing ourselves in our spiritual life and in the practices of our religion
- identifying and developing our gifts; using our gifts to glorify God and serve others.
- enriching ourselves by reading a book, taking a class, learning a hobby; expanding our minds

Ancient Sins . . . Modern Addictions

Summary

The sin of sloth or apathy is far more basic to the human predicament than perhaps we initially thought. It is not one of the exciting sins, like anger, lust, or greed, but it is foundational to the human struggle. Unless sloth is overcome, little else in life is possible. Occasional sloth in the form of rest is a good thing. Sloth becomes the soil for addictions, however, when it is chronic and excessive. It breeds an attitude of apathy, of taking the easy way out, of favoring instant gratification, all of which sustain all of the addictions. Over time, sloth robs us of our natural motivation to learn, grow, and work.

Questions for Self-Reflection

- In general, what motivates me? How motivated am I as a person? Is my motivation primarily external or internal?
- Do I avoid physical work? Do I enjoy work or do I see work as an obligation, unpleasant drudgery, or some kind of punishment? Do I think that the world owes me a living?
- Do I have personal standards of conduct? Am I motivated to maintain those standards?
- In what ways am I spiritually lazy, emotionally lazy, or interpersonally lazy?
- How do I balance work and rest?
- Sometimes life is just plain hard. What challenges do I face or have I faced in my life, and what helped me do the work to overcome them?

Biblical passages related to sloth: Eccl 1:14, 4:4; Matt 7:7; 25:14–30; Mark 13:37; Luke 10:38–42; 15:1–24; 1 Tim 5:8; Jas 1:22–27, 4:17; Rev 3:14–17

6 Greed

A Problem of Excess

In October of 1492, Christopher Columbus, the first widely-known European to "discover" the new world, came ashore and encountered the Native Americans of the Caribbean islands. Columbus met "a gentle, hospitable people with handsome faces who will give all that they possess for anything given to them." They were unfamiliar with the weapons the Europeans carried, and Columbus concluded, "They would make fine servants . . . with fifty men we could subjugate them all and make them do whatever we want."[1]

He continued in his log, "As soon as I arrived in the Indies, on the first Island which I found, I took some of the natives by force in order that they might learn and might give me information of whatever there is in these parts."

What Columbus wanted most, of course, was gold. He was looking for gold to fulfill his contractual obligation to the king and queen of Spain and to fund his next trip. His reports of the presence of gold in the New World were exaggerated. On return trips, Columbus became more desperate, more violent, and more cruel. The pursuit of gold became, for Columbus and his compatriots, an obsession—an obsession that had severe consequences. By some estimates, in the next ten years, on the island of Hispaniola alone, the population of natives declined by three million due to war, slavery, disease, and laboring in the gold mines.

THE CONTEXT OF THE above story is the series of historic initial encounters between two great but very different cultures. Europe in the sixteenth century was witnessing the emergence of capitalism, which was as yet

---

1. These quotes are taken from Columbus's journal of his voyage (Cohen, *Columbus*, 55–59).

unregulated. It was largely for capitalistic reasons that Columbus and other European explorers sailed to the West and into dangerous waters around the world. They were not motivated by an enlightened desire for knowledge, by the lure of a cross-cultural experience, by a search for a better world. They were motivated by profit. They were entrepreneurs. All too easily, the desire for profit became an obsession, an obsession that would demand that all other values—charity, tolerance, peace, and modesty—be subjected to the all-consuming desire for profit. Columbus was a Christian man, sailing under the banner of a Christian nation. How do we explain the abdication of Christian values that led to the enslavement and destruction of so many human beings? This was neither the first nor the last time that human values would be abandoned for the love of gold. I am sure that Columbus thought he was doing the right thing. How do we explain his blindness and ignorance other than by the presence of denial and, by implication, the presence of an addiction fueled by greed?

Greed or avarice is defined as a desire for the excessive acquisition of things or wealth. The key word is "desire." Greed is a strong desire, a craving, an inner motivation. Like the other six deadly sins, greed is a sin of the mind. As such, greed is the first step in or the first component of an addictive process, but it does not become a full addiction until there is a behavioral component—a compulsive behavior that is repeated and repeated. Greed can manifest itself as an addiction in several different ways. Some of the manifestations are compulsive gambling, compulsive overworking, hoarding and compulsive collecting, and "greedy" ambition. And when these behavioral manifestations of greed become out of control and destructive, we can justifiably label them as addictions.

The term "greed" has negative moral connotations in our culture. It is universally considered a bad thing. American literature, myths, and movies—on the TV screen and the big screen—often present greed as the chief cause of an otherwise ordinary person going bad, becoming a villain, and doing hurtful or corrupt things. How many movies can you think of that have to do with the perils of greed, from *Erin Brockovich* to *Wall Street*? Our culture seems to agree with the Bible verse that says, "The love of money is the root of all evil" (1 Tim 6:10). We universally condemn people who take advantage of others in times of crisis by price gouging. We prosecute people who run scams that cheat people out of their hard-earned money. We judge people who make false claims in advertisements or cook the books in order to improve their bottom line. We feel pity for the workaholic who ignores his or her children and realizes too late in life that without meaningful relationships, life is very lonely.

Yet, at the same time, the capitalistic culture in which we Americans live promotes earning a profit, material gain, getting ahead, ambition, and self-interest. Capitalism works, in theory, because every individual is trying to promote his or her own profit, and this motivates us to work harder, develop new products, and provide better service. In a sense, capitalism has institutionalized greed, at least at a low-grade level. And the only consumer safeguard against the untamed greed of a businessperson is "let the buyer beware." In other words, if the salesperson can get away with tricking us into an over-priced purchase, it's the buyer's fault. Another version of blaming the victim, if you ask me!

In summary, we Americans are ambivalent about greed. We don't like it, yet we allow it to motivate us. Then we rationalize and justify our actions so extensively that it is difficult to determine even within our own minds when greed is greed. Personal morality and social pressure are important in terms of helping us clarify, monitor, and manage our cravings for excess. Yet, in an era characterized by the declining influence of organized religion and the increasing privatization of modern life, individual morality and social pressure appear to be less powerful than they once were. These days, it seems that the only mediating influence on greed is government regulation, laws, and legal prosecution. In some ways, one could argue that our whole apparatus of government regulation, as distasteful as it is to some people, is a necessary safeguard against the ravages of greed.

Hoarding, Collecting, and When Is Enough Enough?

Hoarding has received increased media attention in recent years. A reality television show called *Buried Alive* documents real-life examples of hoarding, people whose houses are filled to the ceilings with "stuff." Hoarding is usually understood by clinicians as a type of obsessive compulsive disorder. It is defined as the excessive acquisition of or inability to discard large quantities of objects that most people would view as being useless or having no value. It is estimated that 2 to 5 percent of adults in America could be diagnosed as compulsive hoarders.[2] Normally, we do not think of hoarding as an example of greed, because the stuff that is collected is largely useless

---

2. Pertusa et al., "Compulsive Hoarding," 371–86.

or without value.[3] Yet, if greed is defined as the excessive *acquisition* of things, not just the excessive *desire* for material things, why should we not call hoarding a modern example of an addiction that grows out of greed? Hoarding meets most of the criteria of a behavioral addiction—tolerance, obsessive, out of control, destructive. What is less clear is the mood-altering effects of hoarding or over-collecting.

As a young adolescent I spent several summer vacations with my family in a beach house in southern California. I have fond memories of sun and cool breezes, of swimming and bodysurfing and exploring. After a busy day in the waves, it was relaxing to patrol the surf line with my mother, looking for shells, stones, and similar treasures. As the surf washed over these collectibles, they would sparkle with color, rich textures, and smooth shapes. My mother and I were particularly fond of moonstones, so we searched for the largest, most beautiful of these stones we could find. Yet, the collecting activity also had a compulsive tone. I was driven at times to find just one more stone. And so some days I kept looking and looking for the always elusive prize just out of my sight. I have wondered, in retrospect, did I really need all of those shells or pretty stones? More often than not, I took them home, left them on the patio, and forgot them within a few weeks after our vacation was over. I never got around to building a collection. There are many people who do build collections, of course, of items such as rare coins, stamps, or antiques, but I was not one of them.

When I got older, I embraced the ecological ethic that tells us to "leave only footprints" in our encounters with nature. So, I tried to discourage my own children from collecting souvenirs from nature that they did not need, or at least limit them to one souvenir. In spite of my sermons, my children did collect stuff. There were Cabbage Patch Dolls in the 1980s and Beanie Babies in the 1990s. I suppose that collecting stuff is a natural instinct in humans, given that for millions of years we were hunters and gatherers. The compulsion to collect might have had some evolutionary advantage in earlier eons. There is still a lot of collecting behavior going on among modern humans, both adults and children. We need only look in our closets or our garages. Do we really need everything we collect? Probably not. Most of us would not be labeled as hoarders, but the impulse to collect is pretty universal among us humans.

---

3. The stuff hoarders collect is not always useless, at least not in their minds. A subset of hoarding is the hoarding of pets/animals.

Greed

The problem of collecting too much stuff, which most of us can identify with, and the even more serious problem of hoarding, is made worse in a consumer-oriented culture because we are encouraged to get our needs and our wants confused. Marketers are constantly trying to persuade us to treat every want as a need, every optional purchase as an essential purchase. An excited teenage girl exclaims, "I need it. I need. It's so awesome. I just must have it!" Does she really need that new outfit or that cell phone or that latest CD? I doubt it. But in her mind, her wants have become needs. All of us do this kind of "stinkin' thinkin'" some of the time. Our thinking is distorted. If we turn wants into needs, even if just in our minds, then there is no limit on our needs. Every want becomes urgent. Optional wants become necessary needs. This kind of urgency drives the addictive process. If most of our wants are turned into needs, then we come to have many, many more needs than we can realistically fulfill. We live with a sense of desperation because we think our needs are not being met. We become demanding and frustrated and turn into what the young people call high-maintenance people.

Ambition: Possessing, Not Possessions

Wilber Smith was a popular student in high school and was elected president of his graduating class. He was naturally friendly, had a big smile, was good-looking, and had a way of making everyone feel included. In addition to going to school, he worked part-time, participated in his church, and volunteered. He was chosen most likely to succeed by his classmates. After high school, as a National Merit Scholar, he attended college, where he joined a fraternity and again gravitated to leadership positions, and when he was given a chance to represent student grievances, he did so. While not quite an official Rhodes Scholar, he did study abroad one year at Oxford. He attended Stanford Law School, where he worked hard. He achieved one accomplishment after another and graduated with honors in four years. He passed the bar on his first try and was given a job in a County District Attorney's Office. Over the years, he continued to work hard, preparing tirelessly for each case; his percentage of convictions was high, and he was promoted. At the young age of thirty-six, he ran for and was elected District Attorney. He championed an anti-corruption campaign and made the evening news regularly for an investigation revealing corruption in government contracts. In the meantime, he married a lovely woman, and together they had two young children. His family regularly appeared with him as he ran for public office. On the night before his re-election, he was given a white hat as a symbol of his role as a knight doing battle against the greed, corruption, and scandal in government. He won re-election, and two years later he was appointed by the governor to head the state's anti-corruption task force.

On a particular fateful day in October, an investigative newspaper reporter uncovered a madam in a nearby town who reportedly revealed that Wilber Smith was a regular patron of her escort services. She cited days and places over an eight-year period. When the story broke, Smith denied it most fiercely. Yet, as the evening news ran the story night after night, more facts began to emerge. Eventually, a woman gave an interview in which she described her love relationship with Smith and his efforts to compensate her in ways that discouraged her from ever going public. Then questions arose about where the money for the pay-offs came from. Then there was another woman and another set of stories. On the sixth week after this scandal broke, Smith resigned from the state's justice department. Two months later, that justice department filed an ethics complaint against Smith with the state bar association.

On the surface, this may sound like a case of sexual addiction, and maybe it is. That is how the press played it. "Moral crusader succumbs to temptation." "Smith gives new meaning to hypocrisy." "Mrs. Smith devastated!" I suggest that this story might also be a case of greed. Greed is not just about the insatiable acquisition of material possessions. Greed can also take the form of an insatiable acquisition of achievements, titles, positions, status, and accomplishments of various kinds. Ambition can be addictive. We use the phrase "greedy ambition" or "blind ambition" to suggest such a concept. It might also be understood as over-collecting and a problem with excess.

We don't recognize ambition as addictive or as an expression of greed because, as I have said, greed is a socially acceptable sin in our capitalistic world. We admire the high achiever. We are blind to the down side of compulsive achievement. But addiction is addiction is addiction! Addictions tend to cluster together. Those addicted to greed do tend to also be addicted to sex. Sexual conquests are just another form of achievement, another acquisition. Of course, in Smith's case, sexual activity may also be an escape, an escape from the stress of the primary addiction, which is greed. Addicted people tend to exchange one addiction for another or use one addiction to compensate for another.

The contemporary world shapes the sin of greed into different expressions than the cultural context that originally identified the Seven Deadly Sins. I am inclined to think that greed is a universal temptation, but the expression of greed varies from culture to culture. One modern American variation on greed is that greedy people do not just love their possessions. . . . they also love possessing. They love the process of possessing, acquiring, and collecting. Our slavery is not to things per se, but to the process of acquiring those things. As soon as we have secured some prized possession, we become restless and begin again to focus on the next thing. We find it difficult to be content with our possessions. Whether our possession is a prized work of art or a sailboat, when we are consumed with greed, we do not take time to enjoy our possession, to relish it or use it to facilitate other non-materialistic goals. All too soon we become bored and are ready to move on to the next acquisition. So it is, then, that one of the modern expressions of the sin of greed is over-work. Isn't it interesting that we employ a term from the world of addiction—workaholic—to describe this version of greed?

Greed is addictive. The word almost implies it. Like all of the addictions related to these deadly sins, the addictive process starts in the mind, in a pattern of obsessive thinking. When we are caught in greed, we think a great deal about money, about acquisitions, about what we need to do next. Our thinking consumes our energy and distorts our values. Our addiction is satisfied when the desired acquisition is secured. "I got it! I won!" That is the high, the adrenaline rush that comes when we finally acquire a desired object or achieve a desired success. Recent research by neuro-economist Brian Krutson at Stanford University indicates that it is not just adrenaline, but more precisely a dopamine rush in the brain that provides us with this high.[4] According to Krutson, the high occurs not just at the time of acquisition, but also in the anticipation of the acquisition. Thinking about the "big score" or an unusual investment opportunity makes our dopamine levels rise, and this change in brain chemistry is exactly the same change caused by drug addiction! Now do you believe me when I say that greed is addictive?

By the way, lest we deceive ourselves, greed is not a sin of the rich alone and is not necessarily limited to material things. The rich and the

---

4. Zweig, "The Thrill Is Wrong," 76.

successful appear to be better at marshalling their greed than the rest of us, but all of us can be consumed with possessions, personal gain, and/or the collection of credentials or even information. If greed is a sin of the mind and is more focused on possessing than possessions, then a person of any income level can be vulnerable to greed. It is not *having* possessions that makes one greedy, but *loving* possessions or, if you will, the love of possessing. It is not how much we own that makes us greedy; it is our attitude toward our wealth. Whether or not we actually acquire wealth is almost secondary, although clearly greedy people tend to become rich in part because they put so much energy into it. In theory, however, greed is possible among people of any economic class because greed is not about the amount of possessions but the love of possessions or, as I have just suggested, about the love of possessing.

Is Work Addictive?

A colleague of mine claims to have coined the term "workaholic" in his 1971 book, *Confessions of a Workaholic*.[5] The term has caught on, in part because Wayne Oates was pointing to a growing phenomenon, not just in himself, but in all of us. In the economic uncertainties of the twenty-first century, it seems that workaholism has become standard fare. Employers expect and employees have come to feel compelled to work as many hours as they can in order to avoid the dreaded layoff.

Denny Miller was in a serious auto accident that resulted in the tragic death of the passenger riding in the car, a man who was his neighbor and friend. Ironically, they were returning from playing golf and having a few beers when the accident occurred. I say "ironically" because Denny rarely took time off to play at much of anything. In the accident, Denny suffered a brain injury and a shattered right hip and leg. Although Denny wasn't a member of my church, I was encouraged to visit Denny because he was having difficulty adjusting to his new life. Now in his seventh month of rehab, Denny was beginning to realize that his life would never be the same again. He recounted the initial shock and trauma of his injuries, when he was just thankful that he was alive, and then he went through the "I am going to overcome this just like I've overcome everything else in my life" phase. Now he was in the third phase, realizing that his life might never return to normal. In a series of short conversations over several weeks, Denny recounted

5. Oates, *Confessions of a Workaholic*.

Greed

his work career, how he inherited his start-up computer company when his partner sold him his share, and how he worked his tail off 24/7 to make the company a success. The days went by in a haze of compulsive activity, moving from event to event, phone call to phone call, letter to letter, and project to project, and he often worked fifty to sixty hours per week. It was quite exciting those first twelve years. Then the company was purchased by a German software firm and the activity level stepped up another degree or two. Now there were early morning conference calls across the Atlantic and occasionally overseas trips as well.

"It was addictive, you know," Denny said one day. "The work life was addictive. As I look back on it now, it was such a rat race, such a slavery to success at any cost . . . and then it all came crashing down."

"I feel like I am now in recovery from work, not just my injuries. I used to find vacations, when I did take them, so difficult. I was always thinking about work and checking messages, sometimes behind my wife's back. Even as late as a few months ago, when I had recovered enough to get on the phone, I was calling in, asking questions, giving orders. . . . I do not know if I made much sense because I was still recovering up here [pointing to his head]. I just could not believe that they could survive without me there . . . and yet they are apparently doing quite well without me. We all think that we are indispensable, don't we, pastor?"

As our conversation deepened, Denny began to see more clearly than ever how addicted he was to work. Sometimes that is the way it is with addictions. Once we break free, we realize how trapped we really were. Workaholism is such a tempting addiction because over-working is so socially acceptable. The material rewards are great. Everyone praises and even depends on the over-achiever. We are a nation of doers. Two months later, Denny asked to talk to me again. It was now clear that he was not going back to work, at least not to his previous job, and he had begun to prepare the paperwork for disability retirement. He insisted that his wife be present at the meeting.

"I want to say this in front of you, pastor, kind of in front of God, that I am so grateful to Jenny [looking straight at her] for putting up with me all these years. I was not much of a husband and father for most of our marriage. She could have and should have walked away. I spent way too much time at work and missed a lot of years watching my kids grow up and all."

Jenny responded, "I would not be so quick to take me off the hook. You were hard to live with during those years, and it was just as easy for me to have you at work, instead of behaving like a caged animal at home."

Later, Jenny continued, "We are learning to live on a lot less. I have sold the boat and the time-share (we never used it much anyhow). We have gotten into Denny's retirement funds, but it is all good. I got my husband back. We'll get by."

I responded, "Yes, and you'll do more than get by. You are going to flourish in this new life together."

In some ways, Denny was the lucky one. He was forced to hit bottom and begin recovery. Other workaholics never reach bottom, and they destroy their marriages or kill themselves before ever getting any help. Still others have alcohol problems that ultimately force them into recovery.

Is over-work an addiction? It certainly can meet the criteria in some people: mood altering, habit-forming, and tolerance building, characterized by obsessive thinking and out-of-control behavior, and destructive to self and others. Is there an element of greed in work addiction? Certainly, greed is the craving, the mental portion of the addictive process. But the craving in this case is not just for more possessions, but an obsession with getting things done, an addiction to accomplishment and doing. It is an addiction to checking off items on one's to-do list. It is a life that favors doing over being, goals over process, and things over people. The phrase "idle hands are the devil's workshop" dates back to Chaucer, but it found its zenith in the Protestant work ethic. It was probably a warning against the sin of sloth. In modern times, the opposite is equally true. The devil is to be experienced in the appeal of over-working and in the corresponding lie that our worth is to be found only in our productiveness. Unfortunately, it is a lie that capitalistic cultures reinforce.

Greed and Interpersonal Relationships

When we think of greed we tend to think of a miser, a grouchy old man holed up in a dark room and counting money all day. We tend to think of Scrooge or King Midas or even Howard Hughes, who lived the last years of his life in a private penthouse in a Las Vegas hotel. More often than not, the traditional image of a person caught in the web of greed is one of social isolation. Greedy people are often lonely people, preferring their money and wealth to the company of others. There is a good deal of truth to this image.

Greedy people do tend to use people and love things instead of loving people and using things. Greedy people tend to be poor marriage partners and even poorer parents. Greedy people are lovers of things, not people.

Current manifestations of the sin of greed are not nearly so stereotypical. Another example of a greedy person is not the miser, but the overspender. The modern expression of the sin of greed is not just the socially isolated individual, but also the socially active person who enjoys showing off his or her wealth. The modern media image of wealth, especially among the nouveaux riches, is someone with lots of friends—after all, riches can buy friends. The attitude is, "If you got it, flaunt it" (the other side of envy). The focus is not just on the acquisition of wealth, but also on the spending of wealth by traveling, eating, and entertaining, thereby securing fame and friends as well as fortune. These days the sin of greed is blended with the sin of pride (narcissism and self-indulgence) and the sin of gluttony (over-consumption).

People who are addicted to greed tend to see the world in terms of possessions and possessing. They want to possess. They like to consume, acquire, and control. This possession style spills over into all arenas of life. They treat people as if they are commodities to be possessed and controlled. They view spouses and children as trophies, not loved ones. They approach others with questions such as, What can this person do for me? How can this friendship advance my goals? Greedy persons have a difficult time with friendship for friendship's sake. When they do love, they often have a very possessive, insecure style of love, prone to jealousy and fits of rage if the loved object threatens to escape or to make a free choice. As I said, people caught up in the sin of greed usually make very poor marriage partners and even poorer parents because they often over-indulge and/or over-push their children.

Treating people like commodities is nowhere more obvious or painfully repulsive than in the case of human slavery, whether it be the slave trade of the sixteenth through the nineteenth centuries in North America or the sexual slave trade that is still going on today around the world. In human slavery, slave owners treat other human beings like possessions, something to be owned and used for their ability to produce or to give pleasure. Slaves are literally bought and sold at auctions, not unlike livestock, a used car, or a bushel of apples. They are evaluated according to their ability to work or breed more slaves.

Slavery goes back to the dawn of human civilization, if not earlier. Wherever slavery has existed, it has often been interwoven with the capitalistic motive, and with the advent of modern capitalism in the sixteenth century, slavery was taken to new heights. I would argue that slavery should be understood as a manifestation of greed because in slavery profit is elevated higher than life, welfare, and basic morality. In the vignette that opened this chapter, it is all there! Columbus's initial impression of the natives of the Caribbean is one in which he is sizing up their value to his business goals. They are not human beings, in his eyes, but commodities to be used and exploited. It was then a short jump from seeing them as commodities to seeing them (and others) as slaves. Could the institution of slavery be understood as a form of collective addiction, like our modern addiction to oil? And does denial in its various forms and the lure of excessive profit keep these unjust systems in place, then and now?

In all fairness, however, we should also note that the tendency to treat people as commodities exists on a continuum. Slavery is certainly at one extreme, but discrimination, sexism, and racism can also be understood as part of this same continuum. The continuum is really about the objectification of people, and it ranges from slavery to prostitution to employment. If you doubt this link between capitalism, greed, and the objectification of people, pause a moment and look at what is happening to our children.

In 2010, the American Psychological Association issued a report on the sexualization of girls. This report defined sexualization as portraying a girl's value as coming primarily from her sexual appeal. It found increased sexualization in magazines, in advertisements, in music lyrics, and on television, a situation that causes "harm to the sexualized individuals themselves, to their interpersonal relationships, and to society."[6] Sexualization leads to lower cognitive performance and greater body dissatisfaction. The report also connects sexualization with eating disorders, depression, and physical health problems.

Objectifying women is not new, but the sheer amount of messages that girls get these days is astonishing. Some estimate that, on average, girls view nearly five hundred advertisements a day. It is reported that today 18 percent of girls ages eight to twelve use mascara; 43 percent of girls ages six to nine use lipstick and lip gloss; and 81 percent of ten-year-old girls fear getting fat.[7] Retailers now sell padded bras in the children's aisles of

---

6. Zurbriggen, "Sexualization of Girls," 2.
7. Clean Cut Media, "Unnaturally Beautiful Children."

department stores. Of course, this is not about sex. It is about marketing, and it is about profit. If little girls are convinced to want to become sexier, marketers have opened up a whole new group of consumers for cosmetics, clothes, hair products, accessories, and shoes.[8] Marketers do the same thing with violence and little boys, selling boys on being "powerful" by purchasing action toys, guns, aggressive sports computer games, and the like. So, we are making boys more violent and girls more sexy. Why are we doing this? To my mind, this activity qualifies as greed and maybe even as a collective addiction. Treating one another as commodities, whether it be through slavery, classism, or objectification, is a symptom of the sin of greed, and it is certainly deadly. It is also highly addictive to individuals and to entire institutional systems.

Some of you who are a part of the Baby Boomer generation will remember the name Martin Buber, who was a Jewish mystic and philosopher prominent in the mid-twentieth century.[9] Buber argued that we humans essentially form two kinds of relationships: I–It relationships and I–Thou relationships. This distinction was embraced by existential philosophers, theologians, and psychologists. In an I–It relationship, we relate to another person or life form in terms of its function, its role, or its usefulness without knowing the other personally or in depth. I–It relationships comprise the vast majority of relationships in the modern world. I–Thou relationships, in contrast, are with persons whom we relate to personally, intimately, and vulnerably. We value these relationships for their own sake, not for their usefulness. Buber's discussion of this distinction is more complex than most people realize, but the terms caught on because, I believe, they articulated the growing objectification of people that was taking place in the modern world. Further, I would argue that the growth of I–It relationships is one of the consequences of the pervasive influence of capitalism upon modern societies. The more the mental sin of greed infiltrates our consciousness, the more we tend to objectify one another.

I bet you have not read the story of King Midas in decades. Is it really just a story for children, though? Out of his desire for more gold, Midas is granted his wish that everything he touches will turn to gold. But at last, in his greed, he gets carried away and touches his daughter, who turns to

---

8. The term "age compression" refers to the contemporary phenomenon of younger children adopting patterns once reserved for older youth.

9. The most recently published translation of Buber's classic book is *I and Thou* (2000).

stone-cold gold. The story illustrates very well the addictive nature of greed and the way that people who are caught in the sin/addiction of greed tend to destroy human relationships.

Gambling and the Lure of Easy Money

Gambling is not new, but it has certainly risen to new heights in modern times. Gambling takes many forms in our society, from informal games of poker to horse racing, sports betting, and lotteries. In more recent times, governments at various levels have sponsored several forms of gambling in the hopes of securing new sources of needed revenue. Today forty-eight out of the fifty states have some form of legalized gambling. The gambling industry—and it *is* an industry now—appeals to our desire to have something for nothing, to get rich quick. Isn't this hook basically an appeal to greed? Perhaps this would be another good definition of greed—the desire to have something for nothing. Greed is greed because it reflects the desire to have material gain without work, without cost or sacrifice. Material gain is not bad in itself, but it becomes sinful when it is secured without work. In a sense, then, we might connect greed with sloth.

Have you ever purchased a lottery ticket? Recently Mega Millions was advertising a $650 million pot. A great number of Americans, in spite of the well-publicized odds, bought tickets in the hope of striking it rich. I have on occasion purchased a ticket, when I am feeling lucky. What usually happens then is that, as I am driving down the freeway or exercising on the treadmill, I find myself dwelling on how I will spend my potential winnings. Sometimes, within a few hours I have all of my millions already spent—mostly on charitable causes, of course. I really do not have much chance of ever winning a lottery, especially since I only buy an occasional ticket. So in a sense it is entertainment more than it is gambling. I can entertain myself for hours, planning how to spend my millions. Great fun . . . but even in this small example, I am struck by how obsessive my mind can become. For a time I can think of nothing else except how I am going to spend those millions. It frightens me to become that preoccupied, that consumed. How easy it could be to keep on buying lottery tickets. Fortunately, I have never won.

Gambling can certainly be harmless entertainment, but for some people gambling becomes an addiction. The addictive lure of gambling depends in part on the type of gambling. Some people get addicted to the high of winning; others enjoy the focused concentration of trying to beat the system; still others enjoy a relived fantasy or the trance-like elements of the experience. If one type of gambling could combine all of these highs in one activity, it would probably be more alluring than gambling in its varied forms already is. Scholars estimate that there are about two million compulsive or pathological gamblers in the United States and maybe another eight million who could be classified as problem gamblers.[10] A problem gambler might have one or two of the symptoms associated with compulsive gambling but not all or most of the symptoms necessary to be diagnosed as a pathological gambler. With the increased opportunities for gambling in our society, most clinicians expect to see an increased incidence of problem gamblers.[11] We now have a twelve-step program for problem gamblers called Gamblers Anonymous (GA), and the parallels of this program to the program for alcoholics are striking. Like alcoholics, compulsive gamblers show symptoms such as preoccupation, tolerance, withdrawal, escape from feelings, lying, loss of control, and negative consequences. Like alcoholics, GA people understand compulsive gambling to be a progressive illness that cannot be cured but that can, with the application of their spiritual principles, be arrested. People who are compulsive gamblers cannot stop thinking about their next bet, the possible big prize which is just around the corner in the next ticket, race, game, or hand of cards. The high associated with this addiction is probably due to higher dopamine levels in the brain. Then there is also the adrenaline rush that comes when one wins or is on a winning streak. The thrill, the excitement, and the fame that comes from having beaten the system are all a part of the appeal of gambling. As most psychologists will tell you, the occasional reinforcer is actually more powerful than the consistent reinforcer. The gambler wins just enough and just often enough to feed the lure of the next winning jackpot.

There is an element of gambling or risk in every investment. Wise investments are supposed to be well thought out, well researched, and rational in nature. Yet, every now and again, temptation gets the best of us. We are tempted to over-extend—to invest money we cannot afford to be without. We may make speculative investments in hopes of making a killing in the market. Then, we panic and sell everything, failing to have the

---

10. Petry, *Pathological Gambling*, 15.

11. This anticipation is based on research that has found that the incidence of "disordered gambling" has increased with the spread of legalized gambling in the last twenty years (ibid., 32).

Ancient Sins . . . Modern Addictions

patience of a long-term investment strategy. So, why are we all prone to such foolish blunders? Why do so many people make investment decisions based on either greed or fear? Like all addictions, greed has a strong element of self-deception. Few people acknowledge that they are being greedy, even when they clearly are. Most of the time, greedy people have justified, rationalized, or denied their true motives, the risks involved, and the consequences of their actions. Greed, like all addictions, has a way of sneaking up on us. It creeps up on us, one little rationalization after another, until one day we wake up and wonder, What have I become? Those who ask this question are actually the lucky ones.

Greed and Corruption

Recently, in the state where I live, a well-known congressman was convicted of corruption, tax evasion, and taking bribes. He was convicted of taking over $2.4 million in bribes from defense contractors and evading more than $1 million in taxes. His eight-year prison sentence was considered the harshest penalty ever meted out to a former member of Congress in a corruption case. When the judge read the sentence, he said, "The word 'avarice' is an antiquated word. But I think that it applies here." This case was particularly baffling to outsiders because the congressman was a war hero who had served his country with distinction and received a Navy Cross. How could someone who apparently lived by a code of honor, service, and sacrifice display such arrogance, dishonesty, and outright greed? The popular phrase "What were you thinking?" comes to mind, and that is precisely the point—greed has a way of distorting our thinking.

It seems like greed and bending the rules go hand in hand.[12] Many people who are intensely enslaved by greed lie, cheat, steal, and otherwise violate common values in order to satisfy their lust for things or money. This observation is consistent with the earlier definition of greed—that greed is greed because it sacrifices other values for material gain. Sometimes the addiction to the acquisition of wealth becomes so strong that otherwise sane people sacrifice loved ones, health, and/or personal integrity to get their fix.

12. Eryn Brown of the *Los Angeles Times*, in an article entitled "Study: Greed Drives Rich to Bend Ethics," recounts the results of several studies at the University of California, Berkeley, that suggest that the higher one's socioeconomic status, the more likely one is to bend the rules at traffic intersections or at the check-out counter. This is an interesting study, but my view is that greed, as a mental craving, affects people of all socioeconomic levels.

They cheat to gain advantage, to gain more money or access to power that will create wealth. Generally, they rationalize their addiction with phrases like, "Everyone else does it," or "That's how things are done here in Washington," or "I'm just trying to get ahead in a competitive business climate."

Greed does have a negative connotation in our culture, so when it comes to light that a person might have engaged in dishonest activities in the name of greed, that same person sometimes lies, cheats, and steals all the more—but now in an effort to cover up his or her previous misdeeds. I guess, at a certain level, they are embarrassed by their own behavior and, in their heart of hearts, know it to be sinful. The trouble with this secondary lying—lying to cover up lies—is that it does get hard to remember what the truth is. Lying gets very complicated very fast.

One can have a "greedy" thought or two from time to time and even use such thoughts to motivate oneself to work harder, but, like I said, greed has an addictive quality if allowed to have its way. Over time, greedy thoughts can burn in our minds just like unspent money burns a hole in our pockets. All too soon greed, if not balanced by a strong personal morality, drives the individual to bend the rules, and then over time it leads to corruption. Stealing and lying are often the natural consequences of the sin of greed, as surely as adultery is the natural consequence of lust.

In What Sense Is Greed Deadly?

Greed leads people to take shortcuts on the job that put others at risk. Greed leads people to take bribes that destroy the democratic process. Greed leads corporations to pad their bottom line with dishonest accounting, which ultimately costs investors profit and employees their benefits.[13] Individuals and corporations have destroyed the environment, rare species, and natural beauty in their mad pursuit for gold or oil or coal. There is a correlation between the greed-based addictions and suicide ideation and suicide attempts. Greed destroys, either indirectly or directly, those who are addicted and those who love or depend on the addicted person.

13. The term "corporate greed" is used in the media these days in reference to America's economic crisis. I am not sure that the term makes any sense. Corporations are supposed to be greedy—the point of a for-profit corporation is to make money. Greed implies moral agency, and corporations have no consciousness to make moral decisions apart from the decisions of its executives. It is true, however, that corporations have their own cultures and that some corporate cultures can be very addictive and addiction-promoting for their employees.

Ancient Sins . . . Modern Addictions

Most spiritual traditions warn against the evils of greed. In the Christian tradition, one out of every ten verses in the Gospels refers to money or a related subject. Jesus had a lot to say about mammon or wealth and its impact on our souls and the human community.[14] He saw the love of material wealth as one of the most significant barriers, if not the most significant barrier, to faith in God. In the Gospel of Luke, where money is referred to in one out of every seven verses, Jesus says straight out, "No one can serve two masters. . . . You cannot serve God and mammon" (Luke 16:13). Or, on another occasion, he stated, "It is easier for a camel to go through the eye of a needle than for a rich man to enter the Kingdom of God" (Mark 10:25). Why? In the mind of Jesus and of many early Christian leaders, greed was essentially a problem of idolatry. Greedy people were loving money instead of God—they were making money into a false god, an idol. Greedy people were trusting in their wealth instead of trusting in the living God. In a sense, then, the commandment that may relate most to the sin of greed isn't "You shall not steal" (Exod 20:15) but "You shall not make any graven images . . . and bow down to them or serve them" (Exod 20:4). The destruction of one's mind or soul is also a kind of death, a deadly result of the sin of greed.

Greed, like the other six deadly sins, has an addictive nature. Greed feeds on itself; the more one is greedy, the more one is greedy. It then sets up or leads to a variety of addictions. Greed as an addiction does not have a single behavioral manifestation. There can be a variety of manifestations, ranging from over-work to gambling, hoarding, participating in scams, shopping, and even sexual addictions. Those addictions in turn lead to a variety of deaths. So greed comes by its status honestly as a deadly sin.

How to Help Ourselves

The traditional antidote for greed is mercy or charity. The more we practice charity toward others, the more we are insulated from the sin of greed. How can mercy or charity be an antidote for greed?

As noted earlier, people who are caught up in greed—and we all are to some extent—see people not as people, but as objects, commodities, assets,

---

14. The fact that the perils of greed were of such concern to Jesus and other spiritual pioneers as long as two thousand years ago suggests that greed is one of the oldest of the human addictions. When we think of addictions, we think first of drugs and alcohol, which in their present form are certainly products of the modern world. But greed and gluttony also have a long and ancient history among humans.

or tools to be used. If someone cannot produce, we have no need for them. Mercy requires that we look at people as unique human beings who have needs and that we value them apart from what they can produce. Mercy requires that we see ourselves as human beings, too, not value ourselves based only on what we can produce.

Generosity, another word for charity, is also an effective antidote for greed. By being generous, we keep our focus on the needs of others, not on our own wants. By being generous, we are also not allowed to get too attached to our wealth. The reason most Christian churches collect an offering each week is not just because the institution needs money to pay its bills. A weekly offering gives congregants the opportunity to practice generosity and, in so doing, fortifies them against the temptations of greed.

A third antidote for greed is gratitude. Cultivating gratitude as an attitude helps us focus on what we do have, not on what do we not have. In recent years, gratitude as an attitude has received some scholarly attention among psychologists, and the universal conclusion is that gratitude contributes positively to our mental, physical, and spiritual health.[15]

We can practice the virtue of generosity and mercy by doing the following:

- giving regularly to our church and to charities; visiting our favorite charity and seeing its human face
- traveling lightly through life; sorting regularly through our possessions, recycling items that are no longer of use; passing things along now while we are able to enjoy the giving
- sharing our time; taking the time to listen to loved ones, friends, and colleagues who are hurting
- developing a friend or two who are just friends, nothing more—not business contacts, not vendors, and not even within our line of work
- meditating, which is an effective tool for the overly active mind that obsesses on doing; participating in contemplative prayer, which emphasizes being over doing; making regular space in our week for activities that affirm our value as who we are rather than what we do
- attending a funeral once a year to help us remember we will all die and to keep our values and priorities in perspective; noticing that

---

15. See Emmons, *Thanks!*

most people are eulogized for the character of their lives and their relationships

- seeking alternative ways of measuring our net worth besides our material wealth
- making lists of our needs and our wants and reflecting upon these lists
- reducing our needs; focusing on desiring less rather than making more
- cultivating gratitude as a daily attitude

Finally, one of the time-honored spiritual approaches to the problem of greed, found in various Western religious traditions, is emphasizing that each of us is a moral agent. This is a fancy way of saying that each of us makes choices every day of our lives and these choices are based on values, whether implicit or explicit. Greed has a way of lulling us to sleep, but through value clarification exercises, we can reflect on our choices and make them conscious, and then we can choose clearly and healthily and morally. If we fail to make our choices conscious, we tend to move through life as mere materialists or robots, reacting to whatever social pressures or internal needs are strongest in the moment.

Jesus took this approach. He often confronted people with their choices and by so doing made their implicit values explicit, so they could then clearly choose. In his confrontation with the rich young ruler (Luke 18:18ff.), for example, Jesus forces the ruler to choose between his riches and discipleship. In so doing, the ruler comes to recognize his love of money—his greed—and even though he chooses against discipleship, he makes a clear choice. In the parable of the rich fool (Luke 12:13ff), Jesus lays out the consequences of one's choices regarding the use of wealth. We must choose and be constantly aware of our choices. Again and again, Jesus is forcing choices. This method—which we might term a value clarification exercise—is a good one and is still applicable in our time as a safeguard against the temptation of greed. Greed is a subtle, self-deceiving dynamic, especially in this culture. So we must be constantly and regularly reflecting upon and examining our values. The more we are aware of our choices and the values upon which those choices are made, the more we can turn away from greed before it becomes addictive and potentially destructive to our lives, relationships, and very souls.

Summary

In summary, greed is a prevalent sin in capitalistic societies because in many ways capitalism encourages and justifies greed. More specifically, American culture seems to be ambivalent about greed. On the one hand, we admire those who achieve great wealth and we celebrate the prevailing ethos that "more is better." On the other hand, we recognize in the arts and government regulation the destructive elements in too much greed. The line is fine between these two views. But clearly, greed surrounds us in contemporary culture. Psychologically, greed is the desire for acquisition, a craving to collect or possess money, things, people, achievements, and even accomplishments. But greed reflects not ordinary acquisition, but acquisition in excess or, if you will, craving in excess. Greed can lead to or support a variety of addictions, from over-work, over-ambition, hoarding, and gambling to various forms of slavery. The greed-based addictions are often associated with corruption, distorted values, and the dehumanizing of human relationships. In all of the manifestations of greed's addictive nature, destruction comes when we unknowingly choose material values over human values and trust more in material security than the living God.

Questions for Self-Reflection

1. Do I consider myself to be a materialistic person or a non-materialistic person?
2. Do I measure my worth by my wealth? Do I like new things?
3. Have I ever been called a workaholic? Am I a type-A personality, competitive, driven, tense? Is it difficult for me to take time off?
4. When and how has greed gotten me into trouble?
5. Am I tough-minded when it comes to my business? Am I freely generous or do I tend to expect something in return for my charity?
6. Do I like to gamble? How do I manage to keep my gambling in check?
7. What do I do to cultivate generosity and gratitude in my life?

Biblical passages related to greed: Matt 6:24; Mark 11:15–19; Luke 12:13–21; 18:18–30; Phil 4:10–13; 1 Tim 6:9–10; Heb 13:5

7 Gluttony

Being Hooked on Consumption

Frank: How is my blood work, doc?

Physician: To be quite frank, not good. Your cholesterol is high, as are your triglycerides. We talked last year about altering your diet and increasing your cardiovascular activity.

Frank: I get plenty of exercise every day, crawling under houses and pulling pipe.

Physician: And your alcohol consumption?

Frank: I enjoy a nice cold one after a hard day. Don't you, doc? What stresses me out, if you want to know the truth, is the damn traffic. It gets worse every year. I must spend a third of the day on the road. That's not good for business.

Physician: Actually, my major concern, Frank is your sugar levels. These numbers indicate that you are what we now call pre-diabetic. I think we need to consider a more aggressive approach to this problem.

Frank: I don't like the sound of that, doc.

Doctor: You need to start taking your health more seriously, Frank. The way you are going, you are not going to live much past your retirement party. Wouldn't you like to enjoy that retirement you have worked for all these years?

Frank: You are right, of course, doc. But who can afford to retire these days?

Gluttony

THE CONTEXT OF THIS conversation is a doctor's office. The scene is a familiar one for all too many Americans, adults and even children. Increasingly, people with gluttony issues are ending up in hospitals, clinics, and medical offices. Frank Johnson is a fifty-seven-year-old husband, father, and owner of a small plumbing business. Like many people, he has a stressful job. He talks a good talk about joining a gym and losing some weight, but he really does not think he should have to join "any damn expensive gym"—work is hard enough. Weekends are spent on the lake in the summer and taking care of household chores the rest of the year. But a good portion of every weekend is spent drinking beer and binging on snacks in front of the big-screen television where the latest professional sports event is being shown. Frank is overweight by at least sixty pounds compared to those "unrealistic" (according to Frank) charts on the walls of his doctor's office. Frank thinks of himself as having a good life but, in fact, he is gradually killing himself. He is about to pass a milestone in that journey to destruction by becoming diabetic. After the above conversation, Frank will try again to make some changes. He will go on a diet and maybe bowl some on weekends. How long do you think this diet will last? Why is it so hard for Frank and millions of men and women like him to maintain a healthy lifestyle? Could it be that there is an addiction operating here? And if so, an addiction to what?

Is the sin of gluttony a problem today? Absolutely, and maybe more now than at any other time in the history of humanity because we have so much food and drink available, at least those of us in the developed nations. Nearly one third of the adults in the United States are obese by commonly accepted standards.[1] Currently, nearly fourteen million Americans, or one in every twelve adults, abuse alcohol.[2] In recent years, there is more attention being paid to the growing problem of childhood obesity and the resulting growing incidence of health consequences like childhood diabetes.[3] By any contemporary measure, the sin of gluttony is alive and well.

What drives such over-consumption? Certainly, affluence is the economic background that makes such over-consumption possible. We have more food and drink than ever before. It is readily available and affordable for most of us. In some ways, we are victims of our own success. In

---

1. Ogden et al., "Prevalence of Obesity," 6.
2. National Council on Alcoholism and Drug Dependence, "FAQS/Facts."
3. One in every six children is considered obese in the United States, as reported in the film *The Obesity Epidemic* (National Center for Chronic Disease Prevention and Health Promotion). The same source reports that from 1974 to 2000, the number of children who are overweight tripled.

addition, our modern lifestyle is more sedentary than ever before. Officials report that the majority of Americans get no exercise on a daily or even a weekly basis.[4] We are less physically active than our ancestors were. The other factor in such over-consumption is the economic system in which we all live and work. We have become a consumer-oriented society. We have all been trained to be good consumers, to consume more—believing that more is better, we consume bigger portions, bigger houses, bigger meals, and bigger cars. The convergence of all of these forces has created an environment in which gluttony can easily evolve into one or more addictions.

The sin of gluttony has traditionally included both the over-consumption of food and the over-consumption of alcohol. In modern times, we might extend the list to include various legal and illegal substances. Gluttony has to do with ingesting something into our bodies, repeatedly and abusively. Gluttony has to do with over-consumption—period!

Gluttony as Craving

On first impression, gluttony sounds like more of a behavioral sin. We overeat, over-drink, and over-consume; these are behaviors. Should gluttony be defined as over-consumption? Suppose that our spiritual forebears understood gluttony first and primarily as a sin of the mind. How would we define gluttony then? I propose that gluttony be defined as a craving—the craving to eat, to drink, to consume, to fill ourselves with something external, something that promises to make us happy. We experience this craving largely in our minds. Sometimes there are physical symptoms, such as restlessness, anxiety, lethargy, or irritation, but mostly the craving is mental. Our mind thinks about the desired substance. We dwell upon it. We relish the taste, smell, and sensation of it. Our minds are consumed with thoughts of when and how we are going to get our next fix.

We all experience cravings. We all experience hunger and thirst. This is universal and normal. Craving occurs when we are hungry or thirsty over a prolonged period of time. In earlier eons, cravings drove humans to seek food and water relentlessly, thus enabling them to survive! The craving mechanism worked. In modern times, the addictive process has hijacked the normal mechanisms of hunger and thirst. Now we desire food or drink

---

4. More precisely, a 2001 study found that the majority of those living in the United States do not engage in physical activity consistent with the minimum standard of thirty minutes per day (Centers for Disease Control and Prevention, "Prevalence of Activity").

when we are not hungry or thirsty. Or we desire chemical substances that act like food or drink, although their effect is intensified. Thus, the craving gets out of control and leads to compulsive behaviors that are then reinforced with a high, and the addictive cycle is repeated and repeated. There are two addictions traditionally associated with gluttony: compulsive eating and alcoholism. But by using this definition of gluttony as craving, we can add drug addiction in its multiple forms and degrees of legality to the list of gluttony-related addictions.

This view of gluttony as the mental aspect of addiction is consistent with what alcoholics tell us—that alcoholism needs to be defined not just by behavior, but also by what goes on in the mind. They tell us that drunkenness per se or how many drinks one drinks in a certain period of time is not the chief criterion of an alcoholic. Alcoholics who have been sober for twenty years still introduce themselves at their weekly AA meeting with the words, "I am an alcoholic." Being an alcoholic has more to do with what goes on in the mind than with what one is doing or not doing. Alcoholics crave alcohol. They think obsessively . . . about alcohol, about their next drink, about the smell, taste, and social context of drinking. It's the craving that makes them alcoholics.

How Is Gluttony Addictive?

Unlike the other Seven Deadly Sins, with the exception of lust, the sin of gluttony is rooted in and tied to our physiological needs. In the words of St. Paul, gluttony is a "sin of the flesh." It is a sin that is tied to and based on our fleshly existence as human beings. Further, the consumption of food and drink is enjoyable. It tastes good. Most of us like to eat and drink. Much of our social life is structured around eating and drinking, further reinforcing this activity. Food and drink are great social lubricants, loosening up people who otherwise might be socially inhibited or awkward, and this facilitates conversations and self-disclosure. And, of course, eating and drinking satisfies our bodily needs. For all these reasons, the addictive dynamics associated with gluttony are stronger than those associated with most of the other sins. All of our bodily needs, tastes, and senses compound and intensify the addictive process. So, the addictions associated with gluttony are that much easier to fall into and harder to get free from.

In recent decades, medical researchers have been able to identify the mechanism of addiction. In the brain there is a complex system of various chemicals that are called neurotransmitters. There may be as many as ten to fifteen of these neurotransmitters. Some of the names of the more common ones are familiar to us—norepinephrine, dopamine, epinephrine, serotonin. The relative levels of these neurotransmitters and their stability over time influence overall brain efficiency, health, and functioning. Various neurotransmitters influence moods such as excitement and depression, the ability to handle pain, sleep patterns, sense of peace and well-being, and so on. The neurotransmitter that is associated with the pleasure of consumption is dopamine. In very simple terms, eating raises the level of dopamine, and when we haven't eaten for some time, the dopamine levels fall, giving us the sensation of hunger. Ingesting various artificial substances, like alcohol or drugs, also increases the level of dopamine, giving the user a temporary high in the form of pleasure or satiation.[5] Addiction occurs when we ingest substances repeatedly over time. In such cases, the body's regulatory system sends a signal to various glands telling them to produce less dopamine because the body already has so much of it in its system. So, the body slows down or even stops making dopamine. When the person ceases to ingest those substances, the brain is literally momentarily starved for dopamine. This starved state is experienced as a craving for the desired substances. When the individual tries to quit, the craving, driven by this deprivation, is initially quite strong. In most cases where the substance abuse has been short-term, the body will start making dopamine and the related neurotransmitters again and in time we will return to normal or pre-abuse physiological functioning. In other cases, when we have abused substances for long periods of time and/or abused multiple substances, there may be permanent damage to the body's ability to produce dopamine, and then we experience a constant craving and an inability to experience genuine pleasure from ordinary food and drink.

The regular over-consumption of alcohol, for example, builds up a physiological tolerance in the drinker's body. With each repeated binge, or with chronic abuse, it takes more alcohol to get the same desired effect. The body has reduced its own levels of production of dopamine, thus requiring more alcohol to achieve the same buzz. At the same time, when we attempt to stop drinking altogether, we experience a craving. The craving can be quite physiological, if we have been drinking a lot and/or over a long period

---

5. Or in some cases, if the individual's dopamine levels are naturally low or unstable in the first place, the use of some substances actually makes the individual feel "normal," maybe for the first time in his or her life.

of time, but the craving can also be of a psycho-social nature. This is the addictive process, so familiar to millions of alcoholics in and out of recovery. A similar process occurs in food addictions. Carbohydrates addiction is defined as "a physical imbalance that leads to a compelling hunger, craving or desire for high carbohydrate foods, an escalating, recurring need for starches and sugars."[6] By some estimates, 75 percent of those who are overweight and have high blood pressure or risk-related blood fats could be defined as carbohydrates addicts.[7]

Because gluttony is based on our brain chemistry, the sensation of craving is much stronger compared to the craving associated with behavioral addictions alone. The gluttony-related addictions are the true addictions. These addictions are intense; they are the heavyweights in the world of addiction. Like no other, the addictions associated with gluttony lead to destruction—the destruction of lives, families, careers, and souls. Often, for persons caught in these addictions for years and years, the physiological damage to their bodies and the chemical changes in their brains have become relatively permanent. The craving, or gluttony, as I call it, has become institutionalized. So it is that many recovering alcoholics and drug addicts recognize that the cravings never go away. There is no cure; there is only recovery.

This deep connection between the addictions associated with gluttony and our physiological nature has a couple of implications. First, a severe or long-term addict may need medical assistance to take the first steps in recovery. Recovery may require more than spiritual practices and more than psychological and group support. Some food addicts, for example, need medical monitoring before they change their eating regimen. Some drug addicts need a medically prescribed substitute to reduce the powerful physiological cravings enough to make a recovery program possible. Another implication of this link between the addictions associated with gluttony and our physiological nature is that there may be genetic variables influencing our unique vulnerabilities to various addictions. Some of us may be naturally inclined to experience hunger more intensely than others. Some of us may have more sensitive taste buds. Some of us may have fast or slow or overly sensitive metabolic systems that make us process food and drink differently than most people. Thus, some of us are more vulnerable to weight gain or compulsive eating behaviors. Research has confirmed this

6. Heller et al., *Healthy Heart Program*, xvii.
7. Ibid.

observation, suggesting as well that there are probably genetic predispositions to alcoholism.[8] AA people point to this when they say that alcoholics have "an allergy to alcohol."[9] What this means is that some of us might be more vulnerable to one or several of these addictions, not just because of our psychology and spirituality, but also because of our physiology. It is just the way we are wired. This genetic influence is most apparent in the gluttony-related addictions.

Food Addictions and Compulsive Eating

The traditional image of a glutton is of a person who is obese. In fact, the term "glutton" pretty much describes a fat person, a person with an oral fixation, a person consumed with feeding their face. Yet, if gluttony is primarily to be defined as the mental component of addiction, as I am doing in this chapter, then we must ask the question, Is every obese person suffering from the sin of gluttony? The answer is, not necessarily! There are various reasons why people may be overweight or even obese. As noted above, sometimes there are medical, genetic, biochemical, and lifestyle reasons for obesity. Obesity is not good, regardless of the cause. I am not defending obesity. It is not healthy, and theologically it is a denial of God's good gift of life. Yet gluttony is not obesity per se but, more precisely, the mental component of obesity. Gluttony is a sin of the mind. Gluttony is our obsession with or our craving for food or drink, which in turn leads, more often than not, to an over-consumption of food and drink. So, given this view of gluttony, not every obese person is a glutton, and it is possible that a thin or normal-weight person might be battling gluttony all the time. Gluttony has to do with what is going on in our minds, not just what is going on in our bodies.

How do we know, then, if we are suffering from the sin of gluttony? Well, we must examine our mental processes. People who struggle with gluttony think about food all the time. They are regularly thinking of their next meal, planning their next several meals. They are savoring food in their minds—the taste, smell, look, and texture of food. They consume (excuse the pun) mental energy thinking about eating, about portion sizes,

---

8. This link was first established in 2004 by psychiatrist Subhash C. Pandey of the University of Illinois at Chicago, as reported in Davis, "Researchers Identify Alcoholism Gene." This research has since been duplicated and extended many times.

9. *Alcoholics Anonymous*, xxviii.

diets, choices of food items, etc. Eating takes on an importance far larger than the mere consumption of food to sustain life. Eating comes to mean so much more. When this kind of mental process occurs, we can safely say that gluttony is present. Our mind is craving.

In the literature of addiction studies, we find two terms that describe the addictions related to food and eating. One is the term "food addiction" (or "food addicts"), and the other is the term "compulsive eating." In a sense, these are referring to different aspects of the same disorder. Food addiction emphasizes the chemical or physiological component, the effect a particular food has on the body and our brain chemistry. In everyday conversation, we refer to being addicted to chocolate, or pastries, or coffee. These foods do something to us. The consumption of certain foods does change the chemical makeup of our brains and create cravings that lead to and reinforce addictive behaviors. The operative neurotransmitter appears to be dopamine. It appears that over-eating, or the over-eating of calorie-dense foods, dampens our dopamine levels, thus setting up a craving for more, which leads to more over-eating and more craving.

The term compulsive eating has also come into everyday language. Compulsive eating emphasizes the behavioral component of food addictions. It points to how we eat, to the process of over-eating or to the problem of binge eating. Remember, eating is not a bad thing. It is necessary and natural. The bad thing is over-eating, eating more than we need. Compulsive eating also highlights the speed of eating, which is often related to over-eating. It emphasizes the growing problem of binge eating, gorging oneself on certain foods, often in a social context. In this view, what is addictive is the behavior, not necessarily the food.

In recent years there has been a wealth of new research that suggests that sugar plays a powerful but previously hidden role in difficulties related to compulsive eating or food addiction. Some scholars go so far as to describe sugar as a toxic substance, an addiction-causing substance. Sugar in its various forms and disguises, from sucrose to high-fructose corn syrup, may be the addictive substance in all food addictions. Referring to research on the effects of large amounts of sugar on rats, Princeton University research associate Nicole Avena says, "With sugar, there's neurological and behavioral evidence of dependence.... And the changes are similar to what you'd expect to see if the animals were dependent on drugs of abuse, not just eating tasty food."[10]

10. Nicole Avena worked with the late Bart Hoebel, who studied food addictions at

Sugar alters our brain chemistry in ways that make us feel more alert, energized, and happy (giving us a "sugar high"). As with all addictive substances, our brains can over time build up a tolerance to sugar, thus requiring more and more of it, year after year, in order to experience the same high. And, as previously noted, some of us, because of our genetic make-up, may be particularly vulnerable to the addictive effects of sugar. Unfortunately, sugar shows up everywhere. It surrounds us at every corner. It is in candy, sweets, and desserts. It is in soft drinks. It is the hidden ingredient in processed foods, packaged foods, and fast foods. It even is in alcohol![11] Do you think that the processed food industry knows that sugar is addictive?

Indeed, we Americans are overweight. Many proposed solutions have focused on the need for us to alter our compulsive behavior by eating less, eating more slowly, and exercising more. This is certainly part of the solution. But suppose that there is also a chemical addiction going on here.[12] In addition to sugar in its many forms, our bodies process white flour and other carbohydrates as if they were sugar. More specifically, these foods trigger an over-production of insulin in our liver, which in turn accelerates the production of fat cells. Gary Taubes writes in a recent *Newsweek* cover story critical of the current approaches to obesity reduction in America, "The problem is not only controlling our impulses, but also changing the entire American food economy and rewriting our beliefs about what constitutes a healthy diet."[13] We will not be able to successfully maintain a healthy weight until or unless we all get unhooked from sugar.

From my perspective, I would say that all this sounds awfully similar to a chemical addiction. This is why some writers and TV talk-show guests use the term carbo-holic (carbohydrates addict) to point to the dynamic. This food problem has led to soaring rates of obesity and diabetes, not to mention an assortment of other health challenges, all of which are directly related to the over-consumption of sugar-carbohydrates. Yet, it seems that we humans have been programmed through eons of evolution to seek out

---

the Princeton Neuroscience Institute and conducted pioneering research on the brain chemistry associated with obesity. This quote is taken from an interview with Nicole Avena in Liebman, "Food and Addiction," 6.

11. To be precise, refined sugar and ethanol have similar chemical compositions.

12. If refined sugar and ethanol have similar chemical compositions, maybe—at least for some people—sugar acts on the brain as alcohol does, altering the dopamine levels and creating tolerance. This reinforces the perspective that food addictions are really chemical addictions.

13. Taubes, "New Obesity Campaigns," 33.

sweetness. Apparently, at one time this had some survival value. In contrast, too much sugar is now contributing to our destruction—individually and collectively. Maybe our approach to the problem of obesity in America needs to embrace an addictions model that places this problem within the larger context of the gluttony encouraged by a culture that promotes over-consumption.

The concept of comfort food is also a common term in the world. This phrase points to the emotional component of food addiction or compulsive eating. When we over-eat in general or even binge on certain foods, we are often eating to reduce tension, to calm our anxieties, to self-soothe. We also eat when we are angry, when we are depressed, when we are lonely, and even when we are bored. Eating can meet several different emotional needs. All three of these terms—food addiction, compulsive eating, and comfort eating—speak to the same addiction! For the sake of brevity, I will refer to this addiction as food addiction.

In contrast to alcoholism, the other addiction traditionally associated with gluttony, food addiction cannot be treated with abstinence. Alcoholics can become sober, but food addicts cannot eliminate food entirely. We can eliminate certain foods, of course, but we must eat. We cannot go from one extreme—over-eating—to the other extreme—no food. The standard treatment of choice for over-drinkers—abstinence—is not possible for over-eaters. Food addicts must find another path, a middle path, a moderate path. This fact alone makes recovery programs for food addicts particularly challenging.

Earlier in this book, I suggested that each of the Seven Deadly Sins is a distortion of a basic human need. Food addictions illustrate this truism like no other addiction or sin. What is a normal, healthy need—the need to eat to sustain physical life—is distorted and twisted into an addiction. What starts out as a good part of God's creation becomes a part of our destruction. The sin of gluttony uses our natural need against us, so to speak. To the severely addicted among us, it actually seems that their body has betrayed them, is foreign to them, alienated from them, at odds with them; there is a battle within between their flesh and their spirit. Recovery, then, includes a process of reuniting our spirit with our body, allowing us to become whole again.

Ancient Sins . . . Modern Addictions

Alcoholism: Is It a Disease or a Sin?

Along with food (or sugar), alcohol is certainly the most widespread, socially acceptable, and easily available substance among the gluttony-related addictions. Social drinking is common today in the halls of Congress and the halls of churches and temples. It is promoted in all of the media outlets in billion-dollar advertising campaigns. Drinking, particularly having a good glass of wine with dinner, is now a sign of social distinction, far removed from the traditional negative connotations associated with the local wino or town drunk. Yet, this society's view of alcohol is ambivalent. Despite the widespread social acceptance of drinking alcohol, government agencies and scientists regularly warn the public of the dangers of such things as driving drunk, binge drinking on college campuses, and fetal alcohol syndrome. We certainly get mixed messages. Or, more precisely, the message is to drink responsibly. But this message is drowned out by the overwhelming promotion of "spirits" across the board. Abstinence is really never the message.

Because alcohol consumption is so socially accepted and alcohol is so easily accessible, alcohol abuse and addiction is co-present with many of the other addictions. People who use drugs often abuse alcohol as well. People who are sex addicts or work addicts are often problem drinkers. People who over-eat often over-drink as well. People gamble when they are impaired with alcohol. People who hold a cigarette in one hand often have a beer in the other hand. One of the consequences of this is that alcohol abuse is often the entry point for many people traveling down the path of multiple addictions. Many people start drinking and over-drinking in their teens, and then as the years pass they either learn to drink responsibly or become progressively more addicted and/or graduate on to other addictions in their adult years.[14] The result is that alcoholism is the common thread, the common addictive dynamic, running through many otherwise varied kinds of addictions. Often by treating the alcoholism, one can indirectly treat many of the other addictions as well. But what is alcoholism, exactly?

Over the last hundred years or so, we have changed how we understand alcoholism. It used to be viewed primarily as a sin. People who drank too much were perceived as morally weak and correspondingly were

---

14. By the twelfth grade, 80 percent of youth in the United States have used alcohol. Ericson, "Substance Abuse."

treated with disdain and even contempt. (People who over-eat or who are obese still experience some of this same kind of social stigma.) In more recent years, health care professionals have come to embrace the view that alcoholism as a disease.[15] As a disease, alcoholism has its inception, its progression and predictable stages, its physiological components, and its risks. Yet alcoholism, if it is a disease, is not a disease like any other disease. Some people say it is a "social disease." I say that it is a whole-person disease, a disease that involves the whole person and often the whole family. The disease of alcoholism includes a diseased body, diseased familial relationships, and even a diseased soul. Successful treatment for this disease thus may require interventions with all of the components of the disease. Medical interventions alone will not usually be sufficient.

The disease model of alcoholism has done wonders for improving the treatment rates for those suffering with this addiction. The disease model has taken the stigma off of alcoholism. It has brought the problem out into the open and has normalized the problem. The disease model has opened up the problem to medical services and to health insurance that helps cover the costs of treatment services. All this has increased the success rate for the treatment of alcoholism.[16]

The disease model, however, has its downside as well. I see at least three limitations of the medical model understanding of addiction. First, the very idea that alcoholism is "just" a brain disease reflects a materialistic or reductionist view of addiction and human nature in general. Clearly, addiction is more than a brain disease. It is also a psychological disease, a social disease, and a spiritual disease. It is, as I said earlier, a disease of the whole person. Second, the medical model often assumes that for every disease there is a cure, a pill, a surgical procedure, or a course of treatment that will fix it. Once cured, we can then go back to life as usual. In the case of an alcoholic, we can go back to drinking as usual, or in the case of a food addict, we can go back to eating as usual, or in the case of a compulsive gambler, we can go back to playing the ponies, as long as we drink responsibly, eat in moderation, and limit our gambling to what we can afford. These assumptions do not fit with the experience of millions of recovering addicts nor with the spiritual understanding of addiction posited in this

15. The disease model of addiction for alcoholism reached its zenith recently when the American Society of Addiction Medicine redefined addiction as "a primary, chronic disease of the brain" ("Definition of Addiction," 1).

16. This success rate may not be easy to observe, however, because the incidence of alcoholism and various other addictions continues to rise in our society.

book, which is that addiction is not curable. It is a condition that we can arrest but not fix. And certainly, once clean and sober, an addict cannot go back to drinking or using drugs as usual. I suppose that it is possible that some day medical science will come up with a pill that will take away our addictive cravings, but will the cure be another aspect of the disease? I affirm that through recovery there is healing, but not a cure.

Third, the medical model can also lead people to think that they do not have any responsibility for or choice in their affliction. It is like having the flu or even cancer. These diseases are often thought of as having to run their course; there is not much we can do about it. We are at the mercy of a virus. Indeed, we often feel overpowered by our physical cravings for food or drink. We feel as if we have become slaves to the bottle or the sugar bowl. Our sense of choice has become dwarfed by these overpowering urges and by the disease model itself. Sometimes this helplessness is revealed in the language we use. People with addictive disorders of whatever kind often use the language of helplessness. They say things like, "You made me get angry"; "She made me drink"; "I just had to have that extra piece of cake"; or, "I cannot help myself." The language of "make me" is reflective of the powerlessness or lack of responsibility that many people caught in these diseases experience. The disease model tends to reinforce this kind of attitude, which, in my opinion, actually sustains the disease.

The sin model has several helpful features when it comes to understanding the addictions of gluttony, which I have defined as alcoholism, drug addiction, and food addiction. First, the sin model emphasizes a more holistic approach to the problem, including a spiritual approach. Medical science can help us detoxify, but the underlying problem, the addictive personality, must be dealt with through an array of psycho-social-spiritual methods. Second, the sin model emphasizes that we are moral agents, that we are free, that we have gotten into this situation in part because of our poor choices, and that we can get out of this situation by making better choices. For people caught in these addictions, it does seem like all freedom of choice is gone. Often the path to recovery must begin with a full admission of the loss of control, a full admission that our life is out of control. All remaining sense of free choice or willpower must be surrendered before we can get better. Reclaiming the sense of having a choice in the midst of slavery is the path to recovery. From a spiritual point of view, as well as a psychological point of view, the reclaiming of our ability to make a choice is an important ingredient in the recovery process. People in treatment programs are often told to rephrase their language, to stop using the language of helplessness and start using the language of choice, even if they do not yet believe they actually have a choice. Fake it until you feel it.

Most addicts have a hard time with issues of choice and control. As the Serenity Prayer says so well, "God grant me the serenity to accept the things I cannot change; courage to change the things I can; and wisdom to know the difference." The last phrase seems the most crucial and tricky for most addicts, if not most people in general. How do we discern what we can rightly control and what we cannot control? At the same time, we must both let go of our need to control what we cannot control and also control what we can control.

When one becomes a slave, one no longer has many choices. The path to freedom begins by first acknowledging that lack of choice. Then the path continues toward reclaiming the choices that are ours to make. Second, we must use the language of choice: "Today, I choose not to drink." The very act of saying it this way empowers us to realize that we are making a choice. Third, we empower people and ourselves to make choices, even if those choices are initially poor ones. The very act of choosing will empower us with confidence and responsibility. Fourth, we must accept that all choices are made only on a here and now basis. Choices are available to us only in the present moment, one day and sometimes one hour at a time. The act of choosing is the first step out of slavery.

Alcoholism and all of the gluttony-related addictions are both diseases and sins. Each perspective on these addictions adds to our understanding and treatment of these addictions.

Why Has the War on Drugs Failed?

Drug addiction is as big a problem in the United States as it ever was. Alcoholism and drug dependence are America's number one health problems, according to a 2001 Report commissioned by the Robert Wood Johnson Foundation and conducted at Brandeis University.[17] Drug addiction includes a wide variety of substances, from marijuana to heroin, crack cocaine, and methamphetamines. The degree of legality varies from cigarettes (legal), prescription painkillers (semi-legal), to methamphetamines (illegal). The degree of addiction is reflected in the terms use, abuse, dependency, and addiction, the latter being the most severe. Our newspapers and newscasts

17. Ericson, "Substance Abuse."

are filled with headlines such as "13 arrested in drug raid," "Children placed in custody when parents arrested," "ODE burns marijuana farms in state park," "Doctor arrested for pushing pills," and "Drug cartel murders city officials." It is easy to forget that this large-scale problem with illegal drugs is a relatively new phenomenon in the Western nations. It is really a product of the twentieth century. What are the cultural, psychological, and economic forces that have given rise to such a dramatic development?

President Nixon launched the War on Drugs in 1971 when he said to Congress, "Narcotics addiction is a problem which afflicts both the body and the soul of America."[18] The first drug-fighting budget was $100 million. Every American president since Nixon, whether Republican or Democrat, has reaffirmed and often expanded this campaign. Today, the budget for the War on Drugs is $15.1 billion, thirty-one times Nixon's amount even when adjusted for inflation.[19] In addition to the law enforcement efforts, both overseas and within the United States, the war on drugs has given us the memorable phrase "Just Say No," based on the campaign of the 1980s, as well as the fairly popular program for school-aged children called DARE. While there have been some successes here and there, the problem of drug addiction in its many forms is larger than ever. Drug addiction over-burdens the justice system, strains the health care system, decreases business productivity, and continues to destroy families and children. So, we need to ask ourselves, Why has the war on drugs been so unsuccessful? What have taxpayers gotten for their money? Was the primary emphasis upon law enforcement the wrong approach? Did we not learn our lesson from Prohibition about the limits of law enforcement? Perhaps Bruce has an answer.

I met Bruce in the fall of 1992 in southern California. He was a fifty-two-year-old divorced man of mixed European heritage. I was working as a pastoral psychotherapist, and Bruce needed some counseling to maintain his probation. He had grown up a Presbyterian and so was attracted to my counseling office in the local Presbyterian church. He was not my usual kind of client. He had all of the tattoos and attire that are associated with the ex-con persona. He had served time in prison three times in his life; the last sentence was for three years. Each imprisonment was due to drug possession, selling drugs, or drug-related criminal activities. Each time, upon his release, he had difficulty maintaining gainful employment and stable

18. Quoted in Mendoza, "Has the War on Drugs Failed?," A7.
19. Ibid.

love relationships. Bruce was the father of two children from his six-year marriage to a woman who was a recent Mexican immigrant. She divorced him after his second imprisonment. Bruce wanted to see his children and have a constructive relationship with them. His ex-wife blocked this at every turn. Bruce's primary drug of choice was cocaine, but he certainly drank with the best of them and smoked like a weed. He had first tried the "hard stuff" in Vietnam, and to one degree or another he had kept using it ever since, along with alcohol and whatever other drugs he could get his hands on from time to time. The veterans' programs that Bruce participated in helped with medical issues, but they did not make a dent in his addictive behavior. Bruce worked in various semi-skilled labor jobs. He never really acquired any marketable skills other than as a handyman. He did not like school and had barely finished high school before he was drafted.

During his latest prison time, as with his earlier imprisonment, Bruce became clean and sober courtesy of the state. He dried out, as the saying goes. After his latest release, he lived at a transitional home and worked day labor jobs. When funds ran out, he lived in his car for weeks on end. He was trying really hard this time to "do it right." "I am getting too old for this shit," he would say. A few months after I began to work with Bruce, he encountered the Victory Outreach program, which was an evangelical ministry among ex-cons and street people in a nearby town. Through that experience, Bruce "found Christ in his life," and some time later he became a regular at the Assemblies of God congregation down the street from my office. He attended church events several times per week. The stern morality of his church helped him control his cravings. Through his new-found Christian faith, he saw Alcoholics Anonymous differently and began to attend AA meetings more faithfully. At church, he made new friends, got emotional support, and even got connected to a job-training program to become a machinist. He was more hopeful than at any time in his life that this time he was going to beat it and be the good father he longed to be for his children . . . if it was not too late.

Bruce and I were from different cultures and seemingly from different worlds, even though we were members of the same generation and now were both Christians. My Christian faith was thoughtful, calm, and orderly; his Christianity was emotional, moralistic, and powerful. Yet, we came to appreciate one another and learn from one another. He had a powerful conviction that Christ had saved him literally from death and from the hell he was living in. He had a keen sensitivity to the power of evil both in general and in his fellow humans. His walk of faith was a continual battle between the forces of Satan and his Lord, the Deliverer. His favorite passage, which he repeated daily, was: "Put on the whole armor of God so you can stand against the wiles of the Devil" (Eph 6:11–13). Bruce succeeded in kicking his addictions.

Of course, not all drug addicts are helped by religion. One could also argue that Bruce did not find a cure for addiction, but simply substituted a less damaging addiction for his earlier addiction to drugs and alcohol. Nevertheless, I have thought long and hard about why Bruce went down the path he did. Was it the Vietnam experience? Was he predestined by his biology, by his family dynamics, by brain chemistry, by his psychological makeup? Certainly, "just say no" did not work for Bruce. It was hard for him to say no, especially after years of saying yes. The criminal justice system was unable to keep Bruce from drug activities, even after two terms in prison. Maybe the third time was the charm. Ultimately, Bruce's answer came through a powerful spiritual experience. So what can Bruce's story teach us about the War on Drugs?

Why Willpower Is Not Enough

We have been focusing on the more serious addictions associated with gluttony. Most of us are not alcoholics and do not suffer from a drug addiction, at least not in the full definition of these terms. Yet, most of us still do battle with gluttony every day of our lives. Most of us have cravings of one kind of another. Most of us have tried a diet, only to fail. Some of us may have tried to stop smoking, only to fail. Some of us may have tried to stop drinking, only to fail. Why is willpower alone not enough? Let's explore the mental component of gluttony a bit more.

Everyone who has gone on a diet or tried to go on a diet of any kind knows the problem of cravings. We deprive ourselves. We are hungry. Our minds start to fantasize about that piece of cake in the refrigerator, left over from last night's dinner. The cake looms large in our mind. We can practically taste its rich, smooth, chocolate flavor. We become tense, irritable, and restless. Finally, we break down and consume that remaining piece of cake. Did we really enjoy it? Probably not. Probably we ate it compulsively. Then the guilt starts . . . "Oh, I really should not have done that! I'd better starve myself some more to make up for those calories." These thoughts will in turn only make it harder to resist the next temptation. Every one of us who has ever tried to stick to a diet knows the problem of mental obsessions. I kid you not when I say that the battle with gluttony is won or lost in the mind, not in the behavior.

Interestingly enough, as the mind becomes more consumed with eating, drinking, or some other kind of compulsion, the mind also has a way of increasingly justifying and denying its longings. We say to ourselves, "Oh, just one more," or, "I will diet tomorrow," or "Low-sugar deserts are not fattening." Alcoholics play similar mental tricks on themselves—"After all, I can stop after just one drink," or, "I can social drink just like everyone else," or, "I only drink when I am depressed." People with all kinds of addictive problems participate in some version of this stinkin' thinkin'. Our cognitions become distorted and twisted in ways designed to justify our habits and protect us from facing our own weaknesses, thus reinforcing and strengthening the addictive process (surely, pride is in cahoots with gluttony).

A 1998 study reported in *Psychological Science* offers us another perspective on the mental dynamics of willpower. In this research project, eighty-four subjects were asked to hold a pendulum steady.[20] Some were simply told to hold the pendulum steady. Others were told to hold it steady and also not to move the pendulum sideways. The latter group tended to move the pendulum sideways more often than the group told merely to keep it steady. Why do you think this curious dynamic happened? Scientists call this dynamic the "ironic processes of mental control." Simply put, it is our tendency to do the very thing we are telling ourselves not to do, like when we say to ourselves, "Don't spill this," and then we do spill it—the very thing we sought to avoid. Further, this 1998 study documented that this tendency is worse when we are mentally distracted or pressured.[21] Does this study offer us a clue to why we cannot lose weight, why willpower is not enough? In going on a strict diet, we think about food or about not consuming food so much that we are actually activating the parts of our brain that are focused on food. And then, if we are actually hungry as well, our craving becomes worse. The man who keeps telling himself "I really do not want to eat that pizza" ends up obsessing so much about not eating it that he creates tension and anxiety and eventually ends up eating the pizza.

20. Wegner et al., "Mental Control of Action," 196–99.
21. The explanation is that thinking about *not* having to move the pendulum sideways actually activates the brain neurons and the very muscles that move it that way. The intention and counter-intention effects arise from the same control system in the brain.

It is a wonder that any of us ever lose weight through dieting! Trying to control our thoughts, especially in perfectionist or obsessive ways, sets us up for failure. This is the nature of addictive thinking. Maybe, instead of dieting, we need to think recovery.[22]

The real battleground with addictions is the mental one, even though the gluttony-based addictions are physiologically grounded. In this sense, recovery is a spiritual process, not just a physical one. We must win the battle of the mind. Recovery must be the process of taking back control of our mind and our thinking. There are many psychological and spiritual methods that can be employed to help us with this mental battle. Let me discuss just one now. I will mention others at the end of this chapter.

Meditation is becoming increasingly popular as a way of quieting the mind, centering the mind, and gaining distance from obsessive thoughts. In particular, many people find the practice of mindfulness helpful. Mindfulness comes out of the Buddhist tradition, but there are parallels in other religious traditions, including Christianity. Mindfulness is first and foremost helpful because it helps quiet the mind's clutter by focusing the mind initially on breathing, on being aware of the present moment. By so doing, we lower our anxiety and experience inner calm. It is a way of disengaging the paradoxical processes of mental control referred to above in relation to the pendulum study. In addition, a typical mindfulness exercise then leads practitioners to shift consciousness or the conscious self into an observer role. By being in the ego state of "inner observer," we can more easily observe our cravings rather than being overwhelmed by them. Each obsessive thought or craving, however frightening or compelling, is received, thanked, and released. Taking this observer stance on ourselves helps us stay grounded and see our cravings as alien to us. We observe them; they do not possess or overwhelm us. It takes some practice to master this method, but it is well worth the effort if we are struggling with addictive thoughts or cravings.

The problem of obsessive thinking is common to all kinds of addictive behaviors. Workaholics are chronically preoccupied with thoughts about their work. The minds of sex addicts are consumed with fantasies about their sexual encounters. People who are filled with hurt and hatred are obsessive about their plots and strategies for revenge. Even everyday worry,

22. For Christians, this dynamic might remind us of St. Paul's own frustration with the perils of moral legalism that he described so dramatically in Romans 7:15–24. St. Paul was focused on religious legalism, which also can be a type of behavioral addiction. The dynamic is the same: sometimes the more we try to be good, the more we aren't!

something virtually all of us are familiar with, is a type of obsessive thinking. Chronic worriers spend too much mental energy dwelling on possible negative future outcomes. The more they think about it, the more they think about it. Worry, like all obsessive thinking patterns, tends to build on itself. In each of these cases, we do not want to think so much about these things, but we do. It does seem like we have two minds at times: a right mind and an addictive mind, consumed as it is with whatever subject or craving we desire. So the spiritual practices of meditation, contemplative prayer, and mindfulness have a much wider application than just managing our cravings. These are spiritual practices that, if practiced, can both treat and prevent the harmful mental aspects of addictions.

Living in a Culture Based on Consumption

We live in a consumer-driven, consumer-based economy. This over-emphasis on consumption has contributed to the rise in problems related to gluttony and to the incidence of gluttony-related addictions. We are surrounded by media images and media messages that value and promote consumption, even over-consumption. Every night, we are bombarded with television commercials that implore us to eat, drink, and be merry. It is little wonder, then, that as our culture has become more consumer-driven, we have witnessed a rise in the incidence of these addictions associated with gluttony. Addictive diseases have become epidemic in our times. Gluttony is a symptom of our consumption-driven culture, similar to the way that greed is a symptom of capitalism.

I have nothing against consumerism per se. It has obviously helped create one of the most successful economies in the world. Yet, there are several aspects of the intense, multi-media commercialism associated with this over-emphasis upon consumption that are not supportive of sound mental and spiritual health. Let me mention a few of them:

- Our consumer-driven economy has increasingly reframed eating and drinking as entertainment as well as consumption. A night on the town is often thought to be a time to eat and drink. Drinks and various food products are increasingly fashioned to be more entertaining by being more unusual, exotic, and exciting, and they are often coupled with music and theater. We no longer eat for nourishment; we eat and drink to be entertained.

- The over-consumption of food and drink is linked to other desirable values such as happiness, youth, friendship, and success. Commercials promoting eating in a restaurant are usually filled with happy people, a warm atmosphere, and the subtle hint of success. If you come to our restaurant, you will be "family," you will have "home cooking," and you will be embraced by warm, caring friends. In a world that is increasingly impersonal, the appeal is certainly not just the beer, but community.

- The consumption of food and drink is framed as immediate gratification. Fast food. Instant service. No waiting in line. Home deliveries. Repeatedly, commercials portray individuals who cannot wait to eat the desired food or liquid product. I've got to have it—now! This emphasis upon immediate consumption leads to compulsive eating, in contrast to the slow and enjoyable eating of food that is carefully prepared and healthier for heart and soul.

- Finally, when it comes to food and drink, the commercials often present over-consumption as a good thing. Restaurants advertise bigger portions, all-you-can-eat options, and plates filled to the brim with good-looking food. One portion is not enough. Do you remember the commercial that ran for years with the verbal dare, "Bet you cannot eat just one?" In a recent beer commercial, a "magic" refrigerator, filled with beer, appears accidentally in the apartment of three young men. They do not take just one beer and thank their lucky stars, but frantically try to fill their arms with as many beers as they can hold. One beer is not enough. (And when the refrigerator disappears, they bow down and worship the "magic refrigerator.") No wonder college students have a rising problem with binge drinking. The food and drink industry sell us on over-consumption.

It is very difficult to overcome the sin of gluttony or the addictions related to gluttony in a culture that promotes over-consumption as our birthright. In recent years, scholars and even some government officials have been highlighting the long-range and hidden costs of the sins of gluttony. Alcoholism and obesity cost American taxpayers millions every year in medical costs and lost productivity.[23] Increasingly, the message is being heard that maybe,

---

23. One study found that the medical costs attributable to obesity rose to 10 percent of the total medical expenses in the United States from 1998–2006 and that the medical costs attributable to obesity rose to as high as $147 billion in the United States

just maybe, our over-emphasis on consumption is not always a good thing for this nation. But this message begs the question, what can we do about gluttony? Indeed, what *should* we do about gluttony?

Gluttony has had a very interesting history in the halls of legislatures—both religious and secular—over the centuries. Trying to outlaw sin does have its complications and frustrations. When temperance was legislated in the 1920s in the United States, it seemed like the opposite result was created—more alcohol consumption, not less. There is something alluring about the forbidden. Whenever we Americans are told "no" by an authority, especially a governmental or religious authority, there seems to be a rebel deep within us that rises up in defiance, even when we know that the "no" is good for us. Yet, in my opinion, the current atmosphere of non-regulation is not working very well either. We have more problems related to alcohol today than ever before, even when the statistics are adjusted for increased population. I would argue that this is true not because we like to rebel, but because the culture has created an addictive dynamic based on an economy of over-consumption. Human (or at least American) nature is potentially very addictive. It is part of our inborn nature. We need our cultural institutions to help control our addictive vulnerabilities rather than encourage them.[24]

Gluttony's Antidote

The traditional Christian virtue that has been presented as an antidote for the sin of gluttony is abstinence. Certainly in the case of drug addiction, abstinence is the preferred and sometimes the only effective approach. For some people, abstinence is also the only option in terms of alcohol consumption. In terms of over-eating, abstinence is not possible, although one can abstain from certain foods. A better antidote here might be moderation. While moderation is effective in the long run for compulsive eating, it is certainly a more challenging and ambiguous path than simple abstinence.

(Finkelstein, "Attributable to Obesity," 822). Similar data on the cost of alcoholism and drug dependence are available through the National Council on Alcoholism and Drug Dependence (see "FAQS/Facts").

24. The same argument is being made currently in relation to the possible legalization of marijuana. Would we have less or more problems with marijuana if we decriminalized it instead of continuing to try to restrict its use?

Christians and members of other religious traditions practice periodic fasting from food and drink. On a weekly basis, Friday was the traditional day on which Christians fasted, which corresponded to the view that believers were most tempted by the sin of gluttony on Fridays. Seasonal fasting is common in many religious traditions. In the Christian tradition, Lent has been the traditional period for some form of selective or modified fasting. Fasting is understood as a way of drawing close to God, but also as a way of keeping our bodies, our gift from God, in good health. From an addictions perspective, it is also a way to break the addictive cycle and re-establish the body's normalcy, even if only for a season. One should not enter into even periodic fasting, however, without medical permission and guidance.

We can practice the virtue of abstinence by doing the following:

- learning to live one day at a time; knowing we have the power to choose healthy alternatives in the present moment
- learning to avoid situations in which we will be unduly and unfairly tempted to over-eat or over-drink; knowing what it means to pray to God to "lead us not into temptation" (the Lord's Prayer); remembering that we are not given temptations without there being a means of escape (2 Cor 10:13)
- meditating; strengthening our inner observer, which helps us have some distance from our cravings
- taking responsibility for our issues and holding ourselves accountable; if appropriate, allowing others to also hold us accountable
- finding other ways to comfort ourselves or cope with our problems instead of eating or drinking for emotional reasons
- using the art of distraction to divert our thinking about food, drink, or alcohol onto a different, alternative subject (I find songs very powerful diversions)
- remembering that it takes twenty-one days to form and establish a new habit; being realistic but knowing that new habits can be formed
- considering mealtimes sacred occasions; sitting down for a meal together with our loved ones; using meals as times for fellowship and relationship, not just consumption

- praying over our food and reminding ourselves where food comes from—the earth, other living creatures, and the Provider; pausing to be grateful for our food; slowing down the eating process; remembering that our bodies are wondrous gifts

Even though I have been arguing for a spiritual recovery-based approach to addiction treatment, let me say that there is a place for a harm reduction approach, too, particularly as a first step toward recovery. This is especially the case with the powerful gluttony-based addictions. Abstinence is not always possible or wise. If we cannot stop using illegal drugs entirely or if we cannot stop over-eating entirely, maybe we can switch addictions—adopt an alternative, less harmful substance that satisfies our craving. Or maybe we can embrace a so-called positive addiction as a way of channeling our addictive impulses in a new direction. But harm reduction measures or even abstinence are basically behavioral interventions for a disease that is essentially spiritual. Our ultimate goal must always be to engage in a spiritual recovery program that addresses both the addictive behavior and the underlying mental obsessions, i.e., the sins of the mind.

Summary

In this chapter, we have discussed the addictions associated with the sin of gluttony. I have defined gluttony as cravings for food, drink, and drugs and have suggested that the real battle for all of these addictions begins with the mental struggle to master the cravings. These addictions are powerful and destructive, in part because they are so deeply rooted in our brain chemistry and physiology. Various spiritual resources are available to us. They can be effective tools in our efforts to manage our addictive thinking.

Questions for Self-Reflection

1. Do I have trouble limiting my eating or drinking to moderate levels? Do I have trouble stopping with just one drink?
2. Has over-eating or over-drinking gotten me into trouble at home, at work, or with the authorities? Has over-drinking or over-eating caused health problems?
3. Is there an emotional pattern to my over-consumption?

4. Do I have a drug problem of any kind, including cigarettes, caffeine, marijuana, prescription pills, coke, speed, or amphetamines? Be honest.

5. Have I ever attended an AA meeting, even just as a visitor? What did I learn? What aspects of the meeting were appealing or not so appealing?

6. When in my life have I felt free from cravings, even for a short time? What state of mind or spiritual practice helped me get free? If not a spiritual practice, what has worked for me in becoming or remaining free from cravings?

Biblical passages related to gluttony: Matt 6:25–26; 22:1–10; Mark 6:41–44; 8:1–10; Luke 22:14–23; 1 Cor 3:16–17; 8:8–9; 10:13; 11:33; Gal 5:19–20

8 Lust

An Obsession with Sex

School Superintendent [SS]: I've placed George Williams, a teacher at Rock View Middle School, on administrative leave until we can complete our investigation of his use of school computers to view pornography. According to the district's policies, I have convened the Board of Education in this special session to receive my report, to interview Mr. Williams, and to determine how to proceed. Also, in the hallway are a crowd of parents and a couple of representatives from the press.

Board member: How did you come to learn of this behavior?

SS: A parent whose child told her about it brought it to my attention. Last year, I suspected that Bill was using his computer for personal use. I drew to his attention the regulation that district computers are for educational purposes, not for personal use. Now, with this offense, his desk computer was confiscated. Our IT people tell us that this activity has been pretty regular the last six months or so.

Board member: So we have the evidence, the hard evidence, that teacher Williams was using school property to view pornography during the school day. The teacher's day is not so busy?

SS: Each teacher has a prep period during the day, and then apparently Williams was on the computer after school hours as well and exchanging information with his home computer.

Board member: Do you have any evidence that he involved any of the children in this activity?

Ancient Sins... Modern Addictions

SS: No. So far, no children or parents have come forward with that accusation.

Board member: Did he send photos to any children or, God forbid, take any photos of our children?

SS: There is no evidence of that either . . . at least not yet.

Board member: Do you think he is a pedophile? How can this be, that a teacher with thirty-two years of experience in this district is a pedophile?

THE CONTEXT IS A meeting of a local school board, where a long-time, trusted school teacher is about to be confronted by an angry school board and members of the community. His name and a photo of his face will be splashed all over the local newspaper the next morning. One board member has already asked whether the teacher is a pedophile. Could there be another explanation? George Williams, forty-eight years old, was the first person from his family to attend college. He is a father, husband, and Sunday School teacher at his local church. He has worked hard to earn trust and the reputation as a qualified and effective teacher. How can he throw it all away with such foolish behavior? Some might say to George, "If you have to do this kind of thing, why not limit yourself to the privacy of your home?" In fact, George did do that for many years, but after several confrontations with his wife, he shut down most of this activity at home. He just could not stay away from pornography, however, and began viewing again during the workday. George had lots of justifications: "I won't get caught," "It lowers my stress level," and "Nobody gets hurt." We will see how well his justifications will hold up when he goes through the door and meets with the Board of Education.

Like the other Seven Deadly Sins, lust is primarily a sin of the mind. Lust by itself is not an addiction, but it is the mental soil in which various sexual addictions grow. There are a variety of sexual behaviors or problems that fall within the generalized label of sexual addictions. Some of these problem behaviors include: 1) cybersex, pornography, compulsive sexual relationships, over-masturbating, and prostitution; 2) exhibitionism and voyeurism; and 3) sexual abuse and sexual assault.[1] What makes any of these behaviors an addiction is the repetitive, compulsive, and self-destruc-

---

1. This classification of levels of sexual addictions is drawn from Carnes, *Out of the Shadows*, 37.

Lust

tive nature of the behavior. Some of these sexual behaviors are really not motivated by lust, per se. Some of them are more about power, inflicting pain, and dependency than about lust. In this chapter, I will limit the discussion to those sexual addictions primarily motivated by lust, which are largely "level one" addictions in the above noted classification.[2]

What is lust? I define lust as prolonged and excessive sexual desire. As with the other Seven Deadly Sins, I believe that lust distorts and corrupts a basic human need, the need for sexual intimacy. Sexual desire is normal, good, and pleasurable. It is part of our God-given human nature. Sexual intimacy is a wondrous, loving, and intimate expression of love. Sexual desire is an essential element in most loving relationships. Sexual desire becomes lust when it is prolonged and excessive. Lust is a problem when it becomes a craving that haunts our minds and drives us to do risky and stupid things. Lust is a problem when it compels us to act out repeatedly and in destructive ways.

Cultural scholars generally believe that the United States has passed through a sexual revolution in the past sixty years or so. The positive side of that revolution is that we are more open, more tolerant, and less moralistic about sexuality than our grandparents were. At the same time, most scholars agree that there has been no reduction in the number of sex crimes per capita in the last sixty years. However, there has been an alarming increase in the incidence of sexual addictions. This is the dark side of the "free love" revolution that began in the 1960s. The only explanation I can offer is to place the growing problem of sexual addictions within the larger context of the growing problem of all kinds of addictions, which is occurring across the board! Capitalistic, media-driven, and consumer-oriented cultures, like that of the United States today, are addiction-promoting environments.

The Uniqueness of Sexual Addictions

Sex is similar to a drug. Like drugs, sex certainly offers a high, a change in mood, and a momentary escape from reality. But how are sexual addictions different from other addictive disorders? How is the sin of lust similar to and/or different from the other Seven Deadly Sins and their related addictions? While there are many forms of sexual addictions, there are a number

---

2. Most of these varied forms of sexual addiction have been classified as immoral by religious organizations, and some of these sexual behaviors are also illegal. These behaviors can be looked at through a legal lens, a religious lens, or a disease lens.

of common characteristics that make lust-related addictions particularly challenging.

First, like the sin of gluttony, lust is deeply rooted in human physiology. We humans are deeply and universally sexual creatures. We have powerful natural instincts to search for a sexual partner, to mate, and to have sexual relationships. This is who we are, and it has served us well over the eons of human evolution. Does it still serve us well? Sexual orgasm is for the most part very pleasurable, one of the most pleasurable and strongest reinforcers possible. At the time of orgasm, the body releases naturally occurring opioids that act on the brain in ways not unlike drugs. It is easy to see how sex has the natural potential to be addictive. The desire for sexual union is always there in us. The highs associated with sexual behavior are powerful. Sexual addiction, therefore, is a problem rooted in our bodies, rooted in the misuse or dysfunction of our bodies. It is the classic "sin of the flesh."

As with our discussion of the sin of gluttony, the physiological nature of lust raises some interesting perspectives. First, sexual desire varies from individual to individual and in the same individual across the course of his or her lifespan, according to his or her biological needs. Persons with strong sexual desires are potentially more vulnerable to sexual addictions. Some sex addicts justify their behavior by saying that they are "over-sexed." There may be some truth to this statement. Similarly, each of us is more vulnerable to sexual addictions during our younger adult years, when we are at the height of our sexual energy. In theory, older adults are generally not as vulnerable to the new onset of sexual addictions.

Because sexual desire is a natural need, there is a debate within the field of sex addictions about what constitutes sexual sobriety.[3] Some argue that abstinence is not appropriate for sex addicts. Like food addicts, sex addicts should not be forced to eliminate all sexual behavior. It is impossible. The best approach is some sort of moderation. Others argue that sex is a drug and that sex addictions are progressive, just like all the other addictions. They argue that for the true sex addict, there is no appropriate resolution other than abstinence. Indeed, this has been the time-honored stance of most religious traditions. Abstinence for a season and celibacy have both been traditional religious approaches to the problem of people wanting too much sex.

---

3. For a good discussion of this issue, see "Defining Sexual Sobriety" by the Society for the Advancement of Sexual Health.

Second, sexual addictions are different from other addictions because sexual desire is more reliant on visual cues than any other craving. Certainly, alcoholics and drug addicts can see, smell, and feel what they long for. Food addicts can similarly smell, see, and taste what they crave. Sexual desiring uses all of the senses too, but sexual desire is primarily stimulated by sight. What this means is that the role of visual fantasy is heightened in sexual addictions. When we crave sexual activity, we can see it in our minds. We fantasize it. We anticipate it. We enjoy it almost as much in advance of the encounter as we do during the actual event. The actual sexual activity may even be disappointing compared to our fantasies. There is a certain high in the form of sexual excitement that comes with anticipation. The sexual encounter can also be relived again and again after the fact through fantasy, a dynamic that usually only increases our desire for another encounter. This intense visual element makes the sex addiction cycle unique and, in some ways, more powerful than the other addictions.

The strong visual aspect of lust makes it more difficult to manage because the media surrounds us with erotic images and stories. Living in this culture is a nightmare for a recovering sex addict. Many recovering sex addicts must literally keep away from magazines, television, movies, the Internet, and music, lest they start fantasizing about sex and thus trigger another round of the addiction cycle. Sexual addictions have been described as "the athlete's foot of the mind." They never go away. In time, we can get alcohol or drugs out of our systems. But the visual images, according to sex addicts, are in their memories and are activated every time they see a model wearing erotic clothes or a commercial with sexual overtones or hear music with erotic lyrics.

Third, shame and secrecy play a stronger than average role in the dynamics of sexual addictions. All addictions have an element of secrecy. Alcoholics hide their bottles. Drug addicts hide their paraphernalia. Workaholics hide the fact that they are secretly checking their email while on vacation. Food addicts hide their candy wrappers. Secrecy is an element in all addictions, but in the case of sexual addictions the secrecy is more pronounced because of the higher level of shame. At some level, sex addicts are embarrassed by their behavior—in some cases for good reason, because the behaviors are illegal or immoral. But more profoundly, our sexuality involves us in intimate relationships with spouses or partners or friends, and at some level sex addicts often feel that their sexual behavior is a betrayal of their love commitments. Indeed, many spouses are deeply hurt when they find out that their partner is behaving in sexually addictive ways. Like no other addiction, sexual addictions are interwoven with the complexities of family and marital relationships. Little wonder that some chronic sex addicts live in isolation, cut off from normal human contact in favor of the fantasy world of sexual intrigue and excitement. At the same time, recovery from sexual addiction is facilitated by a restorative and healing intimacy, which is often the unconscious, distorted goal of addictive sexual behaviors.

Cultural Influences

In the 1976 presidential campaign, Jimmy Carter was asked by *Playboy* magazine if he thought he was superior to other Americans because he was a Christian. Carter quoted the passage from the Sermon on the Mount wherein Jesus says that the sin of adultery begins in the heart. Carter admitted that he had felt lust for some women he had known but had not committed adultery. There was an avalanche of criticism in the media and from political opponents. Within a week, Carter lost ten points in the polls. In my view, Jimmy Carter was simply presenting the standard Christian viewpoint, which is that all have sinned, that all people—including Carter—have lustful thoughts, and that having lustful thoughts is normal, even inevitable. The important thing is to not let those thoughts get obsessive and lead to sinful acts, like adultery or fornication. This view, that a sin is not a sin until it is a behavior, is a standard Christian viewpoint.

This incident illustrated dramatically the double standard and contradictory messages American culture proclaims about lust. The term "lust" has a negative or moralistic connotation in our culture. Yet, if I use the phrase "erotic thoughts," suddenly there isn't the same moralistic connotation. Sexual urges and erotic thoughts are a part of all of us, to a greater or lesser extent. Sexual desire is not a problem, but lust—prolonged and excessive sexual desires—*is* a problem. Lust has a negative connotation in part because lust implies strong or obsessive erotic thoughts. And that is where Carter got hung up . . . people thought his lustful thoughts were obsessive and therefore inappropriate or even sick.

Because of Carter's self-disclosure, he was soundly criticized. He was criticized by moralists who found his self-disclosure to be an admission of sin. Even the liberal media, which otherwise promotes sexuality 24/7, made political hay of his "scandalous thoughts." Some wanted to interview

Rosalynn regarding how she felt about her husband "lusting after other women."

Clearly, our culture has mixed feelings about sexual desire and, therefore, lust. On the one hand, there is a moralistic tendency that treats anything sexual as repulsive, shameful, and taboo. Yet, on the other hand, sex, sexuality, and even immoral sexual behavior are everywhere, on just about every sitcom, advertisement, billboard, and Internet site. On the one hand, we prosecute people who make inappropriate sexual remarks under sexual harassment laws. Yet, on the other hand, we can see the same remarks night after night on prime-time television, often placed in the context of the humor of a sitcom. On the one hand, we over-protect our daughters, and on the other hand, we see male sexual activities as proving masculinity. On the one hand, we promote free love, but on the other hand, journalists go into a media frenzy over a politician caught in an act of free love, proving the point that love is not free. In such a cultural atmosphere, the results of lust—adultery and fornication—are widely talked about, forgiven, and accepted as facts of life. Yet, society condemns the rapist, the sex offender, and child pornography, without realizing that the same atmosphere that creates sexual freedoms for consenting adults also encourages sex offenders. Isn't this a mixed message? Can we not have one without the other?

In spite of our ambivalence, most scholars agree that sex in the media has become more frequent and more explicit over the last sixty years.[4] The advent of cable television accelerated the sexual revolution, but primetime TV is close behind. Relying on the lure of sex, advertisers use sexuality to sell everything from automobiles to perfume. Soft porn is everywhere—in clothes catalogues, song lyrics, and television sitcoms. Because we are inundated with so much erotic imagery, the management of lust is more and more challenging for all of us. Correspondingly, we are seeing more and more people who, for whatever reasons, cannot successfully manage their lust. We are seeing a rise in problems related to sexual abuse, sexual harassment, sexual assault, sexual misconduct, and sex-related sins such as

---

4. A study by the Kaiser Family Foundation released in 2005 reported that 70 percent of all TV shows include some sexual content and that these shows average five sexual scenes per hour ("Sexual Scenes on TV"). Some other studies suggest that the rate of increase of sexual content has leveled off since 2005. The most dramatic increase was, of course, from 1970 to the present. From my perspective, these data are only half of the story. Sexuality is much broader than sexual relations; "sexuality" in this broader sense is also pervasive in TV commercials, which gives the impression that sex is everywhere on TV these days.

adultery. Many of these growing problems fit the criteria for a behavioral addiction: habit-forming and characterized by obsessive thinking and out-of-control and destructive behaviors.

Cybersex

With the advent of the VCR, the personal computer, and the Internet, pornography of all kinds is more readily available and more widely accepted than ever before. Pornography is perhaps the most pure and most pronounced form of lust in our culture, because it is largely something we do in our minds. The vast majority of individuals who view pornography regularly limit their activity to just that, viewing. Sometimes, however, viewing can be only the first step. Some viewers masturbate while viewing or use the viewing as sexual stimulation for a sexual encounter with their partner. Others will graduate to chat rooms, and still others will use online pornography to hook up with local prostitutes. All of these activities together are termed cybersex. Cybersex is the fastest growing form of sexual addictive activity.[5] Some surveys have indicated that sex is the most frequently searched topic on the Internet and that as many as 30 percent of online users visit pornographic sites.[6] One study suggests that as many as nine million Americans have been identified as compulsive in their use of cybersex. Cybersex is a multi-million-dollar industry. Those who log on to view various kinds of pornography on the Internet include both women and men, and all too often teens and children.[7]

Cybersex qualifies as a type of sexual addiction. It is true that not everyone who views pornography on the Internet becomes a problem viewer or a sexual addict, but the potential is high. The viewing is so visually stimulating, so real and so obsessive. The material is so accessible, just a click of the mouse away. It is available on our home computer, cell phone, and iPad. Someone has called cybersex the crack cocaine of the porn industry because it is so accessible and so graphic, and therefore so

---

5. A colleague who serves as a military chaplain reports that in today's military, it is not drug addiction, but sexual addiction that is the fastest-growing problem among military personnel. This is so, in part, because sexual material is accessible, portable, and powerful. Like all addictive behaviors, cybersex is a means of escaping and coping.

6. An MSNBC survey conducted in 2000 found that 60 percent of all website visits are sexual in nature (Blazing Grace, "Porn Statistics").

7. Carnes (*Out of the Shadows*, 83) cites the research of Stanford University's Al Cooper, which found that 40 percent of the most extreme cybersex users are women.

Lust

instantly addictive. The primary barriers to this activity—the fear of shame and judgment—have been dramatically reduced by its ability to be done in isolation. People who previously would have been too embarrassed to walk into an adult bookstore are now able to view such material in the privacy of their home. Thus, more people from religious or morally conservative backgrounds are showing up in clinics and the offices of professionals with these problems. As a result, some churches are providing programs that address this previously unheard-of problem among their congregants.

How is cybersex addictive? Clearly, for all of the above reasons, viewing pornographic material on the Internet can become compulsive and progressive. Anyone who has a teenager knows the power of the computer to create a trance-like state in which you lose a sense of time and become absorbed in stimulating material of one kind or another. In addition to the trance-like state, there is also the high of sexual excitement that releases various pleasurable chemicals in the brain. Then, if one has an orgasm during the viewing or as a result of the viewing, the high is all the more powerful. Finally, cybersex is habit-forming and therefore repetitive. Patrick Carnes and his colleagues, in their book *In the Shadows of the Net*, have identified an addiction cycle related to cybersex that is not too dissimilar from the addiction cycles associated with alcoholism, violence, or drug abuse. They identify the stages of this cycle as: Preoccupation (obsessive thinking or fantasizing about sex); Ritualization (repetitive patterns of behaviors); Compulsive Sexual Behaviors (viewing and related arousing behaviors, leading to climax or climaxes); and Despair (over failure to live up to one's expectations).[8] Based on their outline, I have fashioned a wheel of cybersex addiction (see Figure 5).

Like all the addiction wheels, this one has predictable stages, a mix of behavioral and chemical components, and a sense of doom. Those who are caught in the web of this particular sexual addiction repeat this cycle over and over again. So, by the criteria of what constitutes an addiction described in chapter 1, cybersex can become an addiction, particularly if it becomes out of control and is repeated in spite of negative consequences. In fact, it may be the perfect temptation and the perfect addiction—it is easily accessible, gives a strong natural high, has a strong mental/visual component, is low-risk, and is done in isolation. What has been described here in terms of cybersex is certainly applicable to the boarder range of addictive sexual behaviors.

8. Carnes et al., *In the Shadows of the Net*, 48–49.

Figure 5
Cycle of Sexual Addiction

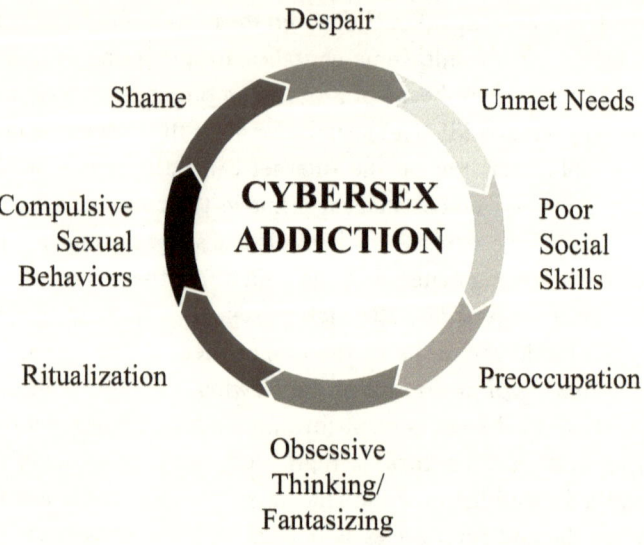

RATIONALIZATIONS AND DELUSIONS: WHY IS LUST DANGEROUS?

It is 2 a.m. on a work night. Bill Anderson is still up in the study. His wife and children have long gone to bed. Bill is in his fifth hour of viewing various pornographic websites. He is transfixed, going from scene to scene. One site leads to another.... There are so many new ones every month. Bill regularly masturbates two or three times per sitting. His wife is aware of his viewing. In fact, she has joined in occasionally. It is actually kind of fun at times. The pornography gets them both more sexually excited and gives their love life a spark that is sometimes not there after fifteen years of marriage, two children, three dogs, and a pile of bills. Bill's wife is not aware, however, of how much time Bill is spending viewing pornography late at night. Nor she is aware that her husband occasionally enters a chat room and talks dirty with various women (she will discover this when she notices some odd credit card charges). But Bill keeps his viewing within bounds. He keeps his viewing limited to once or twice a week. He finds the violent sites repulsive, and he would never actually go and meet anyone he chats with online. In his mind, this activity actually helps him remain faithful to his wife by giving him "a legit outlet."

Many people, like Bill, can see that the extreme forms of sexual addiction are destructive and illegal but look upon cybersex as harmless, at worst a waste of time and at best an enriching experience. People like Bill say:

- "It is a harmless activity. It helps me relax."
- "It enriches our love life as a couple. It makes me a better lover."
- "I am over-sexed compared to most people. I need an outlet when my wife cannot meet my needs."
- "I can limit it."
- "Cybersex is just electrons. It is not real."

Is Bill making some reasonable points, or is he in denial? Bill does not meet the criteria for having a full sexual addiction yet, but he does have a sexual problem or what I would term a lust problem. This would be parallel to not yet being an alcoholic but being a problem drinker, or a recreational drug user who never allows it to advance to the hard stuff. Or is Bill a functional sexual addict? What do we say to Bill?

First, I agree with Bill. A little lust can be a good thing, adding some spice and excitement to a marriage. Yet, like all of the mental sins, if Bill continues to indulge his sex cravings, dwelling on them, with them, and in them hour after hour, he is playing with fire. Lust is, by definition, obsessive and can easily become the first step in the addiction formation process. Maybe Bill can keep limits on it. Maybe he can't. Certainly, the pornography industry will do whatever it can to offer Bill more and more explicit, risky, and expensive activities. He will be offered anonymous phone sex talk. For a fee, Bill can do phone sex or have mutual visual sex. And if he likes that, there are real sex partners available in most cities, with the help of the Internet, on short notice. So, Bill is playing with fire! His lust or mental sexual obsessions will always be pushing him to take the next step.

Second, we know that the dynamics of addiction are such that our minds come to distort reality, using various justifications and rationalizations to support the continuation or advancement of the pleasurable activity. Bill needs to check some of his rationalizations against reality. He needs to have a real conversation with his spouse and with some other guys who have "been there." Maybe he is more addicted than he thinks.

Third, pornography focuses strongly on the genital aspects of human sexuality at the expense of the relational or emotional aspects of lovemaking. The goal of achieving the ultimate orgasm can become a tyranny associated with pornographic material. Like all addictions, the dynamics of sexual addictive activities tend to push us to be in a hurry, speeding us through the activity in order to get to the orgasm as soon as possible. Human sexuality and lovemaking is better when it is a balance of technique and process and not focused just on the end result.

Fourth, pornography over-focuses on appearance. It is a very visual medium. Over time, we come to view the other as an object, not as a person—as an object like all the other material objects that are there to meet our needs. Over time, we come to measure a person's value by his or her appearance. Over time, we come to transfer that template to the real people in our lives, comparing them to our fantasized images and expectations.

Fifth, if lust is indulged, it takes over more and more of our heart, pushing genuine love aside. Or, to paraphrase, people like Bill begin to confuse lust and love. Genuine love is the desire to give pleasure; lust is the desire to get pleasure. Lust is not love. Further, genuine love is selective. It focuses on a particular person. Lust is indiscriminate; anyone will do. Love binds partners together. Lust actually undermines love relationships because one party is essentially using the other party. Is Bill confusing love with lust?

Lastly, as Bill himself said, pornographic activity or lust is a form of escapism, helping us escape from negative or uncomfortable feelings. A fuller and more meaningful life can be found by facing those uncomfortable feelings, whatever they are, and working them through to constructive conclusions. Many times, one of the chief feelings that sex addicts or people with problem sexual behaviors are escaping from, oddly enough, is intimacy. Yes, they are actually avoiding intimacy! Intimacy requires emotional vulnerability, and for many people that is a scary dynamic and/or they lack the tools to negotiate that intimacy. It is easier to indulge in the pseudo-intimacy of a pornographic encounter where there is no risk, no vulnerability, and no love.

So that's what I would say to Bill. What would you say?

Addicted to Romance?

Are lust and the related sexual addictions more of a male sin than a female sin?[9] The statistics suggest that men are more prone to sexual addictions than women, but not universally so. Women are a statistical presence in all of the sexual addictions.[10] Nevertheless, female sexuality is different from male sexuality, and because of this women maybe more vulnerable to certain forms of sexual addictions than men. Interestingly, Patrick Carnes defines sexual addictions as a pathological relationship to "a mood-altering experience."[11] By so doing, he adopts a wider viewer of sexuality and sexual addiction than just genital sexuality. Under this definition, one can also be addicted to romance as a mood-altering experience in the context of a pathological relationship.[12] Is this the female version of sexual addiction?

Nancy had been through three marriages and two unmarried cohabitations. Each one lasted from six months to six years. I first met her when she was fifty-five years old. She was beginning to question the whys and wherefores of this pattern. She said that the pattern was not getting her what she wanted, which was a lasting, stable, loving relationship. On first glance, she blamed this pattern on her poor choice of men. All of the men she fell in love with, with the exception of her first husband, were "bad boys." They were alternative types, unstable, risk-takers, and "sexy as hell." They were exciting men to fall in love with. The lovemaking was passionate, frequent, and at times exotic. One of the fellows had considerable money and so, for a time, all this passion was augmented by travel and a lavish lifestyle. These men drank a lot, and a couple of them were drug addicts. Nancy's relationships with them were full of conflict and verbal fights, which led to "great sex." In time, though, this roller coaster ride got too hurtful and tiring, and when it broke up, it usually broke up with a "bad scene." As Nancy talked and talked over a series of weeks, she began to acknowledge

---

9. This question could, of course, be asked about all of the Seven Deadly Sins. The list was originally compiled by white European men. Is the entire list of sins more reflective of male sins than female sins? Or are these seven sins true of all humans but manifest themselves differently according to gender?

10. Cultural norms play an important role in shaping how free women are about expressing their sexual needs. As women are allowed or encouraged to be more assertive about their sexual needs, the percentage of women diagnosed with sexual addictions may increase.

11. Carnes, *Out of the Shadows*, 14.

12. It is interesting to note that one of the earliest forms of a twelve-step approach to sexual addictions was called Sex and Love Addicts Anonymous (SLAA).

Ancient Sins... Modern Addictions

that the problem was partly hers. She was addicted to a drug, too, the drug of passionate sex and intense romance. It was an incredible high. Some psychologists might have labeled Nancy as borderline or histrionic, but I think that the addiction model has as much to say about Nancy's problem as the diagnostic labels of psychiatry. If any label fit, it would be that of "compulsive love relationships." When these relationships ended, the withdrawal symptoms included rage, violence, self-blaming, depression, and drunkenness. Each time, she went into a period of despair before finding a new fix.

When Nancy was in love, she *felt* loved ... but was it love, or just lust, or romance? In Nancy's words, she "loved being in love." She began to question what love really is. Women like Nancy are the subjects of movies such as *Who's Afraid of Virginia Woolf?*, *Fatal Attraction*, and *Play Misty for Me*, to name just a few. Susan Forward, in her 1991 book *Obsessive Love: When Passion Holds You Prisoner*, speaks of this kind of addiction as "obsessive love." She says,

> In reality, obsessive love has little to do with love at all—it has to do with longing. Longing is wanting something you don't have. Even when obsessive lovers are in a relationship, they don't have enough of what they want. They always long for more love, more attention, more commitment, more reassurance.[13]

That sounds like a craving or, dare I say it, a sexual craving (with "sexual" being defined broadly). John D. Moore, in his recent book *Confusing Love with Obsession*, has suggested that there are stages people like Nancy go through, an "obsessive love wheel."[14] Its stages include: attraction, anxiety, obsession, and destruction. What is interesting about Moore's wheel, of course, is that it sounds similar to the sexual addiction cycles and, for that matter, the addiction wheels that have been documented in all of the major addictions. There may be more going on here than lust, in the narrow sense of the word.

The concept of "relationship addiction" was introduced to the public by Robin Norwood in her 1985 best-selling book, *Women Who Love Too Much*. She pointed to the addictive dynamics present in pathological love relationships and said that often "one addiction feeds another," that is, women who were "man junkies" often had drinking problems or had other compulsive behaviors.[15] A similar concept has been evolving in Al-Anon,

13. Forward and Buck, *Obsessive Love*, 9.
14. Moore, *Confusing Love with Obsession*, 131–32.
15. Norwood, *Women Who Love*, 198.

Lust

the self-help organization for the spouses of alcoholics. Al-Anon is built around the concept of co-dependency; the spouse or partner of an addict is dependent on the addict even as the addict is dependent on his or her substance. In recent years, the Al-Anon world has increasingly come to see co-dependency itself as a type of addiction, an addiction to a dysfunctional relationship. Earlier I mentioned the term co-addict in the context of sexual addictions. These days I am hearing the term used more broadly as a substitute for co-dependent. It speaks to the reality that dysfunctional relationships can be addictive.

Men can definitely be romance/relationship junkies, and women can be hooked on genital sexual addictions. Are these separate addictions or two sides (a stereotypically male side and a stereotypically female side) of the same addiction? All of us—men and women—are vulnerable to sexual addictions. Which form of sexual addiction we fall prey to may have more to do with idiosyncratic differences than our gender.[16]

Lust Is Not Love

My years of work as a therapist and counselor have convinced me that there is a lot of confusion about the nature of love. People tend to confuse love with a host of other feelings and impulses. If genuine love is what most of us are looking for, then I might say, "We go about looking for it in all of the wrong places." The problem lies in part in the English language, which uses one word, love, for a multiplicity of feelings. For example, we use the word love to cover the diverse feelings reflected in statements such as, "I love hot dogs," "I love my husband," and "I love this weather." These are very different kinds of love.

A lot of people confuse lust (intense and prolonged sexual desire) with love. This confusion is the source of many a heartache. Just because someone is "hot" for you, it does not necessarily mean that he or she loves you. That is an easy mistake to make. Similarly, you can't get someone to love you by being sexually available. Lust can actually get in the way of developing a loving, long-lasting relationship.

Second, genuine love is not obsessive love. Someone who is obsessed with you does not necessarily love you. Obsessive love (is this an

---

16. Like many psychologists, I understand gender to be a continuum. Thus, I see specific individuals, regardless of their biology, are vulnerable to the full range of sexual addictions discussed in this chapter.

oxymoron?) desires to possess the other person, control the other person. Obsessive love is jealous love. Romantic love often has an obsessive flavor. The lyrics of love songs often say things like, "I can't stop thinking about you. . . . You are on my mind night and day!" While it is nice to feel so wanted, over time the affections of an obsessive lover become oppressive and controlling. In the end, obsessive love destroys that which it loves by driving the loved one away.

Third, dependency is not love either. Just because someone needs you, it does not necessarily mean that he or she loves you. Many people think that because they need someone, they must love him or her. We do need someone when we come to love him or her, but we do not love them because we need them. Over time, needy love can become smothering and controlling and can easily flip into jealous love.

In these three cases, the antidote is genuine love or caring for another. Genuine love is not the same as lust; neither is it the same as obsessive love nor the same as dependency. Genuine love is free from addictive processes. Genuine love is freely given (not an obsession); freely expressed (not a compulsion); and freely received (a gift). Few of us, apart from the saints among us, embrace pure love. But where and when it shows up in our love relationships, it is a rare gift from above to be cultivated.

Based on my professional work with couples, I would say that genuine love includes elements of sexual desire, altruistic caring, and mutual friendship. These three types of love are a mixture, and getting this mixture right is a delicate and life-long task. The ratio of this mix may change over the lifespan of a long-lasting relationship or over varying kinds of relationships. Often sexual addicts or people with lust problems get this mixture out of proportion. Their love is limited to lust or dominated by lust. There is little or no friendship or altruistic caring.

It isn't that love is selfless and lust is selfish. Erotic love has a natural and important place in all romantic relationships. All healthy love relationships are a mixture of our needs, our partner's needs, and our needs as a couple. The problem with lust is that it is addictive. It drives us to make our sexual needs the most important thing all of the time. The normal healthy balance of love gets out of balance. Ultimately, lust and its related addictions will destroy a healthy relationship, not because lust is selfish or immoral, but because it is addictive.

Having said all this, I have found as a therapist that an important component in treating sexual addictions is helping the addict and his or her partner to nurture more intimacy in their sexual relationships. I usually advise the person with the sexual problem to both stop the "wrong" (addictive) sexual behaviors, often with the help of a twelve-step group, and at the same time to implement a plan for cultivating the "right" kind of sexual behaviors. I invite couples to make a date night, slow down the process and timing of sexual relations, and enjoy more conversation, mutual pleasuring, and full-body awareness. Building intimacy and a balanced kind of love often works to treat at least one of the underlying needs or causes of sexual compulsivity.[17]

Lust's Antidotes

The traditional antidote for lust is chastity or celibacy. The solution offered by chastity is self-restraint, which is a good solution as far as it goes.[18] Yet, as with the prescribed solution for the sin of gluttony, which is abstinence, it seems like it is not enough. Chastity does nothing to help the believer gain a new and more positive understanding of sexual love, nor to deal with the mental aspects of the addiction.

Fidelity, or faithfulness, gets a bit closer to being an effective antidote. Genuine sexual love—sexual love at its best—is expressed best within the context of fidelity: two people together over time, in the context of a commitment expressed publicly as marriage. Within the context of marriage, a little lust can be a good thing—binding spouses physically as well as emotionally and spiritually—as long as it is within the larger context of and under the authority of the rule of love.

Another meaning of the word faithfulness is promise-keeping. Love grows best in a garden bed of kept promises. In such a context of kept promises, there is the security that allows trust to build, which in turn allows for mutual vulnerability, which in turn helps love mature. Trust and vulnerability help love move beyond dependency, lust, and obsession.

Besides fidelity, modesty is another antidote to the sin of lust. Modesty is still practiced in more traditional or religiously conservative cultures.

17. Donald Capps, who has assigned each of the Seven Deadly Sins to one of the developmental stages of life, has assigned lust to the early adult years, when most people are learning how to be genuinely intimate and are tempted to substitute lust for intimacy. See Capps, *Deadly Sins and Saving Virtues*, 52–57.

18. St. Paul proposes chastity throughout his letters. And, if self-control fails, he advises single believers to get married (1 Cor 7:9).

Modesty in dress and social behavior goes a long way toward reducing the amount of visual sexual stimulation between the genders, which in turn makes it easier for all the parties to resist lustful thoughts. Modesty addresses the mental aspects of lust, which is often where sexual problems start. As with the sin of gluttony, the sin of lust is very difficult to outlaw by legislation, whether religious or secular. Another limitation to the modesty solution to the sin of lust is that it requires the cooperation of the opposite sex and in some ways limits his or her freedom and individuality, all of which runs contrary to the value of individual freedom that Americans love so much. Perhaps all we can do is to embrace modesty within our own lives and, most importantly, within our minds.

We can practice the virtues of chastity, modesty, and fidelity by doing the following:

- being modest in dress, language, and actions, particularly in public; dressing down if our clothing is going to make our brother or sister stumble
- being modest in our thoughts; avoiding sexual humor or dirty jokes
- avoiding pornographic material—it's addictive!
- seeking a therapist if our marriage needs help in the sexual area
- modeling modesty for our children; teaching our children appropriate sexual morals and behavior so they don't learn their morality from the media

Another traditional Christian approach to the management of lust—in fact, to the management of all of the Seven Deadly Sins—is the avoidance of temptation. If placed in a compromising situation, who among us could resist sin forever? So it is better, whenever possible, to not even place ourselves in situations that we know in advance are going to weaken our resolve or test us severely. For example, if you are single and wish to stay celibate until marriage, and if you are also a sexually passionate person like most humans are, do not allow yourself to get into a compromising situation. Set your limit long before you get into the back seat of a car or are alone together in his or her apartment. Go slow. Allow love to flourish first, and then lust will find its natural place.[19] Avoid situations that tempt you.

19. In medieval times, these Seven Deadly Sins were aligned with the seven days of the week. Lust's day was Saturday. Supposedly, Christians were more tempted by the sin of lust on Saturday than any other day of the week. So, I guess the advice would have been to avoid Saturdays.

SUMMARY

In this chapter I defined lust as excessive and prolonged thinking about sex. While lust drives some people into sexual addictive behaviors, lust is actually a battle for all of us. We are all created, to a greater or lesser extent, with sexual desires. Then, on top of these natural instincts, the media-dominant culture in which we live incessantly bombards us with erotica and provides various easily accessible ways to fulfill the very lustful cravings that they have intensified within us. The end result is that sexual addiction has become one of the fastest growing types of addictions in the Western world, and sexual addictions have contributed, although they are not the only cause, to the rise in sex-related crimes. I have discussed some traditional and non-traditional perspectives on the problem of managing our sexual desires. As with most of the Seven Deadly Sins, the spiritual path is one of recovery, not cure. Our task is to find a balance, in the case of lust, a balance that allows us to enjoy the good gift of sexuality while managing its excesses or, to put it more succinctly, sexual desire in the service of loving intimacy, not as a replacement for love.

QUESTIONS FOR SELF-REFLECTION

1. Do I have trouble managing my lustful fantasies? Do my lustful thoughts interfere with my relationships at work?
2. How much time do I spend viewing sexual material? Be honest.
3. Do I have a secret life? Do I hide my sexual activities or interests from loved ones?
4. Do I engage in sexual activities in order to feel better about myself? Are there times, however, when I feel lonely or in despair after my sexual activity?
5. Do I engage in sexual activities that are harmful, destructive, or risky? Do I feel that my sexual desires or activities are out of control?
6. Do I force sexual activity upon someone else?
7. Do I tend to confuse lust and love? What spiritual insights or practices have helped me the most?

Biblical passages related to lust: Judg 13–16; 2 Sam 11:2–5; Prov 7:24–27; Song (entire); Matt 5:22–30; 1 Cor 7:1–5; 10:33; 13; 1 John 1:15–17

9 Some Concluding Thoughts

IN THIS BOOK, I have argued that our spiritual ancestors identified the Seven Deadly Sins as deadly because each of these sins contributes to or sustains the addiction process. The advent of the modern study of addictions has illuminated this ancient truth. Over the centuries, spiritual leaders in the West have developed various spiritual practices to help prevent and overcome addictions by winning the battle for the mind caused by each of these sins. Most of these practices have fallen by the wayside in our rush into modernity. I believe that this lapse in spiritual practices is one factor, but not the only factor, in the rapid rise of addictions and addiction-related problems among Westernized people. Other factors contributing to the rising incidence of addiction include affluence, technology, the capitalistic economy, and the eroding of personal discipline.

Spiritual practices are not easy. They are not a quick fix. They take practice. Unfortunately, many of us do not embrace the spiritual path until we have to.

THE SPIRITUAL BATTLE

Some people can drink socially and never become an alcoholic. Some people can gamble and never become a compulsive gambler. Some people can work hard and never become a workaholic. And some people can view pornography or engage in other light-weight sexual activities and never become a sex addict. What is the difference? Why do some people fall prey to addictions and others do not? One explanation lies in the sins of the mind that we have been discussing in this book. If we can manage our mental processes, we can prevent and avoid addictions. If we allow our minds to dwell upon, enlarge upon, and obsess on lustful thoughts, angry thoughts, lazy thoughts, envious thoughts, greedy thoughts, or cravings for food, drink, or drugs, we will gradually become addicted. The particular form of our addiction is almost secondary. The issue is mental and spiritual slavery. In short, then, the real battle against addictions has to begin in the mind. This battle is essentially a spiritual battle or, if you prefer, a psycho-spiritual battle. I do not resonate with the language of spiritual warfare, but after years upon years of working with persons caught in addiction, I sympathize with it completely.

This book suggests a wide variety of spiritual insights or practices that have been proven to be helpful to many people in this universal struggle. I invite you to select the ones that fit your needs and commit yourself to their implementation. The spiritual path is not an easy one, but it is a time-honored and effective way of preventing addiction and rescuing people from the slavery of addiction.

The Value of Acceptance

One of the great spiritual truths of addiction work surrounds the importance of acceptance, not only as a means to recovery, but also as a preventive measure to keep us healthy and whole. We need to learn to accept our addictive impulses. Alcoholism, drug addiction, compulsive gambling, sexual addictions—all these addictions and more thrive on fear, judgmentalism, secrecy, and self-incrimination. Beating up on ourselves for our sinful thoughts or failures in relation to our addictions only makes matters worse. Hiding the truth from ourselves and our loved ones only makes things worse. Getting things out in the open, as painful as that can be, is the first step in recovery. Recovery begins with acceptance.

Ultimately, addictions are not curable. There is no full recovery from a severe addiction like alcoholism or sexual addiction. Such people are only one drink or trick or binge away from a relapse. Ultimately, we are all potential addicts because we all live with one or several of these Seven Deadly Sins. We all struggle with our own addictive thoughts, even if we never do develop a full-blown addiction. We all have "feet of clay." We all get by in life by the grace of God. The more we try to deny our vulnerability to sin, the more we make ourselves vulnerable to sin. But if we accept our vulnerability, accept it and even embrace it, we are given the strength to overcome it day by day. Is it easier to drag a heavy weight on a chain behind you or to pick it up and walk with it, holding it close? Acceptance is part of the reason why twelve-step programs work. Acceptance allows us to make friends with our addictive impulses, accepting them as part of our life and as part of the human condition and finding ways to carry our impulses and transform them rather than dragging them behind us on a chain. Acceptance means learning to live with sin, not eliminating it. Acceptance means not trying to over-control our addictive processes lest they actually gain more power over us. Acceptance means acknowledging our addictive impulses . . . and then releasing them to our Redeemer (or if you prefer, our Higher Power). Achieving acceptance and sustaining it through the recovery process is a spiritual process. Another word for acceptance might be grace. Through grace we learn to live with our sins, our weaknesses, and our vulnerabilities, thereby allowing God to transform them into strengths.

Questions for Self-Reflection

1. Now that I have read this book, do I agree with the author's contention that the term "deadly" in the phrase Seven Deadly Sins refers to the fact that each of these sins is addictive and thus often destructive in a variety of ways?

2. Referring back to Figure 4 in chapter 5, do I agree that each of these sins is a distortion of a basic and natural human need? What is my personal experience with this chart?

3. How would I alter or edit the classic list of Seven Deadly Sins? Does this list still hold up after fifteen hundred years as an accurate reflection of human vulnerabilities in the Western world? Or, would I like to edit the list for the twenty-first century, or make it more cross-cultural, or add an eighth or ninth sin?

4. What have I learned about my personal struggles? Has my mind changed, or have I gained a new insight or a new perspective? What will I do differently as a result of reading this book?

5. What feedback, additional information, or personal stories would I like to share with the author?

You are welcome to contact the author via e-mail at: ssullender@sfts.edu.

Theological Postscript
What Is Sin?

WHAT IS WRONG WITH humanity? Why is it that we humans are so self-destructive and so destructive of each other and the natural world? This journey through the world of addictions, particularly as they show up in the Seven Deadly Sins, has provided us with a graphic and powerful perspective on this eternal question. Nowhere else do humanity's self-destructive tendencies manifest themselves more obviously than in the world of addiction. I have spent thousands of hours with people caught in bondage to various addictions, listening to their long tales of misery and heartache and watching the almost inevitable destructiveness of the addictive process. This has convinced me—like no theology textbook ever could—of the power of sin.

In the Christian tradition, the concept of sin is the answer to the age-old question about what is wrong with us. Traditionally, sin has primarily been understood as a moral failure or as a breaking of God's laws. The metaphor has been framed in either moral or legal terms. But what if we look at sin through the framework of addiction? Will the modern understanding of addiction offer us another metaphor for understanding what we mean by sin? With millions of people struggling with addictions in one form or another, is such an understanding of sin more relevant to the twenty-first century?

I believe that using the framework of addiction adds greatly to our understanding of sin. The main points and questions raised by such an understanding of sin include the following:

- Sin understood as addiction focuses not on sins as deeds, but on the power of Sin. The problem is not that we have made occasional mistakes, broken God's law, or done a wrong thing and are now estranged

Ancient Sins... Modern Addictions

from God by guilt and shame. The problem is that we cannot stop sinning. In ancient times, people were focused on the question, "How can I be saved from the consequences of my sins?" In modern times, most people are asking a new question, "How can I stop sinning?"

- In the legal or moral metaphors for understanding sin, free choice is central. In the addictions understanding of sin, human free will is at best partial, and if we are struggling with an addiction, which includes most of us, most of the time, our free will is in bondage. So how can we be held accountable for our sin when we cannot make choices, or at least when our choices are compromised?

- The Christian prescription for sins has been confession, forgiveness, and repentance. People who struggle with serious addictions experience the confession-forgiveness-repentance process as a failure. They try it, but it does not take. They sin again and confess again, only to sin again and confess again... and again and again. Maybe confession and forgiveness frees them from guilt, but it does not free them from Sin with a capital S. We need to be saved from Sin, not from our sins.

- The experience of persons with addictions is that the power that overtakes them and holds their wills (and minds and souls) in bondage is alien to them. Some experience this power as coming from outside of themselves, taking them over, and if the addiction worsens, the power comes to possess them, replacing their right mind with an addict's mind. The imagery of demons and Satan is an appealing way of describing this experience. Could it be that the ancient concept of Satan is simply a personification of addiction? If that is the case, it gives new meaning to the classic story of Faust, who was offered eternal youth in exchange for his soul. Addiction offers us a similar bargain—bliss in exchange for bondage.

- Sin as addiction highlights the deceptive nature of sin. As the addiction process progresses, our thinking gets distorted. We deny the reality of our condition. We justify, rationalize, and blame others for our addictive behaviors. Understanding sin as addiction helps us see more clearly the deceptive nature of sin.

- Understanding sin as addiction helps us see, as Jesus suggested in the Sermon on the Mount, that sin begins in the mind (or heart). There is a continuum between thought and deed.

- Understanding sin as addiction emphasizes the universal reality of sin. Every one of us is vulnerable to the lure of an addiction in one form or another, and for the most part every one of us has an addiction. No one is free from addiction, although some manage their addiction(s) better than others. We are all universally vulnerable.

- The addictions perspective on sin gives a new dimension to the Pauline phrase, "The wages of sin is death." Indeed, addictive sins lead to literal death, sometimes dramatically, sometimes slowly—but death is clearly a consequence of sin. Yet, the addictions understanding of sin also highlights the many other kinds of death: death of relationships, careers, spiritual life, and even the death of one's soul, if we want to use that traditional term.

- Seeing sin as addiction highlights the idolatrous nature of sin. Addicted persons give energy, devotion, and trust that would otherwise be focused on God to their addiction. Their addictive substance or activity becomes a substitute for God. In this way, addictions create idolatry and drive us away from faith in the living God.

- Sin as addiction helps us understand how good things or natural needs get transformed into evil things. For example, the normal need for sexual intimacy can be transformed by the power of addiction into destruction. St. Paul made a similar argument about the nature and function of the Law, which was originally intended to help humanity overcome sins but through the power of Sin (addictive processes) becomes itself a "slavery" (a new addiction, i.e., religious legalism).

- If sin is best understood as addiction, what then does it mean to be saved from our sins? The traditional moral or legal metaphors for sin and salvation talk about Christ's death on the cross as saving us from our sins. Most addicted persons who are in recovery affirm that they have not been saved from their sins. The potential to sin again is "ever before them." Sin as the power of addiction is still present. They are not *saved*, but they are *being saved*. Sin cannot be cured or fixed, but it can be managed, one day at a time. Understanding sin as addiction opens up the idea of salvation as process, not fact.

What I have said here is only very brief and suggestive. I invite my colleagues and friends who are trained theologians to join me in rethinking our understanding of sin. It seems to me that the traditional moral and legal metaphors for understanding sin are no longer meaningful to millions

Ancient Sins . . . Modern Addictions

of contemporary Christians living in Western societies where addictions are rampant. Increasingly, our answers to the main question raised by sin—What is wrong with humanity?—differ from the answers proposed by our spiritual forebears. Let's listen to each other and reframe our understanding of sin and addictions in a way that helps free us from the power of the addiction process.

Bibliography

AAA Foundation for Traffic Safety. "Aggressive Driving: Research Update." 2009. Online: http://www.aaafoundation.org/pdf/AggressiveDrivingResearchUpdate2009.pdf.
Administration for Children and Families. "Child Maltreatment 2010." U.S. Department of Health and Human Services. Online: http://archive.acf.hhs.gov/programs/cb/pubs/cm10/cm10.pdf.
Alcoholics Anonymous World Services. *Alcoholics Anonymous*. 4th ed. New York: Alcoholics Anonymous World Services, 2002.
———. *Twelve Steps and Twelve Traditions*. New York: Author, 1953.
Allport, Gordon W. *The Individual and His Religion: A Psychological Interpretation*. New York: Macmillan, 1950.
American Psychiatric Association. *Diagnostic and Statistical Manual of Mental Disorders (DSM-IV-TR)*. 4th ed. Washington, DC: Author, 2000.
American Society of Addiction Medicine. "Public Policy Statement: The Definition of Addiction." August 15, 2011. Online: http://www.asam.org/docs/publicy-policy-statements/1definition_of_addiction_long_4-11.pdf?sfvrsn=2.
Beattie, Melody. *Codependent No More: How to Stop Controlling Others and Start Caring for Yourself*. New York: Harper/Hazelden, 1987.
Bien, Thomas, and Beverly Bien. *Mindful Recovery: A Spiritual Path to Healing from Addiction*. New York: Wiley, 2002.
Black, Donald W. "A Review of Compulsive Buying Disorder." *World Psychiatry* 6, no. 1 (February 2007) 14–18. Online: http://www.ncbi.nlm.nih.gov/pmc/articles/PMC1805733/.
Blazing Grace. "Porn Statistics: Statistics and Information on Pornography in the USA." 2012. Online: http://www.blazinggrace.org/index.php?page=porn-statistics.
Brown, Eryn. "Study: Greed Drives Rich to Bend Ethics." *Santa Rosa Press Democrat*, February 28, 2012.
Buber, Martin. *I and Thou*. New York: Scribner, 2000.
Capps, Donald. *Deadly Sins and Saving Virtues*. Philadelphia: Fortress, 1987.
Carnes, Patrick. *Out of the Shadows: Understanding Sexual Addiction*. 3rd ed. Center City, MN: Hazelden, 2001.
Carnes, Patrick, et al. *In the Shadows of the Net: Breaking Free of Compulsive Online Sexual Behavior*. 2nd ed. Center City, MN: Hazelden, 2007.
Centers for Disease Control and Prevention. "Prevalence of Physical Activity, Including Lifestyle Activities Among Adults—United States, 2000–2001." *MMWR*, August 15, 2003. Online: http://www.cdc.gov/mmwr/preview/mmwrhtml/mm5232a2.htm.

Bibliography

———. "Adult Obesity Facts." August 13, 2012. Online: http://www.cdc.gov/obesity/data/adult.html.

Ciarrocchi, Joseph W. "Spirituality for High and Low Rollers: The Paradox of Self-Esteem in Gambling Recovery." In *Addiction and Spirituality: A Multidisciplinary Approach*, edited by Oliver J. Morgan and Merle Jordan, 173–92. St. Louis: Chalice, 1990.

Clean Cut Media. "Unnaturally Beautiful Children: Image and Beauty." 2009. Online: http://www.cleancutmedia.com/advertising/unnaturally-beautiful-children-image-beauty.

Clinebell, Howard. *Understanding and Counseling Persons with Alcohol, Drug and Behavioral Addictions*. Rev. ed. Nashville: Abingdon, 1998.

Cohen, John M., ed. *The Four Voyages of Christopher Columbus*. New York: Penguin, 1969.

Davis, Jeanie Lerche. "Researchers Identify Alcoholism Gene: Alcohol Addiction, High Anxiety Linked to Same Gene." WebMD. 2004. Online: www.webmd.com/mental-health/News/20040526/researchers-identify-alcoholism-gene.

Devlin, Michael J., and B. Timothy Walsh. "Eating Disorders and Depression." *Psychiatric Annals* 19:9 (September 1989) 473–76.

DiClemente, Carlo C. *Addiction and Change: How Addictions Develop and Addicted People Recover*. New York: Guilford, 2003.

Domestic Violence Statistics. "Domestic Violence Statistics." 2012. Online: http://domesticviolencestatistics.org/domestic-violence-statistics.

Emmons, Robert A. *Thanks! How the New Science of Gratitude Can Make You Happier*. Boston: Houghton Mifflin, 2007.

Ericson, Nels. "Substance Abuse: The Nation's Number One Health Problem." U.S. Department of Justice, Office of Juvenile Justice and Delinquency Prevention, Fact Sheet #17. May 2001. Online: http://www.jjcmn.com/forum/usb/14_Successful%20Minnesota%20Prevention%20and%20Intervention%20Models/fs200117.pdf.

Flora, Carlin. "The Measuring Game: Why You Think You'll Never Stack Up." *Psychology Today* 38:5 (October 2005) 42–50.

Forward, Susan, and Craig Buck. *Obsessive Love: When Passion Holds You Prisoner*. New York: Bantam, 1991.

Foundation for Traffic Safety. "Aggressive Driving: Research Update." Automobile Association of America. April, 2009. Online: http:www.aaafoundation.org/pdf/AggressiveDrivingResearchUpdate2009.pdf.

Finkelstein, Eric A., et al. "Annual Medical Spending Attributable to Obesity: Payer and Service Specific Estimates." *Health Affairs* 28:5 (2009) 822–31. Online: http://content.healthaffairs.org/content/28/5/w822.full.html.

Friedman, Meyer, and Ray Rosenman. "Association of Specific Overt Behavior Pattern with Blood and Cardiovascular Findings." *Journal of the American Medical Association* 169 (1959) 1286–96.

Goodman, Amy. "Romney's 1 Percent Nation under God." *Santa Rosa Press Democrat*, February 3, 2012.

Heller, Richard, et al. *The Carbohydrate Enthusiast's Healthy Heart Program*. New York: Ballantine, 1999.

Insel, Thomas. "Spotlight on Eating Disorders." National Institute of Mental Health. February 24, 2012. Online: http://www.nimh.nih.gov/about/director/index-eating-disorders.shtml.

Kaiser Family Foundation. "Sexual Scenes on TV Nearly Double Since 1998." 2005. Online: http://www.kff.org/entmedia/entmedia110905nr.cfm.

Bibliography

Keating, Thomas. *Divine Therapy and Addiction: Centering Prayer and the Twelve Steps.* New York: Lantern, 2011.

Kessler, Ronald C., et al. "The Prevalence and Correlates of DSM-IV Intermittent Explosive Disorder in the National Comorbidity Survey Replication." *Archives of General Psychiatry* 63:6 (June 2006) 669–78. Online: http://www.ncbi.nlm.nih.gov/pmc/articles/PMC1924721/.

Kuhar, Michael. *The Addicted Brain: Why We Abuse Drugs, Alcohol and Nicotine.* Upper Saddle River, NJ: FT, 2011.

Lasch, Christopher. *The Culture of Narcissism: American Life in an Age of Diminishing Expectations.* Rev. ed. New York: Norton, 1991.

Lewis, C. S. *Mere Christianity.* New York: Macmillan, 1984.

Liebman, Bonnie. "Food and Addiction: Can Some Foods Hijack the Brain?" *Nutrition Action Health Letter* (Center for Science in the Public Interest) 39:4 (May 2012) 1–7.

Luskin, Fred. *Forgive for Good: A Proven Prescription for Health and Happiness.* San Francisco: HarperOne, 2003.

Maslow, Abraham H. *Motivation and Personality.* 2nd ed. New York: Joanna Cotler, 1970.

Mathieu, Ingrid. *Recovering Spirituality: Achieving Emotional Sobriety in Your Spiritual Practice.* Center City, MN: Hazelden, 2011.

May, Gerald. *Addiction and Grace: Love and Spirituality in the Healing of Addictions.* San Francisco: Harper, 1988.

Mendoza, Martha. "Has the War on Drugs Failed?" *Santa Rosa Press Democrat*, June 4, 2012.

Milkman, Harvey, and Stanley Sunderwirth. *Craving for Ecstasy: The Consciousness and Chemistry of Escape.* Lanham, MD: Lexington, 1987.

———. *Craving for Ecstasy and Natural Highs: A Positive Approach to Mood Alteration.* Thousand Oaks, CA: Sage, 2010.

Miller, Todd Q., et al., "A Meta-Analytic Review of Literature on Hostility and Physical Health." *Psychological Bulletin* 119:2 (1996) 322–48.

Moore, John D. *Confusing Love with Obsession: When Being in Love Means Being in Control.* Center City, MN: Hazelden, 2006.

Morgan, Oliver J., and Merle Jordan, eds. *Addiction and Spirituality: A Multidisciplinary Approach.* St. Louis: Chalice, 1999.

Nakken, Craig. *The Addictive Personality: Understanding the Addictive Process and Compulsive Behavior.* 2nd ed. Center City, MN: Hazelden, 1996.

National Center for Chronic Disease Prevention and Health Promotion, Division of Nutrition, Physical Activity and Obesity. *The Obesity Epidemic* [film]. 2011.

National Center for Posttraumatic Stress Disorder. "Report of (VA) Consensus Conference: Practice Recommendations for Treatment of Veterans with Comorbid Substance Abuse and PTSD." U.S. Department of Veterans Affairs. 2008. Online: www.ptsd.va.gov/professional/pages/handouts-pdf/SUD_PTSD_Practice_Recommend.pdf.

National Council on Alcoholism and Drug Dependence (NCADD). "FAQS/Facts." Online http://www.ncadd.org/index.php/learn-about-alcohol/faqsfacts.

National Institute of Mental Health. "Any Mood Disorder among Adults." Online: http://www.nimh.nih.gov/statistics/1ANYMOODDIS_ADULT.shtml.

Norwood, Robin. *Women Who Love Too Much: When You Keep Wishing and Hoping He'll Change.* New York: Pocket, 1985.

Oates, Wayne E. *Confessions of a Workaholic.* New York: Abingdon, 1978.

Bibliography

Ogden, Cynthia L., et al. "Prevalence of Obesity in the United States, 2009-2010." NCHS Data Brief, No. 82. January 2012. Centers for Disease Control and Prevention. Online: http://www.cdc.gov/nchs/data/databriefs/db82.pdf.

Peck, M. Scott. *The Road Less Traveled*. New York: Simon & Schuster, 1978.

Pertusa, Alberto, et al. "Refining the Diagnostic Boundaries of Compulsive Hoarding: A Critical Review." *Clinical Psychology Review* 30, no. 4 (2010) 371–86. Online: http://childrenofhoarders.com/pdf/Pertusa%202010%20Hoarding%20Review.pdf.

Peterson, Christopher, et al. *Learned Helplessness: A Theory for the Age of Personal Control*. London: Oxford University Press, 1995.

Petrochko, Cole. "ADHD Increases Risk of Substance Use Disorders." MedPage Today. 2011. Online: www.medpagetoday.com/Pediatrics/ADHD-ADD/26882.

Petry, Nancy M. *Pathological Gambling: Etiology, Comorbidity, and Treatment*. Washington, DC: American Psychological Association, 2005.

Society for the Advancement of Sexual Health. "Defining Sexual Sobriety." Online: www.sash.net/defining-sexual-sobriety.

Taubes, Gary. "The New Obesity Campaigns Have It All Wrong." *Newsweek* (May 14, 2012) 32–36.

Tocqueville, Alexis de. *Democracy in America*. Vol. 2. New York: Knopf, 1951.

Twenge, Jean M. *Generation Me: Why Today's Young Americans Are More Confident, Assertive, Entitled and More Miserable than Ever*. New York: Free Press, 2007.

Twenge, Jean M., and W. Keith Campbell. *The Narcissism Epidemic: Living in the Age of Entitlement*. New York: Free Press, 2010.

Washton, Arnold, and Donna Boundy. *Willpower's Not Enough: Recovering from Addictions of Every Kind*. New York: HarperCollins, 1989.

Weaver, Andrew J., and Harold G. Koenig. *Pastoral Care of Alcohol Abusers*. Minneapolis: Fortress, 2009.

Wegner, Daniel M., Matthew Ansfield, and Daniel Pilloff. "The Putt and the Pendulum: Ironic Effects of the Mental Control of Action." *Psychological Science* 9 (May 1998) 196–99.

Williams, Janice E., et al. "Anger Proneness Predicts Coronary Heart Disease Risk: Prospective Analysis from the Atherosclerosis Risk in Communities (ARIC) Study." *American Heart Association Journal* 101, no. 17 (2000) 2034–39.

Williams, Redford. *The Trusting Heart: Great News about Behavior*. New York: Crown, 1989.

Williams, Redford, and Virginia Parrott Williams. *Anger Kills: Seventeen Strategies for Controlling the Hostility that Can Harm Your Health*. New York: Harper, 1998.

Woititz, Janet Geringer. *Adult Children of Alcoholics*. Expanded ed. Deerfield Beach, FL: Health Communications, 1983.

Zurbriggen, Eileen L., et al. "Report of the APA Task Force on the Sexualization of Girls." Washington, DC: American Psychological Association, 2010. Online: http://www.apa.org/pi/women/programs/girls/report-full.pdf.

Zweig, Jason. "The Thrill Is Wrong." *Money* 35:2 (February 2006) 74–77.

www.ingramcontent.com/pod-product-compliance
Lightning Source LLC
Chambersburg PA
CBHW030110170426
43198CB00009B/564